Methodological Problems with the Academic Sources of Popular Psychology

Methodological Problems with the Academic Sources of Popular Psychology

Context, Inference, and Measurement

Robert Ausch

LEXINGTON BOOKS
Lanham • Boulder • New York • London

Published by Lexington Books
An imprint of The Rowman & Littlefield Publishing Group, Inc.
4501 Forbes Boulevard, Suite 200, Lanham, Maryland 20706
www.rowman.com

Unit A, Whitacre Mews, 26-34 Stannary Street, London SE11 4AB

British Library Cataloguing in Publication Information Available

Library of Congress Cataloging-in-Publication Data

Names: Ausch, Robert, author.
Title: Methodological problems with the academic sources of popular psychology : context, inference, and measurement / Robert Ausch.
Description: Lanham : Lexington Books, [2016] | Includes bibliographical references and index.
Identifiers: LCCN 2015047363 (print) | LCCN 2015049892 (ebook) | ISBN 9781498524148 (cloth : alk. paper) | ISBN 9781498524155 (Electronic)
Subjects: LCSH: Psychology--Research--Evaluation. | Psychology--Methodology--Evaluation. | Psychology, Applied.
Classification: LCC BF76.5 .A96 2016 (print) | LCC BF76.5 (ebook) | DDC 150.72--dc23
LC record available at http://lccn.loc.gov/2015047363

∞™ The paper used in this publication meets the minimum requirements of American National Standard for Information Sciences—Permanence of Paper for Printed Library Materials, ANSI/NISO Z39.48-1992.

Printed in the United States of America

This book is dedicated to all the incredible teachers I've had in my educational journey, along with my consistently supportive parents and partner who put up with all my grumpiness during the writing process. Most of all, this book is dedicated to my daughters, Mila, Estella, and Lucy, who help me balance my life of the head with a life of the heart.

Contents

Introduction ix

1 The Past and Present Landscape of Popular Psychology 1

2 The Psychology of Cognitive Biases 13

3 Fast Systems and Unconscious Cognition 41

4 Happiness Psychology and Uncertainty 75

5 The Effects of Parenting: Correlations and Causes 111

6 Psychological Measurement: IQ, Personality, and Emotional Intelligence 149

Conclusion: How to Read Pop Psychology (and all psychology perhaps?) 199

Works Cited 205

Index 221

About the Author 223

Introduction

This monograph explores several methodological issues that come up in the translation of academic psychology into mass-market, or pop, psychology. While one can identify a broad range of problems raised by psychological research in general, we try to focus on those that appear to come up in the specific areas of research that makes for good popular psychology. We will introduce them at this point but will have much more to say about them over the course of this volume. The three methodological issues we will focus on are: the problems of context, inference, and measurement, all closely related to each other. All of these are fundamentally about limitations in what can be known and how it can be known.

While some of these are clearly related to the practices of academic psychology itself, a general critique of method in psychology is beyond the reach of this study. Further, there might be many elements of pop psychology worth examining, but this study will focus mostly on very specific areas related to methodology and translation from academic to popular sources, often by the very same authors. Clearly, the styles of academic and popular writing differ from each other, but again, this will not be the emphasis so much as how ambiguous research findings, supported by a tradition in academic psychology that permits them to pass as accepted findings, are then inappropriately generalized into quasi-universal principles about the ways in which human beings think or behave. Thus we will focus on both academic research and published popular psychology when they cover the same basic subject. One principal criterion in terms of focus in this monograph is subfields in academic psychology that have a rich pop psychology literature as well as vice versa. In the next chapter, we will address how we selected the genres of academic/pop psychology we did. We can imagine other authors easily selecting different foci.

As we shall see extensively, these issues are related to the classic philosophical problem of induction: how to generalize from the particular. What we will describe as “the problem of context,” addresses what can be generalized from specific research as conditions change. This is both an experimental issue in the sense of controlling conditions as well as an inferential one in the sense of generalizing from sample to population. Thus, we will look at issues of sampling, both of people and stimuli, randomization, and replication to determine the so-called robustness of findings. We consider both the strengths and weaknesses of the experiment, long held up in psychology as the solution to the problem of induction as well as the doctrine of operationalism, the other side of the equation in the sense that is represents the deductive path from general referent to specific observation or results. Without getting ahead of ourselves, this tends to be a particularly important issue in a discipline like psychology where referents are not always shared and identical terms refer to distinct entities or processes.

Inference is a process often managed in psychological research by the use of statistics. The core process revolves around the relationship between sample and population and the pervasive use of Null Hypothesis Significance Testing (NHST) in the disciplines that make up psychology. As a result of this pervasiveness, the field has encouraged a “one-shot” findings approach where single studies with small effects are accepted as valid, quite the opposite of the case in the natural sciences where well-accepted facts have been subject to far more extensive testing and replication over many years. This then gives psychologists permission to make unfounded generalizations, especially in pop psychology variants. The problem of inference addresses the confidence one can have with respect to research findings but is effected by the sometime tenuous understanding both within the field, and outside the field when it comes to pop psychology, of the meaning behind the statistical techniques that psychologists depend on to do their work. Moreover, the transition from a certain world to a probabilistic one creates problems for some in psychology who still rely on the certainty-based mechanical framework of the previous century to develop theory as well as communicate their findings (Hacking, 1990).

Finally, the problem of measurement addresses the precision of what we can know and is aggravated by an academic culture where quantification is often purchased at any price, including the loss of any real meaning. This is further exacerbated in pop psychology, which accepts one of the contemporary assumptions in much psychological research, that real science requires quantification and measurement. All of these issues have been either resolved much more successfully in the natural sciences or have not caused much concern, but they turn out to be particularly acute in psychology because of both the nature of what psychologists study and the limitations of the methods they have to study it.

The first chapter in this monograph focuses on pop psychology itself: its origins, history, and contemporary state. Following this we will typically introduce a research-based genre of pop psychology as well as its academic sources followed by a set of methodological issues that remain unaddressed in the academic research itself. For example, the second chapter turns to the sub-field of biases in judgment, probably one of the most popular and influential areas within popular psychology. In this chapter, we take up the work of Daniel Kahneman and others to look at how the problem of context is exacerbated through excessive generalization, little consideration of how problems are framed to participants and other "input"-related issues, sampling, and the lack of replication of findings. As we review, this is related to more general problems with induction, experiment, and context in the fields that make up psychology.

The third chapter continues the focus on cognitive psychology but turns to the recently resurgent notion of unconscious processes in cognition and its translation into popular psychology writing about competing mental systems. This will bring us to a central problem in the field itself: the lack of shared referents. Psychologists across different disciplines do not always mean the same thing even when using the same terms. This, as we shall review, is related to the influence of the long-criticized doctrine of operationalism in psychology. Chapter 4 turns to the very popular psychology of happiness, focusing specifically on using differences between the mean scores of groups as a way to make inferences about populations as well as determine the "robustness" of findings. This leads us to an extensive discussion of notions of probability in psychological method, especially that related to null hypothesis significance testing. Chapter 5 reviews a range of well-known findings around effective parenting and its translation into popular psychology. We consider the fact that these derive from correlational research and explore broader confusion as to the relationship between correlation and causation as well as the problems with using regression techniques as a vehicle for identifying causal relationships.

Finally, chapter 6 turns to an explicit focus on the issues of measurement and testing in psychology. It explores the underlying assumptions of psychological measurement as well as issues of validity and reliability in testing and assessment. We examine a range of areas where measurement and assessments have been translated into popular psychology, like intelligence, emotional intelligence, and personality, and ask whether these phenomena are truly measurable. We conclude by trying to tie all these themes together into a general guide for making sense of popular psychology as well as trying to identify some of the broader problems in psychology, especially those related to dealing with uncertainty.

Again, this work is not designed to trivialize either academic psychology or popular psychology. Therefore, especially with respect to academic research, we include fairly extensive literature reviews to make clear our desire to capture both the breadth of the field as well as the fact that many critics in the field itself address the issues we bring up. Our goal is to bring some of these criticisms together into a general guide to the mostly unspoken methodological issues that never get addressed in pop psychology. Because of this, this volume highlights the problems at the expense of the work looking toward solutions. Readers of pop psychology without extensive training in psychological methods are at a disadvantage as claims are presented with levels of certainty that are inappropriate given the findings themselves. Clearly some of these issues reflect deeper, long-term problems in the field itself, but it is beyond the purview of this work to fully consider this given our focus on methodological problems with the academic sources of pop psychology.

Chapter One

The Past and Present Landscape of Popular Psychology

In an interview with CNN's Larry King (2/2002), talk show host/pop psychologist Dr. Phil complains that he is "not sure what pop psychology is, but I don't like it," suggesting he doesn't hold it in high esteem. But if Dr. Phil, presumably one of its most famous practitioners, doesn't like pop psychology or even know what it is, how can one possibly study it? Yet, another of its well-known practitioners, Daniel Gilbert, working in the long tradition of trying to "give psychology away," does seem to know what it is and likes it very much. He explains in an interview in *The Atlantic,*

> Psychology, unlike chemistry, unlike algebra, unlike literature, is an owner's manual for your mind. It's a guide to life. What could be more important than grounding young people in the scientific information they need to lead happy, healthy, productive lives?

Gilbert suggests something about its immense value when he describes it as an "owner's manual" for one's mind. Gilbert goes on in the same interview to say that psychologists are doing a good job of sharing their ideas,

> If you look at the nonfiction bestseller list in the *New York Times*, at almost any point, two-thirds or more of the books are about psychology . . . [the books might be] at different levels. But they're about the science of human behavior . . . people are hungry . . . [for] answers to the deep and enduring questions about their lives.

Gilbert goes on to stress the importance of introducing psychology to the young.

> What could be more important than grounding young people in the scientific information that they need to live happy, healthy, and productive lives. To have good relationships? I can't imagine a course that's more important to teach as early as possible.

Interestingly, McGraw was asked about pop psychology in an interview with Larry King as he was promoting his new book, *Self Matters: Creating Your Life From the Inside Out*, which does sound an awful lot like an "owner's manual" for life. He goes on to explain to Larry that it might seem like they are doing "quickie" cures on his show, but the "real work," as he terms it, is done after the show is over. McGraw goes on to say, "We are not trying to cure anybody in eight minutes with some pop psych answer. What we are trying to do is heighten awareness and point them in a direction."

How is one to interpret the fact that the Harvard faculty member seems more comfortable with the idea of a popular psychology than the talk show host? Gilbert (2014) answers this question in the interview by explaining a vital difference:

> My guess is when most people hear the word "psychology," they think of a person lying on a couch talking about their mother. There's a part of psychology called clinical psychology, which has to do with helping people who are having problems. But that's just a piece of psychology. Other pieces are, by and large, experimental sciences that are studying every aspect of human behavior from the neuron to the neighborhood.

Our focus in this volume will be on the latter type of psychology, the findings of what some term "psychological science" as communicated through mostly mass-market or trade books written for the general public, usually summarizing specific research findings in the field as well as drawing out their implications.

Gilbert's distinctions have much currency, at least in the United States, where university-based psychologists have been fighting against less worthwhile forms of psychology since the start of the discipline in the late nineteenth century. Within the field itself, at least since the rapid expansion of clinical psychology after the Second World War, experimental psychologists have consistently looked to distance their work from that of clinicians, but also various other versions of psychology, even inside the university—think humanists, existentialists, deconstructionists, qualitativists, interpretivists, and the like—who are not doing the proper work of a scientific psychology. University-based psychologists have long felt that spreading the findings of psychology to the public through popular writing is important. Popularization is not a problem, as long as it's of the right type of psychology. In the same interview Gilbert himself alludes to a distinction within popular psychology when he explains that people are looking to psychology for answers but "don't want to get them from people who are flapping their gums and speculating."

The kind of pop psychology we will focus on, then, is quite specific. It is often written by academics and reviews research that was originally published in peer-reviewed academic journals, though sometimes, especially when written by journalists, doesn't describe the actual research so much as tell anecdotes about research and various experiences. A key characteristic of this type of pop psychology is both the source of epistemological authority the authors invoke—*research*, *science*, *data*, *findings*, and *evidence* are some common terms—as well as the intended audiences for the writing, especially we suspect, with respect to education and income.

Critics of pop psychology abound. Reviewing the excesses of most of popular psychology is simply too easy. Take Stewart Justman's (2005) polemic, *Fool's Paradise*. The book has many chapters on pop psychology themes like therapy, self-esteem, and guilt, themes that mostly emerge out of clinical psychology, yet says nothing about any of the areas rich in academic research that we will review. To avoid this, we focus on ideas that are taken quite seriously by academic psychologists yet have made their way into popular psychology, often through the writing of those academics themselves.

THE HISTORY AND FUNCTION OF POPULARIZED SCIENCE

The findings of academic psychology translated into popular forms spread through media, books, and day-to-day conversation, circulate through the institutions of modern life including government, schools, religion, work, and the family. It is a relationship that was first established during the Progressive Era with its embrace of expert culture and has grown exponentially with the growth of the universities in the postwar period. The explosive growth of new media in the past few decades has made this expertise even more accessible than ever before.

Historically, the popularization of scientific psychology has accomplished several goals: (a) the diffusion of findings from the field, (b) introducing the general public to scientific/psychological ideas and ways of thinking, (c) strengthening the influence for and support of psychology as well as science in general among the public, (d) keeping academics in other fields aware of specialized findings, (e) helping to mark off disciplinary boundaries, and more recently, (f) assisting academics secure employment in a job market where drawing students to a particular university makes for a much more attractive candidate.

Some of these themes were central to a popular, general scientific writing tradition that emerged in the latter part of the nineteenth century. One key figure in this new genre was E. L. Youmanns, the founder of *Popular Science Monthly* in 1872. For example, the introduction of the new forms of thinking associated with science as well as the dissemination of scientific findings were central goals of Youmann's work, as he described in the introduction to *The Culture Demanded by Modern Life* (1867), a collection of essays by leading scientists that attempted to explain why understanding science was vital to adapting successfully to modern life.

> Among other imperfections of the prevailing education, in all its grades, one of the most serious is a lack of the study of Nature. . . . In place of the excess of verbal acquisition and mechanical recitation, we need more thinking about things; in place of the passive acceptance of mere book and tutorial authority, more cultivation of independent judgment; in place of the arbitrary presentation of unrelated subjects, the branches of knowledge require to be dealt with in a more rational and connected order; and in place of much that is irrelevant, antiquated, and unpractical in our system of study, there is needed a larger infusion of the living and available truth which belongs to the present time. (p. vi)

As the quote suggests, schools were viewed as key sites for the popularization of science, certainly since the late nineteenth century. These themes about reason and authority go back at least to the eighteenth century and the group of philosophers and writers associated with Diderot's *Encyclopédie* and its battle against religion and superstition. One of the greatest of all nineteenth-century popularizers, Herbert Spencer, explained the essence of scientific thought as conceived by many nineteenth-century writers.

> Every step in a scientific investigation is submitted to his judgment. He is not asked to admit it without seeing it to be true. And the trust in his own powers thus produced, is further increased by the constancy with which Nature justifies his conclusions when they are correctly drawn. (Spencer, 1860, p. 89)

Spencer might have made scientific judgment seem straightforward, but in actuality, given its technical methods and novel findings, a large audience was open to popularized forms of the natural sciences in various forms including lectures, seminars, books, texts, yearbooks, and magazines. These tended to be works prepared for the educated middle classes, as opposed to, for example, the writings of phrenologists and mesmerists, also presented as findings of science, yet explicitly written to speak to a broader and less-educated audience.

In terms of science in general, the work of popularization started in Britain in the late eighteenth century, and began in earnest in the United States after the 1840s. In fact, the term "popularization" itself arose in the 1840s, as only then was the position of professional scientist distinct enough from the rest of the populace to warrant translation efforts (Burnham, 1987). Thus the professionalization of the scientist and popularization tended to go hand in hand. Popularization, as the editor of *Popular Science News* explained in 1883, "means science put into language which can be comprehended; it means science adapted to every one's wants, to every one's necessities" (cited in Burnham, 1987, p. 34). The more technical and specialized science became, the more popularizing organs arose. By the 1870s most major national newspapers (e.g., *New York Times, Harper's Monthly*) had regular science sections.

This work was sometimes done by scientists themselves, but increasingly, it was done by a new class of popularizing writers. This was not always "watered down" science, as their work was often aimed at the educated classes and the function was to fill them in on the latest discoveries, as opposed to convince them of the value of science. But part of the work of popularization was also to firm up the distinction between scientist and layperson and it was during this period that amateur-scientists were no longer to be considered "men of science," a term increasingly used to connote the distinctness of practitioners of science (Dupree, 1963). Men of science commanded a lot of respect in a society increasingly enamored by science and technology, and with the spread of the Progressive Movement, more and more certain that science could be employed to solve social problems.

Popularization was part of the professionalization of science as it established a firmer boundary between professional and amateur science. While the professionalization of science began in Europe much earlier in the century, in the United States, it began in the years following the Civil War. For instance, in 1820s Germany, when the first chemical laboratory was set up in Geissen, the first full-fledged research university, the University of Berlin, had been in operation for nearly two decades. Many early U.S. scientists spent several years studying in Germany and other European centers of science and brought the vision of science they saw there back with them. The earliest "professional," or full-time, scientists were actually looked down upon by many Americans, regarded as lacking interest and ability in practical affairs (Dupree, 1963).

Professionalization required credentials and the acquisition of higher education became a necessary step in participating in science properly. Only experts in science could now comment on it. Professional science required an elaborate system of specialized knowledge, technical methods, and norms of behavior. As was the case with U.S. medicine, professional science had to remove amateurs from its midst, creating long simmering tensions between science and the democratic spirit of U.S. society (Starr, 1983). But it also gave the opportunity for scientists to speak across this "divide" and seek public support, especially as science began to require more and more financial support, first from industry and later from the federal government.

THE ORIGINS AND HISTORY OF POP PSYCHOLOGY IN THE UNITED STATES

For psychology, with long-standing questions about its place in the hierarchy of sciences, popularization has always been very important and, in fact, its early forms took on a long-surviving popular genre—the battle against myth and superstition. The long-running battle with superstition in popularized writing long preceded this period (Burnham, 1987). As far back as 1646, Thomas Browne's *Pseudodoxia Epidemica*, notably written in English and not Latin, warned the public about its misunderstandings of natural phenomena and other popular errors. While Catholics had simply sanctified pagan magic, Protestants sought to stamp it out completely, creating a space for tracts identifying these pagan practices (Thomas, 1971).

Nearly two centuries later, Thomas Dick's *On the Improvement of Society by the Diffusion of Knowledge,* published in 1833, began with chapters on superstition, particularly astrology and witchcraft. Early popularizers of scientific psychology, which by the 1880s and 1890s was increasingly set against a traditional and speculative "philosophical" psychology, took up the role as well. One of the first works of popularization, Joseph Jastrow's (1900) *Fact and Fable in Psychology,* contains chapters debunking all sorts of "occult" phenomenon including psychic phenomena, spiritualism, and folk medicine, so much so that he earned the ire of William James, notoriously sympathetic to psychism and spiritualism. The early popularizers of psychology had to struggle with the fact that for the public, the term "psychology" referred to all sorts of "psychic" phenomena including spiritualism, mesmerism, mind cure, hypnosis, and telepathy. Thus, much of this work involved distinguishing experimental psychology from all these others practices, many of which were also described by the term "psychology" (Leahey and Leahey, 1983).

This reflects one issue for popularizers of psychology in the nineteenth century. It was not yet viewed as a specialized discipline, as was the case with most of the natural sciences by this point, and all sorts of writers felt they had the right to speculate on the nature of the mind. Part of what popularizers of psychology had to do, therefore, was establish the idea that expertise on the mind was limited to those that practiced experimental psychology. Only once this was accepted could there be a distinct enough "general public" to translate findings for. Thus one cannot really speak of a popular psychology until, at least, the late 1880s or so. Furthermore, because academic psychology developed out of philosophy, for much of the nineteenth century, it took on the form of popular philosophy, essentially concerned with telling people the right way to live (Burnham, 1987).

This meant that by the end of the century, popularizers of the new psychology had to work hard to distinguish psychology from philosophy and they did this by highlighting the "scientific" elements of psychology as opposed to simply focusing on the theme of mental phenomena. Psychologists became some of the most vocal defenders of the practices of experimentalism and the scientific worldview in general (Burnham, 1987). This was especially beneficial to academic psychologists in the United States during this period as they were struggling with university administrators over the establishment of independent psychology departments and were seeking well-funded laboratories to do their work. Thus, the expansion of the academic discipline of psychology and popularization went hand in hand.

One of the first bestselling works of popularization of the new psychology was E. W. Scripture's *Thinking, Feeling, and Doing* of 1895. It sold twenty thousand copies in the first five years (Burnham, 1987). The book focused mostly on "psychological facts" as opposed to previous ones focused on the more philosophical "laws of the mind" (ibid., p. 89). Yet, as Burnham notes, its most potent examples came from the demystification of "illusions" in thinking. The same was true of some of G. Stanley Hall's early publications in *Harper's*. In other words, what seemed like "inane" facts about sensation and reaction time, had to be framed as revealing the mysteries of the soul to make it interesting to the general public. This quick and dirty solution to the problem of induction—taking specific findings and turning them into general laws of mind—was necessary to make some of these claims and has long been a part of popular psychology writing in the United States, as has been the battle against superstition and the defense of the scientific worldview in general.

This is still the case. Some of the more popular books of psychology over the twentieth century include Hans Eysenck's (1957) *Sense and Nonsense in Psychology,* making his infamous case that psychoanalytic treatment was no more successful than no treatment at all, but also has the requisite chapters on telepathy and hypnosis. Then there is the more recent as well as very popular, *50 Great Myths of Popular Psychology* (Lilienfeld et al., 2010), which takes on "myths" ranging from the idea that people only use 10 percent of their brains to the notion that low self-esteem causes major psychological problems. There are some that are not quite "myths" as they are not quite as resolved as the authors suggest, like "intelligence tests are biased against certain groups" or "students learn best when teaching styles are matched to their learning styles" (pp. 83, 92). An effect of this was that, in general, as compared to other works of science, works of popular psychology tend to make clear their ground in the "scientific" method and, in fact, can sometimes promote a kind of harsh yet naïve scientism.

The two most influential popularizers of the early twentieth century were Joseph Jastrow and Hugo Munsterberg. Jastrow, the recipient of the first doctoral degree offered by G. Stanley Hall's program at Johns Hopkins, introduced the methods of psychophysics to a wider public through his exhibition at the Chicago World's Fair in 1893. By the early 1900s, he turned away from research and toward popular outlets including commercial lectures and press articles against the growing influence of both behaviorism and psychoanalysis in the field. He was known and well liked for his especially florid style of writing. Munsterberg, in contrast, published claims that were sometimes so sensational that he was even disavowed by his own colleagues, and he eventually became one of the most widely disliked psychologists of his generation—more for his intense German nationalism than his psychology. He was accused by James Mckeen Cattell of opening the floodgates to a lot of very bad pop psychology (Hale, 1980). He introduced Americans to lie detector tests, opposed Prohibition, and exposed fraudulent psychic mediums. Most importantly, Munsterberg combined the reforming scientific spirit of Progressivism with a much more conservative political agenda. Through science he found support, argues Matthew Hale (1980, p. 8), for traditional sources of authority.

Many psychologists participated in the work of popularization. This was even true of the arch-experimentalist E. B. Titchener, who occasionally discussed optical illusions, emotions, and "mob" psychology in his work to extend its popular appeal (Burnham, 1987, p. 94). One venue for the popularization of psychology at the turn of the twentieth century was the mental self-help book. This genre was taken up by psychologists but had a long tradition in American writing starting with Cotton Mather's (1710) *Bonifacius: Essays to do Good* and Benjamin Franklin's (1757) *The Way to Wealth*. Popular examples of this written by professional psychologists included Albert Wiggam's (1928) *Exploring Your Mind with the Psychologists*, which was made up of interviews with leading psychologists including Edward Thorndike, Louis Terman, and James Mckeen Cattell, where they turned their findings into more general advice. For example, Thorndike tried to explain to readers the consequences of his associative view of mind for learning and Terman explained the importance of intelligence testing for children.

It surely was a sign of the times, that most of the interviewees mention intelligence testing at one point or another as by the late 1920s, IQ testing represented one of the most visible forms of psychological research in terms of the general public. Another popular example, Joseph Jastrow's (1928) *Keeping Mentally Fit*, a collection of his nationally syndicated newspaper columns, also focused on IQ testing but included chapters on "keeping happy" (enjoy solitude, he advises), how to choose your job, and "curing" stealing. It is quite clear Jastrow was willing to generalize far beyond any specific experimental findings and present himself as an expert on all things related to the mind, however tangential.

Another venue for popularization related to the growing sub-field of child psychology. G. Stanley Hall was a regular contributor to magazines on this topic. Certainly one of the early successes in this genre was John Watson's

Psychological Care of the Infant and Child (1928) and the strict "behaviorist" regimen he advised parents to stick to. Another popular theme: the underlying instinctual nature of human beings. This was a topic taken up by G. Stanley Hall and William James but most associated with British psychologist William McDougall and his popular *An Introduction to Social Psychology* (1908), which helped to spread theories of instinct to the broader educated public (Craven, 1978). Another well-known popularizer getting his start during these years was Arnold Gesell, a student of Hall's, who introduced mothers to his "milestone" approach to infant development.

By the late 1920s, psychology had established itself both as an academic discipline and as a topic of popularization. Topics that especially commanded the public's attention during these years included behaviorism, psychoanalysis, mental hygiene, and intelligence testing. Psychology was so popular that even non-psychologists began to write about it. Although the 1930s and 1940s provided a temporary lull in popular efforts, by the 1950s the rise of clinical psychology and the growing influence of Freudianism turned the popular psychologist from expert-experimentalist to expert-therapist (Burnham, 1987). It was during these years that psychoanalytically inspired popularizers, like Erik Erikson, Karen Horney, and Eric Fromm, started to have the most influence as well as the work of humanistic-psychologists like Carl Rogers and Abraham Maslow. In fact, in the 1950s, the APA organized a campaign to help the public learn to distinguish between psychologists and psychiatrists because they feared all psychologists were simply viewed by the public as Freudian therapists.

It was also during these years that some of the old high-culture magazines where psychologists had long published their work began to disappear, and psychology began to appear in more "mass" magazines in the form of advice or self-administered tests and quizzes. This development, along with the establishment of the magazine *Psychology Today* in 1967, introduced psychology to new segments of the population. Psychologists, in their quest to be popular, started to become more willing to address whatever fad the public was interested in at a particular moment. Popular topics included sex, the environment, humanistic themes (e.g., growth and self-actualization), parapsychology, media, and politics. One of the consequences of the expansion of topics studied was that some psychologists themselves began to make the argument that psychological laboratories were too divorced from life and that a reductionist approach was not the right one. Another consequence was a divergence between those more concerned with speaking to the public in their own terms and those concerned with disseminating the findings of psychology to the general public.

The list of ideas or terms originating in academic research that have found a way into popular psychology over the twentieth century is quite long. Here is just a brief sample: behavior, intelligence, personality, attitude, trait, attachment, stress, achievement, extraversion, self-actualization, conditioning, identity, cognitive, self-esteem, authoritarian, and so on. Often, successful ideas in academic/popular psychology speak to attitudes already well accepted in a society, often describing them in a new "scientific" language, even when they purport to turn those attitudes on their head. Sometimes this can be quite useful, sometimes not, but it does make certain assumptions, especially those made before the research even begins, difficult to identify and challenge. For example, there are certain well-accepted ideas about children and child-rearing that stem from eighteenth-century Romantic sensibilities that cannot be tested via research but are taken for granted. Just to name a few: early experiences in life shape later ones, development involves increased autonomy and individuality, mature adult-like thinking gradually replaces childlike thinking, and mother's love is necessary and healing (Ausch, 2015; Kagan, 1998). We will find many of these same ideas in today's parenting psychology.

The success of these ideas benefits from the fact that the United States is a society that values expertise. Typically, debate over ideas deemed "scientific" is limited to those that are credentialed to perform science. Today this means acquiring a doctorate degree in psychology and having a university appointment where one performs research, teaches, gives papers at conferences, and publishes in reputable journals. This had still not become the case in the first few decades of the twentieth century, but became so soon thereafter corresponding with the rapid expansion of higher education and its increased control over credentialization (Abbott, 1988). In most fields, over the course of the late nineteenth and early twentieth centuries, amateurs were replaced by those with "appropriate" qualifications, as various fields began to professionalize by policing who got to perform certain kinds of work.

Again, this was especially true of psychology, where mind-curists, mesmerists, spiritualists, phrenologists, and other healers as well as philosophers had long claimed to be practicing psychology and thus had something to say about it. With respect to clinical practice, in the United States at least, this was accomplished by becoming an adjunct of medicine, and with respect to academic psychology, this was accomplished by adopting experimental methods, all this exacerbated by the academic discipline of psychology's long struggle to identify itself as a respectable science in the forms of the more successful sciences. We will explore the intersection of these methodological prescriptions and popular psychology over the course of this volume.

TODAY'S POP PSYCHOLOGY

Just how popular is pop psychology of this type? To answer this we looked at Amazon.com's annual top 100 and the *New York Times* bestseller list from 2010 to 2014.

Table 1.1. Number of Amazon Top 100 books with Pop Psychology Themes

2014	2013	2012	2011	2010
10	13	12	15	9

The figure is roughly 10 percent or so a year, which is in contrast with figures from the mid-1990s, where the figure is closer to 5 percent. While we should not draw too many conclusions from this, these are large numbers given that the bulk of the list is made up of much more popular genres like fiction, autobiography, and children's books. The top sellers that involve academic/pop translation include authors like Malcolm Gladwell, Susan Cain, Daniel Kahneman, Charles Duhigg, the APA publication manual, and the *DSM*. The *New York Times* bestseller lists from 2010 to 2014 include the writings of Gladwell, Cain, Steven Levitt, and Paul Tough, though the overall percentage of pop psych books is slightly lower than was the case with Amazon. We shall encounter almost all these authors over the course of this monograph.

In our cursory examination, we found that books in cognitive psychology and happiness psychology dominated the list. Also dominant were those related to neuropsychology and clinical psychology, though we chose not to focus on either, as they would take us too far afield from the experimental tradition in psychology. In terms of those focused on cognitive psychology, we found two broad areas reflective of two distinct research traditions in the academy. The first argued that humans have certain innate cognitive biases that lead them to make basic errors in judgment, while the second argued that human minds are composed of conscious and unconscious processes, the latter exerting a powerful role on cognition, affect, and motivation. In happiness pop psychology we found a core message: Research identifies what makes human beings happy and can be used in order to improve the quality of their lives.

Parenting psychology was quite popular as well, though the links between academic and popular sources were not quite as direct. Still many of these texts worked under the assumption that research in psychology reveals what children require to develop in a healthy way, especially what they need from their parents. Finally, we selected assessment/testing because much pop psychology seemed to assume that by using various types of assessments and tests, psychology reveals how people differ from each other and can make predictions about their behavior. The question as to whether psychological phenomena are indeed measurable was simply never asked. In fact, the underlying assumption of almost all the work we identified was that findings from psychology, when properly translated, could be used to improve our world and ourselves. In a sense, interrogating this supposition is the central project of this work. Do the findings of academic psychology really give pop psychology writers the grounds to make this leap?

Chapter Two

The Psychology of Cognitive Biases

A quick search of the *New York Times* bestseller list or Amazon's top 100 sellers in recent years for books related to psychology yields two names again and again: Malcolm Gladwell and Daniel Kahneman, both doing something described as cognitive psychology, or more specifically, the psychology of heuristics and biases, and other times described as behavioral economics. A more extensive search reveals several other names again and again: Nasim Taleb, Dan Ariely, Charles Duhigg, Richard Thaler, and Steven Levitt. What these authors have in common is that they are all focused on a "popular" yet well-respected—both inside and outside the university—variant of cognitive psychology arguing, both, that human reason often fails people and that much of its activity takes place outside of awareness. Most argue that these biases can be modified with attention and perhaps some techniques, an argument that tends to show up more in the pop psychology writing as opposed to the academic writing. This chapter focuses on the first proposition and the following, the second. Both of these positions are grounded in extensive university-based academic research. Thus, over the course of the next two chapters, we will review both the mass-market psychology as well as their academic sources. Our focus will eventually turn to some of the problems with those sources, especially specific methodological issues that seem to come up again and again.

Malcolm Gladwell, a journalist and former staff writer for the *New Yorker*, is no doubt the biggest seller in this genre, but when it comes to the psychology of cognitive biases, there is one person whose work has come to define the field like no other, Nobel Prize winner Daniel Kahneman. While Kahneman has published quite a few academic articles, he only recently published a widely heralded "popular" synthesis of his work, *Thinking, Fast and Slow* (2011). The recognition received by the book was enormous. The premise of the work is that human beings are not the rational actors that traditional sociological, political, and economic theories purport them to be, but have developed a host of cognitive "shortcuts"—described as "fast" thinking and usually viewed as products of evolutionary processes—that lead them to solve problems in ways that often ignore basic logical, mathematical, and statistical principles, especially probability and sample size.

For Kahneman, the work began when he and his now-deceased, but long-time collaborator, Amos Tversky, published a series of papers in the 1970s, the most influential of which was "Judgment under Uncertainty: Heuristics and Biases" published in the journal *Science* in 1974. The paper described three of their most influential ideas related to errors in judgments: a representative bias—assuming like goes with like, often at the expense of basic probability; an availability bias—using a singular "available" instance to judge likelihood of a future instance, essentially an error in sampling; and anchoring—using an initial arbitrary value, or "anchor," to judge the value of related items, also a form of sampling error. In a book of the same name published in 1981, they included other biases like overconfidence—people's confidence in their own judgments is greater than their accuracy (a sampling error as they ignore their "misses")—and poor judgment of risk/loss aversion, or people's tendency to avoid losses at the risk of giving up gains (again, an error in the calculation of probability). These latter biases were part of what Kahneman termed "Prospect Theory," a critique of an idea central to economic orthodoxy, the idea that economic actors make decisions based on rational ends. Instead of "optimal" decisions, argued Kahneman and Tversky, people often make decisions based on the potential value of gains and losses to them, for instance, avoiding loss irrationally as losses feel worse than gain feels good. In the 1990s, Kahneman began a study of "hedonic" psychology, focusing on various biases related to estimating future happiness. In 2014, *The Economist* named Kahneman the fifteenth most-influential economist in the world.

For Kahneman and his school, these biases are stable enough that they can yield predictions about how people will behave in the future. People are, as leading figure in this field Dan Ariely titled his 2008 bestselling book, *Predictably Irrational.* Yet, whether or not these biases can be "predicted" or generalized depends on how seriously one takes the effects of the context within which these biases were generated. As we shall see, at times Kahneman and those influenced by him tend not to take the context that seriously at all, meaning one can describe these biases as reflections of universal human failings rather than see them as responses to a particular set of experimental conditions. Yet, when those conditions change slightly, these biases can disappear. In psychology, ignoring the context within which phenomena emerge helps to create seemingly generalizable laws of mind and behavior. This makes for good popular psychology. But alter the context slightly, as a good research tradition with extensive replication must do, and the phenomena can become something else entirely. As we shall see, the findings of the heuristics and biases tradition often do just that. Not surprisingly, psychologists have long recognized these problems with experimental methods, yet overgeneralizing about specific findings seems to go on.

POPULAR VARIANTS

The first successes in this pop tradition were some of Kahneman's earliest collaborators. One example is Thomas Gilovich's (1991) *How We Know What Isn't So: The Fallibility of Human Reason in Everyday Life*. Gilovich focused on the tendency to find order in randomness as well as various confirmation biases. These biases were part of Kahneman's original tradition of identifying how reason fails people. Another early writer in this tradition was cognitive psychologist Robyn Dawes. Dawes published a well-received textbook in the field, *Rational Choice in an Uncertain World*, in 1988 and a critique of psychotherapy, *House of Cards*, in 1994. His *Everyday Irrationality* (2001) was geared toward a popular psychology audience and focused on the prevalence of contradiction, circularity, and self-interest in the way people think.

Another early student of Kahneman, Richard Thaler, who became better known through his popular column *Anomalies* published in the *Journal of Economic Perspective* in the late 1980s, adapted the Kahneman approach to highlight behaviors that violated traditional economic orthodoxy. This work helped to found the field of behavioral economics. Thaler's first success in pop psychology writing, *Nudge* (2008), represented an interesting political twist on behavioral economics. His position was essentially that, given human "frailty," governments must intervene to help guide people into making the correct judgments, a position supported by Kahneman but also leading political figures like Michael Bloomberg, former mayor of NYC (i.e., placing healthy foods at sight level). Conservative critics argue instead that human beings are basically rational as are market forces. Therefore government involvement will only make things worse.

One of the more influential writers in this tradition, Dan Ariely, feels a bit more firmly in the pop, chatty tradition. Ariely was trained as a cognitive psychologist in the 1990s and, at the urging of Kahneman, pursued a doctorate in business administration. His work essentially applies Kahneman and Tversky's research to everyday situations. He offers people strategies for becoming aware of these biases and making better decisions. He followed up *Predictably Irrational: The Hidden Forces That Shape Our Decisions* with two other bestsellers, *The Upside of Irrationality* and *The Honest Truth about Dishonesty*.

Still another influential author in this tradition is self-proclaimed rogue economist Steven Levitt, the author of the wildly successful *Freakonomics*, first published in 2005. Levitt originally established himself in his field with an economic analysis of the finances of a drug-selling gang and by demonstrating, in a much-criticized study, that legalized abortions lowered crime rates. In *Freakonomics,* Levitt and journalist Stephen Dubner explain how incentives, whether intentional or not, affect behavior. In Levitt and Dubner's follow-up, *Think Like a Freak* (2014), they offer to "retrain your brain." What exactly does this entail? The advice is relatively straightforward: Recognize expertise, be open to feedback, and design "experiments."

In one anecdote, the authors tells of working with a large retailer who was spending millions on advertising and never thought to determine if it was effective or not. The solution: Design an experiment and get over your attitude that says "why mess with an experiment when you think you already know the answer?" For those who are "willing to think like a Freak and admit what you don't know, you will see there is practically no limit to the power of a good randomized experiment" (39). It turns out, however, that laboratory experiments are "often fascinating—but not necessarily that informative" as they are "the academic equivalent of a marketing focus group—a small number of handpicked volunteers in an artificial environment who dutifully carry out the tasks requested by the person in charge" (40–1). Doesn't sound exactly like a ringing endorsement for experimentation.

Unfortunately the retailer in question was not willing to think like a "freak," but in other cases the authors describe "experiments" with "hypotheses" and "double-blind" conditions—like food and wine critics who try to determine whether people can tell the difference between expensive and cheap wines but end up with many confounding and meaningless measures—e.g., a "1" rating is "bad," a "2" rating is "okay," "3" is "good" and "4" "great," with an average of 2.2 or "just above okay." Although the term "randomization" is often mentioned, it feels like a metaphor more than anything else. This makes it hard to accept the fairly obvious finding: Most people can't tell the difference between expensive and cheap wines without labels. These "experiments," argue Levitt and Dubner, should be used by governments and companies to test their programs and "incentivize" desired behavior. This fast and loose definition of "experiment" serves as a call to collect lots and lots of "data," as seems to be the trend today in business and government circles, but not much else.

During recent years, two authors writing in this genre handily dominate the bestseller list: Malcolm Gladwell and Nassim Taleb. Like Levitt, Gladwell and Taleb have sold many more books than most of the academic authors we cite, yet have also received far more criticism. Gladwell has published the mega-bestsellers *The Tipping Point* and *Blink* and Taleb, *Fooled by Randomness* and *The Black Swan.* Taleb's *Fooled by Randomness*

(2001) borrowed Gilovich's notion that people find patterns in the world even if they are not really there. Gladwell's *Blink* (2005) borrowed the idea of non-conscious intuitive judgments from his teacher, Richard Nisbett.

In Nisbett and Ross's 1980 book, *Human Inference*, they argued that people often make decisions based on intuitive reasons that are unavailable to them. Nisbett later turned to the study of the effects of the social and cultural environment on decision-making and human judgment, as we shall see in the next chapter. Gladwell views himself as a student of Nisbett and describes his role as bringing the findings of social science to a broader audience. He characterizes his work as exploring the hidden rules that underlie relationships, certainly something that sounds like social psychology. Yet he also describes himself as a storyteller, using science to tell better stories, and reports that he is not too concerned with the same issues academics are. Gladwell went as far as to say in an interview in *The Telegraph* that his readers are not all that concerned with coherence, consistence, and logic!

As Steven Pinker noted in a November 2009 *New York Times* review, Gladwell's work relies on a kind of populism that undermines talent and careful analysis in favor of luck, intuition, and opportunity. He sets up straw men over and over again and then sets out to prove that his counterintuitive approach is the one that works. The lesson of *Blink*, for example, is: Trust your intuition except when you shouldn't, an idea that has made its way into popular media and corporate circles. Yet when one looks at the evidence Gladwell brings to bear on trusting insight, unlike most of the previous writers in this pop psychology tradition who cite research studies, Gladwell tells stories of people making incorrect judgments from first impressions. There is little sense of what an "intuition" actually involves, other than some vague notions of a kind of subconscious information processer.

Critics of Gladwell argue correctly that his work provides great examples of the pleasures of hindsight bias as his stories involve "mistakes" that can only be analyzed after the fact. That is clearly not his point, however. In one case, a museum spends time and money to determine if a work of art is authentic or not, yet when art historians look at it they immediately recognized it as a fake. This is an example of the power of "intuition," says Gladwell, but only, it seems, if one ignores the years of training the art historian required to get to that point. In other words, Gladwell's interpretations are often about proving his point. There is a clear "journalistic" style in his prose: starting from small details and building to grand claim, lots of names and datelines, asking questions and answering them, then repeating the answer and the question again, making those who speak to your position slightly more attractive and moral, etc.

Nassim Taleb's work is much of the same. His principal lesson is that people cannot predict the future of the stock market: a good point. But it is embedded in broader generalizations about humans being "wired" to find certainty in randomness, but as is typical in popular psychology, leaving out exactly what it means for something to be wired. Taleb's more recent writing focuses on the non-rareness of seemingly rare events. Both he and Gladwell prefer anecdotes to coherent narratives, even when reporting the findings of research where they seem to function more like clever illustrations than anything else. But even in the more respected variants of this genre, the interpretations of findings can be a problem.

For example, Gerd Gigerenzer's popular psychology books tend to be some of the more thoughtful ones coming out of this tradition, yet they still have their share of problems. For example, *Gut Feelings* (2007) focuses on intuitive heuristics, or those "biases" that do not actually distort judgment but support it. He offers a range of them, from one that allows baseball players to fix a gaze on a ball and adjust their running speed to catch it, another that allows correct answers to trivia questions, to another that helps a police officer identify drug couriers at LAX. In the case of the latter, Gigerenzer tells us about Dan Horan, who identifies a women coming off a plane and their eyes meet in a knowing glance. He follows her to baggage claim and she turns out to be a drug courier. But such a story about the successful use of intuition never informs us about the unsuccessful cases, a requirement if one is interested in calculating the effectiveness of such hunches. Ironically, Gigerenzer is severely critical of Kahneman for neglecting similar issues. It seems that a "gut feeling" is a gut feeling when the judgment is correct. But people have such "gut feelings" all the time, or feelings that are described that way after the fact.

Gigerenzer then extends the phenomenon to explain the fact that speakers can tell if language is grammatically correct without being able to articulate the underlying grammatical principles. What makes them all "gut feelings," says Gigerenzer, is that they are judgments that happen quickly whose reasons one is not fully aware of, yet are strong enough to act on. While Gigerenzer's examples share these qualities, they are also very different from each other. All of them involve a history of very different types of experience. The language example is a reflection of the ability to detect patterns, the baseball one, to detect physical relationships. These are fairly generic and involve simple principles. The drug courier case instead involves a history of training along with successful drug busts. These principles are much more variable and context dependent. The first two examples are developments of sensorimotor and associative intelligence, the latter something very different. The strength of Gigerenzer's approach is his understanding that gut feelings develop in relationship to a specific environment as opposed to Kahneman, who views biases in a more decontextualized way. In other words, for Gigerenzer, they are adaptations. This means to make sense of them one looks to both mind and environment. It calls into question the usefulness of describing them as "biases." Unfortunately, in his concrete examples, Gigerenzer doesn't always follow through on this—for instance, he never considers that the collective experience of regularity in the structure of spoken language is what creates that "intuition" in the first place. In other words, languages evolved to be intuitive. This problem begins to clue us in to a more general set of problems with these findings, the problem of context. As we shall see, critics of the academic sources of this tradition identify some of the same problems.

ACADEMIC SOURCES

At base, the issue at stake here is whether humans are inherently rational creatures, thus deviating from rationality must involve some kind of misinterpretation of the problem—often described in the field as the "panglossian" position—or whether, for whatever reason, humans make "irrational" judgments just as they make rational ones. This leads to many further questions about what it means to be "rational" in the first place. In the field of cognitive psychology itself, this is often described as the "rationality debate." Historically, studies in deductive reasoning were used as evidence one way or the other. As Jonathan Evans (2013) explains, for much of the twentieth century, the field conflated failure to solve reasoning problems by way of formal logic with irrationality, or in the case of Piaget, immaturity. Deductive inferences are truth-preserving and apply to situations with certain premises (202). Yet this is not often true of reasoning in real life. For example, inductive reasoning in the real world often requires a kind of pattern recognition in which formal logic/deduction is not especially useful (159). We rarely remember all the premises we take for granted, often depend on environmental information to make judgments, and are not especially reliable sources of precise mathematical calculations. Thus humans are perfectly rational yet do not always rely on logicality. One of the problems in the field itself that critics point to has been the tendency for Kahneman and his students to use their findings to advance a specific position with respect to the rationality debates, a position then extended into pop psychology, despite the fact that this position has been questioned by over two decades of academic criticism.

Similar "debates" extend much further back in philosophy. For example, at the turn of the nineteenth century there were two well-laid-out positions on the question of human rationality that seemed irreconcilable, variants of the associative and rationalist schools of philosophy. The latter argued that humans were inherently creatures of reason while the former viewed "correct" thinking as inherently dependent on a history of associations and habits. By locating the source of human activity in the environment, the long dominance of behavioral theories in psychology aligned most of the field with the associative position. Yet, the influence of evolutionary thought posed the question: Exactly what makes something reasonable? Is it following certain principles of formal logic or adaptations to specific contexts?

The immediate history of this tradition in psychology begins in the 1950s during the early years of the so-called cognitive revolution. Research into these types of cognitive biases began with Herbert Simon, the influential pioneer of Artificial Intelligence who developed a general problem-solving program (GPS) along with Allen Newell in the 1950s to mimic the processes involved in thinking. This was pivotal in establishing the idea that the mind works like a computer, an idea that helped to give birth to cognitive science. Simon's doctoral dissertation, later published in 1947 as *Administrative Behavior,* examined the effects of the limits of rationality on decision-making, essentially the program of Kahneman and Tversky decades later. Simon termed these limits "bounded rationality" and suggested that people often rely on similar "heuristics" to make judgments rather than formalized algorithms. Simon also introduced the idea of uncertainty and its role in decision-making into economics, winning the Nobel Prize in 1978. One of Gigerenzer's criticisms of Kahneman is that in Simon's original formulations, these heuristics actually led to better decisions, and in fact, in older introductory textbooks, heuristics are still described as cognitive strategies used by experts as opposed to sources of bias and error.

Still, for much of the middle decades of the twentieth century, a subject's incorrect responses to cognitive reasoning problems, when actually considered, were seen as a result of a "personal" interpretation or a refusal to accept the logic of the task (Henle, 1962). Like Piaget, most psychologists assumed that aside from these "errors," humans were inherently logical thinkers, at least if they were fully developed adults in the West. Studying thinking in other parts of the world, psychologists influenced by Piaget, like anthropologists before them, found culture-wide "lags" in the development of thought. But by the 1960s, some approaches in the psychology of problem-solving began to challenge the premise of such rationalist interpretations. Peter Wason (1966), for instance, devised his own reasoning problems to demonstrate that people are both poor inductivists and deductivists. They instead tend to confirm assumptions that they have already made, prefiguring Kahneman and Tversky's work in the next decade.

Wason's work was criticized at the time for creating cognitive "illusions" (Stanovich and West, 2000). In other words, they were not examples of normal reasoning problems. Critics asserted that correct responses to Wason's tasks were really measures of intelligence or education. His findings were said to be artifacts of the strange content of the problems and context, leaving the premise of basic human rationality intact. But also, his critics argued that actual competence in problem-solving was distinct from described performance. In other words, even though his subjects did not solve the problems correctly, this was an artifact of the strange conditions and not necessarily a reflection of their underlying competence. Force was added to this criticism when later studies showed that subjects performed better in more "realistic" contexts (Evans, 2013).

This pointed to a strange paradox. Though the norms of rationality are devised from human behavior, humans are constantly violating them (Cohen, 1981). Wason responded that such differential interpretations on the part of his subjects, based on the content and context, was characteristic of real-life human reasoning. He also challenged critics on their performance/competence distinction, which he viewed as protecting them from refutation as only incompatibility with their theory requires that performance not be competence. Therefore, he argued, his critics were simply protecting the basic rationality of humans. These are some of the same issues that will come up with Kahneman's work. They remain unresolved, yet are rarely mentioned in the popular faces of the biases paradigm.

For instance, Gigerenzer argues that these errors are part of an "adaptive toolbox," and suggests that humans mostly use cognitive shortcuts advantageously. Thus they do not dispute the idea that humans are rational. As we reviewed, Gigerenzer's popular psychology books tend to focus on the power of these biases, also termed "intuition" or "gut feelings," as in the full title of his book, *Gut Feelings: The Intelligence of the Unconscious*. As we will see in the next chapter, this dispute was partially the basis for Kahneman's recent turn to a "fast and slow" systems approach: The fast approach is efficient but can sometimes turn people into poor thinkers; thus, for rational thinking, we have a slow approach.

CRITICISMS OF THE ACADEMIC SOURCES

One question that critics in economics and psychology raise with respect to these findings is the question of the generalizability of theses biases. There are a couple of issues related to this question. Some are related to experimentalism itself, which we shall review later, but others question how to determine whether these are biases in the first place. The essence of many of these biases is human ignorance of both uncertainty and basic probability. Biases are evident when a subject's judgment on average deviates from a normative response. But who is to say exactly what that normative response should be?

Take the example of the representative bias. Kahneman's best-known example of this problem has been repeated since the 1980s. In this version, Kahneman tells his students about Linda. Linda is described as young, outspoken, bright, and fired up about social justice. Participants are asked what is more probable, that (a) Linda is a bank teller, or that (b) Linda is a bank teller active in the feminist movement. Most subjects answered (b). Obviously, the number of people who are both bankers and active in the "feminist movement" is smaller than the number of people who are simply bank tellers and (b) is therefore less probable. The error, according to Kahneman, is assuming that like goes with like—"concerned with social justice" goes with feminism—and hence is an example of the representative bias. It is also sometimes described as a conjunction bias as respondents tend to ignore the effects of the conjunction on probability.

People use this "heuristic" to solve the problem instead of relying on a fairly simple analysis of probability. About 85 percent of undergraduates get it wrong (Kahneman, 2011, p. 158). Students even justify their incorrect responses after they are debriefed and insist that they thought they were simply being asked for their opinion. Moreover, according to some of Kahneman's students, correct responses to this problem are correlated with SAT scores, thus might even be a measure of intelligence (Stanovich and West, 1998). But even if this finding is correct, interpreting this finding is not as simple as Kahneman makes it out to be. What exactly is being assessed? This is one of the questions raised by Gerd Gigerenzer, perhaps Kahneman's most articulate critic.

First there is the artificiality of the problem itself. Gigerenzer points out that the biases are much reduced if problems are framed in terms of the much more familiar notion of frequency rather than in terms of probability. This means that subjects are asked a question like: To how many of 100 people who are like Linda do the following statements apply: "Linda is a bank teller" and "Linda is a bank teller and a feminist"? Kahneman's version instead looks like this: "Order the following statements with respect to their probability."

When it comes to deductive problems like this, most people are intuitive "frequentists" as opposed to "Bayesians," meaning they have an easier time in these types of cases viewing probability as the relative frequency of an event not as a calculation involving a prior agreed-upon base rate, though to be fair, they often confuse the two as well. Moreover, people do not always mechanically apply the formulas we want them to, unless they understand that this is what they are expected to do. It is not clear that people are "ignoring" the conjunction. Many do not even realize that the conjunction is there in the first place. If attention is called to the conjunction, error rates drop (Poulton, 1994).

Second, one-word terms like "representativeness" and "availability" are fairly vague and say little about the actual cognitive processes that are involved. Gigerenzer calls them "surrogates for theories" or "robust facts waiting for a theory" (Gigerenzer, 1991, p. 86). All they really do is describe the "error" using a clever term. They are fairly flexible and are easy to apply post-hoc to a range of findings. And they are almost impossible to falsify. Good writers in this tradition tend to create lots of new biases that are not always consistent with each other. Other than the general sense that people can sometimes be "irrational" when making judgments, although the "irrationality" in these cases is at base, just a judgment by a researcher, it says very little about how cognition actually works. In other words, why only focus on the differences between judgments? Why not focus on how differing judgments are made in the first place in realistic environments, especially given the unusualness of the problems subjects are asked to solve? In fact, such study would likely reveal that subjects have different ways to come up with the same "error," calling into question that they are part of a singular bias.

By calling them biases one is implying that a subject's performance is being measured against some set of norms. But there are problems with applying statistical norms to real-world contexts. People use contextual cues to determine what kind of reasoning to apply. In real-life judgments, statistical norms do not always fit depending on the person's goals, the information-richness of the environment, and the reliability of base-rates. Furthermore conversational norms often conflict with statistical norms (Schwartz et al., 1991). For instance, after endless variations of the representative bias problem, Kahneman discovered that the more descriptions he offered about "Linda," the more likely it became that his subjects got the probabilities wrong. The less information provided, the more likely they were to get it right (Schwartz et al., 1991). The key lesson for getting the problem right: Ignore the unnecessary details and skip to the statistics. This is a lesson many of us learn when we take high school mathematics and learn to solve word problems. As such, it would not be surprising to find some correlation between success and formal education, as long as the expectations are understood by participants.

In real life, conversational details are supposed to be taken into account. Ignoring them is rude. Listeners expect speakers to provide the information that is required to communicate their meaning, not excess information to confuse them. Speakers are expected to avoid ambiguity and wordiness. What Kahneman's study actually demonstrates is the importance of context (Gigerenzer and Murray, 1987, p. 156). His students are treating an experimental conversation like an everyday conversation. It is not surprising, as Kahneman reveals in *Thinking, Fast and Slow*, that his graduate students at Stanford were more likely than most to get the problem correct. They are more familiar with the context and understand its expectations. Perhaps they even suspect that the language used by Kahneman is intended to deceive them in one way or another. Thus the context shapes the inferences they draw.

In another version of the representativeness problem, subjects are told about a panel of psychologists that administered personality tests to a sample made up of thirty engineers and seventy lawyers. A second group is given the opposite numbers, thirty lawyers and seventy engineers. Subjects were told they would receive a series of several randomly drawn descriptions like "Person X is conservative and ambitious." Based on this, the subjects are asked to estimate the probability on a number between 1 and 100 that the person is an engineer. Naturally, the majority of subjects used the personality characteristics described to determine the probability of the person's occupation rather than base rates provided, making the mean responses between the groups virtually the same. Once again, like seems to go with like.

But as Gigerenzer and Murray (1987) point out, this interpretation of the findings is not so obvious. As long as the descriptions provided were selected at random, the base rate is indeed the most relevant bit of information. But if that were not the case, if the researchers selected cases by their profiles, as could easily be expected when generating a sample, the base rate is irrelevant. Who is to say the experimenters did not select the most stereotypical sample? The term "random" in the instructions was not enough to clue most people into this, and in fact, Gigerenzer discovered that when the subjects selected the descriptions themselves at random out of a vase, the mean responses between the groups changed. Once again, Kahneman is confusing an artifact of the experiment, this time inferences made based on the content of the experiment, with a stable cognitive process.

Kahneman has, over the years, responded to his critics. In *Thinking, Fast and Slow,* he admits to not using experiments in his work because demonstrations are more "powerful" (9). He has also acknowledged that his effects disappear with changed wording (Mellers, Hertvig, and Kahneman, 2001). He mostly explains the disjunctive findings away, and in *Thinking, Fast and Slow* oddly complains that his critics focus on only the weakest elements of his work as opposed to its general thesis (165). But, in fact, it is the generality of the thesis that is the problem. Stanovich and West (2000, p. 663) suggest that differential responses to differing conditions might be a system 1 or 2 issue. In other words, those cases without biases reflect different "fast" system 1 responses that are triggered because of the new frame. This is because these "ecologists"—this is Stanovich and West's term to describe those who see reasoning as context-specific—are looking to find adaptations that already exist and they are simply redesigning environments to elicit them. Yet, they also seem to be using the dual-system framework to shift the context of the disparate findings, just like the so-called ecologists they criticize.

To be sure, such problems are not limited to Kahneman's work. In recent years, some of the research into logical reasoning has focused on the relationship between a subject's response and the way they interpret the problem. As we noted, when subjects understand what is being required of them by altering the instructions provided, their performance improves. On the selection task, for example, when the wording is changed in specific ways, performance improves. This is sometimes called "instructional effects" (Griggs,

1989; Margolis, 1987). Others critics argue more broadly that reasoning is always context-dependent. For instance, some view reasoning as part of a broader social relationship (Manktelow and Over, 1991). Results tend to change if cues are offered that shift the meaning of the relationships involved. For example, if subjects are told that there could be cheating involved, they respond differently (Griggs, 1989).

Also there is the problem of judging responses using a normative theory of rationality that confuses rationality and logicality (Ayton, 2000; Evans, 2013). Critics argue, for instance, that reasoning should be judged by an evolutionarily adaptive logic that would not view variation in responses as a type of bias. Again, we require induction to survive in the world, despite the fact that induction regularly ignores or even violates the principles of formal logic. Typically, the "correct" response is the one of untutored "high IQ" (or high "*g*") respondents in elite institutions. There is a bit of circularity here as what makes them smart is their response, but this is also what makes the response correct (Goodie and Williams, 2000). Part of the issue is that acknowledging some of these differences make the problems more consistent with real-life problems, yet the research mostly remains confined to the laboratory or the college lecture hall.

Elements of this paradigm are reminiscent of Piagetian research and its flaws. In fact, Piaget offered children a problem very similar to the representational one in *The Early Growth of Logic in the Child* (1969, p. 101), essentially a class inclusion task like the "Linda" problem. He found that eight-year-olds got the problem right. He obviously offered a very different interpretation. It is notable that Piaget's language was far simpler than Kahneman's—he asked what there was more of "X" or "X+a." He framed the problem in terms of frequencies as opposed to probabilities (Hertvig, 2000). Yet, in Piaget's classic demonstrations of the absence of concrete operational intelligence in young children, critics argued that his findings resulted from confusion on the children's part (Donaldson, 1978). They did not understand that the experimenter might engage in an irrelevant task, for example pouring liquid from one glass to another. By age seven or so, the children understood this and were more likely to answer the problem correctly. In other words, the error was not a cognitive one, but one involving participants' expectations, social norms, and context. If there is a unifying message in the criticism of the heuristics and biases program, it is the lack of attention to context, which leads to inappropriate generalizations. While the finding that people tend to make poor judgments obviously resonates given the influence of these ideas, the actual research provides little basis for making such broad claims.

METHODOLOGICAL PROBLEMS WITH THE ACADEMIC SOURCES

Clearly, the problem of context when it comes to experimental design is a broader issue in psychological research. Take one vital element of the context, the study itself. Psychologists have long recognized all sorts of factors that can influence the results, including experimenter's expectations and personality, subject's expectations, awareness of experimenter's intent, and awareness they are being evaluated (Rosenthal, 1966). Even the design itself is a factor.

For instance, this type of research utilizes a between-subjects (BS) design in order to call attention to these biases. In other words, groups of individuals are given the identical reasoning problem to solve—the treatment—and in this case the frequency of erroneous responses is simply added up. Yet there is a fundamental problem with a BS design in which the dependent variable is a judgment. In classic psychophysics research, for example, the judgment of whether a stimulus is judged "large" or "small" is far more consistent within the same individual than across individuals. This is why early psychologists utilized a within-subjects (WS) design. For instance, when subjects are asked whether a certain number is large or small, their response depends on the number (Birnbaum, 1999). When one group is asked to rate the number 9 and a different group the number 221, on average, the number 9 is rated larger than the number 221. In other words, if only presented with the number 9, which tends to bring to mind smaller numbers, it is experienced as a large number, while the number 221 tends to bring to mind a larger frame of numbers and is judged "small." Thus the same stimulus, in different contexts, can produce different judgments.

Kahneman's discovery of widespread flaws in reasoning depends on his using a BS design. With a WS design, many of the biases disappear (Birnbaum and Mellers, 1983). Thus, one can arrive at different conclusions dependent on whether one uses a BS or WS design. Furthermore, one cannot typically regard BS responses along an ordinal scale as they might have little relationship to each other. So computing frequencies of erroneous responses, for example, is not so simple. One might be comparing apples to oranges. From a comparison perspective, in this type of research, it would make much more sense to utilize a WS design, as then there is a basis for comparison. Moreover, in biases research, a WS design would give more of a sense of when the errors are made and when they are not, providing more insight into the reasoning processes involved. The problem is that when subjects are asked to make several judgments, the prior ones shape the later ones. The treatments are no longer independent of each other, a requirement for statistical comparisons. The subjects might begin to understand what is being manipulated and respond differently. These are termed the "demand characteristics" of the experiment. Here, too, the context becomes an issue. Thus, psychologists tend to turn to BS design as a way of "avoiding" contextual issues. Though, of course, there is always a context.

To be fair to Kahneman, in his early work, he acknowledged the problems with his BS design but argued that it has more ecological validity, as people in the world don't make the same judgment over and over again with slightly different variations as in a WS design. By randomly assigning subjects to groups, insisted Kahneman, and keeping the conditions identical, judgments in a BS design can be compared to each other (Kahneman et al., 1981). The problem is, this neither changes that fact that the findings are a function of the design nor that BS designs tend to have a higher variance (e.g., range of responses) because different individuals can imagine different contexts (Birnbaum, 1999, p. 246). They are therefore easier to perform statistics on and this is part of what makes them attractive to psychologists. This is despite the fact that the large variability in responses reduces the power of the statistical tests, which should make it more difficult to find significant differences, a point we will return to in a later chapter.

Kahneman himself recognizes the importance of "framing," another way of talking about context, yet doesn't appear to acknowledge this consistently, and certainly not in *Thinking, Fast and Slow.* This is the case even given that in other work he has recognized context, explaining how findings are limited when using a WS design. In his Nobel Prize lecture, for example, Kahneman argues that a WS design pushes subjects into an "S2-based" rather than "S1-based" response, explaining away the divergent findings. Kahneman believes that because people in the world typically make one-off judgments, these issues are mitigated by a BS subjects design, but this ignores that identical "stimuli" are often interpreted differently, so it is hard to say that the identical "bias" is appearing over and over again (Birnbaum, 1999).

Context never goes away, even if its effects are tempting to ignore in order to make generalizations. A typical approach in psychology is simply not to specify context. When subjects are free to "choose" their own contexts, they tend to choose different ones. Typically psychologists have responded by trying to "correct" for these biases via alternate design, but the problem is, these design changes are just as much a part of the phenomenon being studied as the actual task (Birnbaum, 1992). All this is simply a reflection of the limitations of experimental designs in psychology when it comes to making generalizations based in people's judgments. Treatment and context form an indissoluble whole. While this is not an issue when subjects' responses are independently assessed, say scores on an exam are compared, there are other measurement problems that come up.

A REVIEW OF THE METHODOLOGICAL ISSUES AT STAKE (I): CONTEXT AND MEASUREMENT

The historical move from WS design to BS design reflects a broader methodological shift in psychology. The shift from the single-subject designs of early Wundtian introspectionism to comparing group means was a result of the influence of neo-Galtonianism in psychology (Danziger, 1990). The original Galtonian designs had focused on the study of groups, as Galton did in his research into the heritability of talent in the 1880s. It was from these studies that he and his student, Karl Pearson, developed basic correlational techniques. This became the preferred method of applied psychology. These applied studies tended to focus on "natural" groupings. They were defined by the possession of certain qualities elicited by a psychologist's intervention (e.g., intelligence). In contrast, as this paradigm was taken up by laboratory psychologists in the 1920s and 1930s, groups were defined by their experience with a psychological intervention.

As Kurt Danziger notes, in the first case the observed effect is interpreted as an expression of some quality of the subject, while in the latter it is interpreted as an effect of the intervention (125). Error in the new experimentalist framework, which had once referred to variability in individual responses, was reinterpreted as variability in responses between individuals, as it was viewed in intelligence testing. Instead of studying the functioning of individual psychological systems, where variability is to be expected, the goal was to establish a statistical norm from which individual responses were regarded as deviations (127). This compromise between experimental and applied techniques quickly came to dominate psychology.

Contemporary experimental psychologists view generalization in terms of probability rather than causal laws. There are no absolute or necessary laws of mind or behavior as much as there are regularities in thinking and behavior, which, though composed of independent events, can be expressed as averages and variations from that average in terms of probable frequencies. This was the essence of the Galtonian program taken up by intelligence testers in the early 1900s. These relationships can be captured via statistical analysis and used to make predictions. This was also the position of Ronald Fisher in the 1930s and it revolutionized psychology. Yet, the implication of law still exists in popular versions of academic psychology and it is part of what makes the heuristics and biases program so successful. In fact, as Kurt Danziger (1990) argues, a blurring of the distinction between statistical reality and psychological reality gave psychologists the opportunity to blur the distinction between generalizations based on statistics and generalizations that expressed truly generalizable relationships (116). This made replication of findings less important.

If one's goal is counting in some sense, as is any approach based in frequencies, then units of investigation must be "countable." This requires that they be viewed as discrete, unambiguous, and easily separated from their context. We can describe this as reductive in the sense that most psychological phenomena are not actually experienced as discrete, unambiguous, and easily separated from their context. In fact, the case is quite the opposite. To defenders of this view, this type of reductiveness is attractive because it mirrors the similar decomposition of phenomena into their constitutive parts that one finds in the natural sciences. Just as the body is composed of cells, the mind, too, is composed, at least in a functional sense, of types of thoughts, feelings, and so forth, that can be identified given their effects on behavior. Thus there is a mental "bias" that causes certain types of responses in specific tasks or there is a quantity of a certain trait possessed by a subject that causes certain responses on a personality test.

This prompts the question: Does such an approach lose the complexity of the actual phenomenon one is interested in? As well as, how do these statistical categories, that is, categories created so there is something to count, relate to the real-world phenomena one is interested in? This is the question of validity and it tends not to occupy psychologists as much as the development of techniques of measurement does. Whatever one's position, we should accept that the need for countable items creates an incentive to focus on certain types of thought and behavior or certain ways of viewing thought and behavior as opposed to others. Historically, the problem of studying subjective experience was related to the problem of measurement. Conscious experience is not easily measured despite attempts by Fechner, Wundt, and Titchner. This is part of the reason the field tends to focus more on observed behavior and not, as is sometimes argued, simply because subjective experiences are "unobservable"—science studies unobservable phenomena all the time.

Central to the theory of measurement taken up by psychology and key to this statistical view of thought and behavior is that units of investigation are independent of each other. The other key to this view is that observed behavior of these units are reliable, that is, they occur over and over again if the conditions are the same. Critics of this approach in psychology question both of these assumptions. If the context of the units of investigation cannot be divorced from the units themselves because it "acts" on those units, generalizations become questionable. This can happen in a myriad of ways. Shifts in context can alter the thinking or behavior itself or can alter the meaning of the thinking/behavior to the individuals involved. Unlike the case with physical as well as physiological responses, human responses are not dictated by the force of casual laws. Interestingly, this insight has been well integrated into evolutionary biology, which focuses more on probable behavior rather than effects of causes. The problem is that the context is just too important.

Similarly, if the units of investigation are part of the same network of meaning, then it is possible one is not studying two distinct phenomena and can hardly express how they relate to each other statistically.

A REVIEW OF THE METHODOLOGICAL ISSUES AT STAKE (II): EXPERIMENT AND SAMPLE

Historically, one response to the problem of context was control. At first this meant simply control over conditions. The idea of controlling context as a means of isolating causal relationships was one of the key successes of the scientific revolution and, in physics and in chemistry, it is often not that difficult to do. Experiments, therefore, were viewed as key to solving the classical problem of induction. If one can isolate other factors and manipulate one variable in particular, causal knowledge was possible. Such control was historically regarded as impossible with respect to psychology. Because of this, experimentalism came by way of physiology. Both Fechner and Wundt well understood the importance of controlling conditions as well as measurement, helping to explain why they are regarded as seminal figures in the history of the field. Yet as psychology moved away from simple psychophysical phenomena, this kind of control was more difficult to establish.

The "control" group is one way to hold conditions constant when many contextual variables are involved. Pascal used a "control" in 1648 when measuring atmospheric pressure at different heights. John Stuart Mill formalized it the 1840s, calling it the method of agreement and argued it was required to establish a necessary relationship in addition to a sufficient one. This made it required to establish causality. The control added a frame of reference that gave an observation meaning. With respect to human phenomena, one of the first attempts to establish this kind of control was in medicine. In 1747 James Lind sought to determine the effects of different treatments on his crew members afflicted with scurvy. As he divided them into six groups of two, trying to hold other conditions constant, he discovered that those treated with citrus juice saw the greatest improvement. This is often described as the first modern clinical trial. The advantage of this was that effectiveness of treatment could be determined without knowing anything of the precise biochemical relationships involved. In retrospect, however, Lind had no idea what other factors those treated with the citrus juice had in common. This advantage, identifying causal relationships without a sense of the precise mechanisms involved, certainly made this approach attractive to psychologists as well.

Control in the sense of constancy in conditions was key to the introspective methods of Wilhelm Wundt in the late nineteenth century as he studied just noticeable differences in stimulation. Yet, as we have discussed, Wundt was utilizing a WS design. Today, critics of this design argue that the continued repetition of variations on the same task influenced the results and thus there was no constancy of conditions. Instead, he would have benefitted from a control group and a BS design even if that meant accepting that the groups were probably different in certain ways. The English school inspector, W. H. Winch is said to be the first to have used a control group in his studies of mental fatigue and transfer training. Edward Thorndike used the method as well as asked whether learning in one context transfers to other contexts, an argument made by defenders of the classical curriculum. The control group was well suited to education where work was already carried out in groups (i.e., different classes) and success was determined by aggregate measures (Danziger, 1990, p. 14). It was also easier, at least at first glance, to isolate single variables and vary them. Yet, after an initial period of enthusiasm, educational researchers found the control method yielded unrealistic results, however, the method was taken up by psychologists in laboratories where, as Danziger puts it, "it developed into a vehicle for maintaining fantasies for an omnipotent science of human control" (115).

All this was happening just as William Gossett—known by the pseudonym "student" as he was still employed by Guinness beer in Dublin when he published—explained how to generalize from small samples of populations that were not well understood. He offered his *t* statistic, which looks to the distribution of means in small samples utilizing the standard deviation. This was in contrast to the central limit theorem or the normal distribution, which worked only for large samples. As we will review in more detail in a later chapter, these developments went hand in hand. With the notable exception of Skinner, who continued to use single-subject designs and regarded control in the traditional sense as actively controlling conditions, psychologists as a whole began to move in the direction of focusing on differences between groups and a control in the sense of a control group. This made comparing means and significance testing central, an important topic we will explore in a later chapter.

Given the difficulties of identifying all contributing factors, let alone holding them constant when it comes to more complex human phenomena, other strategies for establishing control developed. For instance, Charles Sanders Peirce and Joseph Jastrow used randomization in their research on sensory perception in the 1880s. This was gradually institutionalized in psychology after Fisher advocated it in his classic 1935 textbook. The idea was that random assignment to treatment and control groups mitigated the effects of differential factors so that those other factors were balanced out. If every member of a sample has an equal chance of being assigned to any condition, even if the groups are not identical, the assumption goes, those differences can be regarded as due to chance. Random assignment is so easy to do in laboratory research and so easy to understand, popular psychology writers mention it all the time, although sometimes they use the terms "random assignment" and "random selection" interchangeably even though the latter is a sampling issue. Outside the laboratory is a different story where, contra Leavitt, random assignment is notoriously difficult and often generates conditions so artificial that generalization still remains a problem.

Yet random assignment cannot do the real work of randomization if the sample is already a highly constrained one or a very small one and the point is to make an inference about a population (Krause and Howard, 2003). This was first recognized by late-nineteenth-century survey researchers as they were struggling to generalize from small samples and developed what was then called the "representative" method. It wasn't until the 1930s that random and purposive samplings were defined as distinct from each other by statistician Jerzy Neyman and the value of the former became much more evident.

Too often, random assignment simply functions to give researchers permission to ignore all other contributing factors that are outside of their interest. As we shall see later, psychologists also use regression techniques to compensate for lack of randomization in both sample and assignment, using what are known as quasi-experimental designs, but most of the techniques employed simply do not permit the kinds of causal inferences the researchers are looking to make, leading to findings that are impossible to interpret (Achen, 1986). Certainly, such analysis must begin by modeling the processes by which data were generated. It is probably not an exaggeration to say this problem affects the great majority of regression studies published in psychology. In fact, ignoring how data were generated is probably the single most pervasive methodological mistake in all of psychology and good data always starts with a good sample, at least if one plans to make any inferences about a population.

This problem is not in the research itself, but with the inferences drawn from research with respect to the generalizability of findings. There are perfectly good reasons to do research where generalizability is not the goal (Mook, 1983). Generalization refers to the breadth of the conclusions. The findings themselves might be perfectly valid for the sample being studied, yet the question of whether that sample represents the broader population one is interested in is a more complex question. Generalizability gets to the heart of the problem of induction. Modern approaches view induction as framed through relations of probability. In psychology, the language of significance testing addresses this. This means we can distinguish between statistical generalizability—where estimates from a sample can be applied to a population—and scientific generalizability—where parameters obtained in one population are applied to others. The two are easily confused and randomization is fairly basic to statistical generalization in a way that it is not for scientific generalization.

The key issue in statistical generalization then is not assignment, which is an experimental issue, but sampling, which is a statistical one. If one is interested in generalizing findings, all possible contributing factors in the population should exist in the sample drawn. Selections must be independent of each other. This is the point random sampling. What random sampling does, at its heart, is generate a framework of endless hypothetical replications upon which to base statistical inferences. The point is not to distribute population characteristics "evenly" because patterns arise by chance as well. With respect to generalization, this technique works best if one is dealing with large enough samples and is able to select from all possible members of the population.

Actual "random" sampling only exists in the idealized world of statisticians. It is more realistic to rely on representative or other types of purposive samples. The key to these designs is to understand that they tend to lower variance in a way that is not necessarily related to the phenomenon of interest. There is no more independence in the sampling process. Gustav Fechner understood this and used it to distinguish between random variation and what would now be termed variation due to error (Bennett, 1998). These are issues that tend to come up in the work of survey researchers and pollsters, yet are equally applicable to psychologists. The core problem here is that when one is making a statistical inference, one is making a statement about probability. Without randomization it is not clear what this probability value actually refers to (Berk, 2004).

In the kind of studies described in this chapter, and in fact in most university-based psychological studies with limited resources that mostly rely on volunteer or low-paid college students, few of these conditions are met. As is well known, psychologists often work with "convenience" samples that are, in reality, not samples but populations. When large samples are used, typically poor response and availability rates turn them into convenience samples anyway. Psychologists are notorious for their samples made up of available undergraduates. In 1946, statistician Quinn McNemer described psychology as the "science of sophomores" (333).

Today about 67 percent of psychology studies in the United States use college students, down from about 86 percent in the 1960s (Smart, 1966; Schultz, 1969). But even in the case of better sampling, about 96 percent of subjects tend to be WEIRD (Western Educated from Industrialized Rich Countries) unless the focus is specifically on culture (Heinrich, Heine, and Norenzayan, 2010). Sometimes one can make a plausible argument about the universality of a particular process, especially physiological ones, and therefore argue in favor of undergraduate samples, but it's hard to see how, nearly a century after Franz Boaz, Margaret Mead, and Lev Vygotsky, one can still assume forms of reasoning are universal and make inferences about certain "hardwired" capacities or innate biases. Hilgard (1967, cited in Rosenthal and Rosnow, 2009) found that psychology students are not even representative of college students, let alone humans in general, though some have contested this (Cooper et al., 2011). In most large American universities, psychology students are required to participate in research in order to receive full course credit and yet they are still often described as "volunteers" by the researchers.

There is still another form of randomization that gets ignored in this research, and that is randomization of stimuli or the conditions subjects are exposed to (Gigerenzer, 2000). This was absolutely central to the original Wundtian program but seems to no longer be a requirement in today's academic psychology. To be fair, nothing said here is new or hasn't been said by others over and over again. This is not intended to be an indictment of psychological research. So-called "purposive" samples are used all the time in behavioral research, but they require that researchers attempt to represent a population or at least set limits on generalizations. There are plenty of statistical techniques to mitigate these issues, for one, modeling the sampling and/or assignment process and its possible outcomes, yet they receive no mention as an issue in this work.

A REVIEW OF THE METHODOLOGICAL ISSUES AT STAKE (III): REPLICATION

The simplest path to valid generalization in science is replication, especially across samples, contexts, and conditions (Cronbach, 1982; Cronbach, 1986). Replication takes many forms: Further studies can simply test findings, but they can also vary independent variables, dependent variables, data sets, operational definitions, time points, environment, population, sample, data collection, methods, data analysis, and so forth. Valuable for psychology, then, is not so much a single finding but the variants of findings over time. Replication helps to further support findings, but even more importantly, helps to establish the limits of findings, key to restraining psychologists and the already present tendency to generalize.

This has turned into a big issue in academic psychology, where there are not many incentives to replicate. In fact, there is a much-discussed replication "crisis" in psychology, psychiatry, and medicine, leading some to question the worth of most published findings (Ioannidis, 2005; Francis, 2012). This is the result of several factors including research journals that will not publish replication studies, an underdeveloped culture of making data transparent, absence of incentives to publish findings that do not achieve statistical significance, desire on the part of researchers to publish findings that say something novel—all this connected to funding research, promotion, and tenure in universities—and occasionally outright fraud (Asendorpf, 2013).

For example, one study found 92 percent of publications in psychology contain confirmed hypotheses, a near statistical impossibility given the low power and small effect sizes of many of those studies, suggesting, at the very best, lots and lots of failed unpublished studies (Fanelli, 2010). One way to inflate the rate of success: post-hoc hypotheses and study designs that are basically irrefutable (Asendorpf, 2013). In fact, in a survey of psychologists one study found that the conjectured replication rate for an established finding was roughly 50 percent (Fuchs, Jenny, and Fidler, 2012). In another poll of over two thousand psychologists, respondents estimated that the prevalence of deciding whether or not to collect more data after one has tested for statistical significance occurs in about 60 percent of cases and stopping data collection after one has found significance, thereby distorting the sample, in about 40 percent of cases (John, Loewenstein, and Prelec, 2012).

One recent case illustrates the problems with this. In 2011, well-known social psychologist Darryl Bem published a study in a notable journal that found evidence for extrasensory perception. The journal then refused to publish failed replications of the findings by other researchers, even though Bem encouraged it, because, they insisted, they do not publish replicated studies. In other words, psychology has created a culture of one-shot findings (Schimmack, 2012). This promotes confusion between statistical and substantive significance. Ironically, the one form of "replicability" psychologists do engage in is multiple statistical tests within the same study, though this only increases the likelihood of finding statistically significant relationships that have no substantive significance (Maxwell, 2004).

METHODOLOGICAL ISSUES IN THE BIASES PROGRAM

There is also a tradeoff between replication and generalization—typically, the more replicable the study, the narrower the focus. The heuristics and biases tradition is a revealing exception. There has been much of "replication" yet because the context is typically not specified, especially in popular psychology variants, there is little narrowing of focus. Kahneman knows all this very well. In 2012, Kahneman published an open letter to the research community about the importance of replication, specifically in research on priming. His hope was to restore public faith in psychology. He also argued for the use of larger samples to increase power. Essentially, the smaller the effect size, the larger a sample must be in order to demonstrate it. Atypically, the effect sizes in Kahneman's most famous bias studies are so large, small samples are not a problem. This allows Kahneman and his students to skirt around some of the issues we have been discussing.

In *Thinking, Fast and Slow,* Kahneman confesses that he, too, was often guilty of using small samples in his research and that his intuitive judgments about their reliability was often incorrect. In fact, this problem, the so-called "law of large numbers," was the topic of one of his first papers with Tversky (Kahneman and Tverky, 1971). They describe an erroneous faith in small numbers among researchers in which psychologists have an exaggerated belief in the likelihood of successfully replicating an obtained finding because of incorrect beliefs about random sampling. Specifically psychologists view "a sample randomly drawn from a population as highly representative, that is, similar to the population in all essential characteristics. Consequently, they expect any two samples drawn from a particular population to be more similar to one another and to the population than sampling theory predicts, at least for small samples" (105). This is an excellent point when applied to the specific case of how researchers tend to think about sampling and replication. Whether or not this is the result of a cognitive "bias" is not as easily answered, though the prevalence of these types of errors among psychologists appears easy to demonstrate.

According to Kahneman (Kahneman and Fredrick, 2002), this paper inspired the broader notion of a representative bias where "resemblance" is confused with true representativeness. When his students produce a proposed distribution of coin flips that is virtually even for both heads and tails, Kahneman and Tversky call this same basic bias the "gambler's fallacy," as it happens often in games of chance, perhaps one of their most widely circulated findings. Again, this error in predicted distribution on the part of his students resembles the representativeness bias. In the real world deviations from the mean are not cancelled out so much as diluted. The point is, it is very easy to overestimate the strength of empirical evidence due to the fact that chance is "lumpy." Yet this is precisely what Kahneman then goes on to do.

The problem here is that Kahneman's large effects are a function of his search for "systematic" biases, cases where an answer is so obviously wrong it should never occur as it is viewed as a violation of basic logic. However, as we have reviewed extensively, viewing this as a systematic bias ignores that there are many possible explanations of why subjects respond as they do related to the conditions of the studies themselves including the use of probabilistic as opposed to frequentist language, violating conversational conventions, assuming that base rates must be accounted for, the BS design, and so forth. There is no question if these issues are mitigated the effect sizes shrinks dramatically if they don't disappear altogether. Kahneman's typical response, that modifying the conditions triggers a "slow" as opposed to "fast" response tells us nothing as a "slow" system response seems to be defined here as any response out of sync with Kahneman's theory. The seemingly large effect sizes allow a lack of attention to replication under different conditions. These deceptively simple studies give the illusion that replication is fairly simple and can be done in any undergraduate psychology class.

But simply replicating studies identically when working with large effect sizes is not always useful. Sometimes it can be worthwhile because, surprisingly, psychologists often assume that given certain p values, replication of findings will almost always occur (e.g., $p > .05$ = 95 percent chance of replication), thus ignoring the role of chance and error in all forms of sampling. Again, this is actually a finding of Kahneman and Tversky's early work. In the case of large effects, especially if they are suspect (e.g., are so many people really "irrational"?), a useful strategy is to *modify conditions so as to determine the limits of the findings*. This point is especially relevant when applied to Kahneman's work, where findings tend to easily replicate, and is in contrast with the great majority of psychological research with tiny effect sizes, where one would not expect findings to replicate as often.

The fact that Kahneman's popularized findings, for the most part, seems immune to falsification or even specification suggests their influence might be a sociological and psychological phenomenon, maybe one that is just as important as the findings themselves. Kahneman and his students have developed a new way to do psychology, and no specific criticisms will alter the investment many have in his approach. He is the founder of a school, not unlike Darwin and Freud. He has helped to create an accessible form of hybrid between experiment and anecdote, basic and applied, and academic and popular. It is one that has seemed to turn psychology into a respectable science once again, all the while selling tons of popular psychology books.

The accolades Kahneman receives from his peers testify to the fact that, for many of them, he reinvented psychology. Psychologically, Kahneman's message of pervasive irrationality resonates as Freud's critique of reason did in the early twentieth century and Skinner's did in the mid-century. Generalizations tend to be subject to less scrutiny when they confirm beliefs that already exist and this case is no exception. Dan Ariely describes the essence of this generalization well on his blog when he writes that "from a behavioral economics perspective we are fallible, not that smart, and often irrational. We are more like Homer Simpson than Superman."

Ignoring the context in this type of research can lead to confusion between the world of experiment and the world people actually inhabit. Kahneman is probably correct about people's general confusion around certain types of deductive reasoning, especially those that involve probability, but one does not need an experiment to see that. Kahneman himself readily admits that he doesn't always do, what he terms, "elaborate" analyses but insists that the original, simplified problems are more "charming" (Kahneman and Fredrick, 2001, p. 81). This means he has a theory of human behavior, though not a very extensive one, and that it is demonstrated in dramatic illustrations. He is proposing that what happens there is prevalent in the broader population. This is because these biases are pervasive in everyday life, even "built" into the brain itself. Yet, it is still hard to see on what basis Kahneman and his colleagues can make this leap.

Sometimes, too much successful replication means one has ignored the subtleties of the phenomena at hand. The conditions are not really being controlled and there is little attempt at real randomization. This does not mean that the findings are worthless but only that the types of generalizations one finds in popular psychology versions of this work are not especially reliable given that one cannot depend on the findings given slight alterations in the context. Sometimes, the language of method in psychology helps to elide the context entirely. Simply describing the effects of a treatment rather than the effects of a treatment-setting combination communicates to the audience who the real agent is thought to be (Cronbach, 1986, p. 94). In this case, it is the "bias" that does all the work. It is likely, as we have discussed, that Kahneman's large effect sizes are a consequence of the way problems are "framed." The real work of experimental psychology is the work around randomization, of people, groups, and conditions, and this tends to receive virtually no mention in this variant of popular/academic psychology except, ironically, as a "bias" of generalizing from a limited sample.

Psychologists working in the biases tradition find generalization easy and convincing because they seem to be able to provide their readers with many resonant examples of these "flaws" in thinking. They make great stories. Throw in a couple of clever observations about people and one has a bestselling work of popular psychology. Again, the problem is not so much Kahneman's specific findings, some of which are interesting, even unexpected at times, but the inferences he and others make from them. In fact, as we will argue, in a basic sense people do struggle with probabilistic concepts. This is especially true of psychologists. Calling it a "bias" is uninteresting because the phenomenon is context-specific, but even more importantly, it reveals nothing about the actual cognitive processes involved in these forms of confusion.

Jerome Kagan (1998) offers useful advice as he examines diverse referents of the term "fear" in psychology: Always specify type of stimulus (or agent), particular situation, and source of evidence. In the end, whether or not humans are fundamentally rational or not will not be settled via experimental findings. There are quite a few researchers in the field working to expand the conditions under which these problems are studied, but their work doesn't seem to alter the writings of pop psychology works (Evans, 2013). The most valuable findings of Kahneman and his students are those that are themselves stimulus, situation, and evidence specific, like the fact that researchers tend to struggle with sample size or that gamblers in certain contexts focus more on minimizing losses than maximizing gains. The least valuable are those that purport to identify universal biases in human thinking and develop post-hoc just-so evolutionary stories that exceed available evidence about why this must be so.

Chapter Three

Fast Systems and Unconscious Cognition

It seems fairly straightforward that the functions and activities that compose the mind sometimes take place outside of awareness. Historically, this position has long been associated with Freud and, not surprisingly, it is a position experimental psychologists have long been skeptical of. No doubt, Freud's methods added fuel to their critical fire. One standard criticism of Freud over the years is that he took this obvious fact about mind and mystified it by referring to these processes as "unconscious" or, worse still, "repressed" and built an entire theory of mind around it (Webster, 1995). Skinner (1954) took a position more extreme than most and compared the idea of unconscious processes to the theory of phlogiston and, while sympathetic to Freud's determinism, thought it best to throw out the middleman and focus directly on the relationship between stimulus and response. Yet in a surprising turn of events, the once-disparaged notion of unconsciousness has been resurgent in cognitive psychology. And this turn has influenced recent pop psychology in the cognitive tradition, especially in the case of the writings of Kahneman and his students.

Kahneman's notion of two systems of cognition, implied in the title *Thinking, Fast and Slow* (2011), makes the case for unconscious cognitive processes quite directly. Authors in the biases tradition typically distinguish between one system of thought (S1) that is described alternatively as fast, automatic, intuitive, associative, or unconscious, and a second system (S2) that is careful, deliberate, rational, and conscious. This has been translated into popular variants that, more often than not, encourage people to trust this type of fast thinking (e.g., Gigerenzer, 2007; Gladwell, 2005), though sometimes warn people of its dangers (e.g., Kahneman, 2011). The case for a system 1 and a system 2 is often framed in evolutionary terms, with S1 being the more "primitive" one. Though not always acknowledged, these notions are descended from certain nineteenth-century arguments that viewed the brain as a composite of evolutionarily ancient and recent components, with the ancient ones being more associative, or "reflex-like," and the newer ones being more rational and logical. Thus, in a broader sense, as we shall discuss later, S1 models often resonate with nineteenth-century reflex-based models of mind.

It is unlikely that such philosophical questions, which seem to get at the heart of Western conceptions of mind, will be resolved so easily. The methodological question we pose in this chapter is this: Are all of these authors who defend a dual-system approach to cognition describing the same thing? Do terms like "intuition" and "unconscious" have the same referents across various writers? Do those referents change when talk of unconsciousness enters popular psychology? As we shall argue, these questions are related to the more basic doctrine of operationalism in psychology, which, though mostly rejected on an explicit level, continues to create problems in the field. Talk of a new unconscious offers a perfect opportunity to consider these issues and focus on one of the ways in which psychology differs fundamentally from the so-called hard sciences: Psychologists do not always share the same referents across sub-fields, yet talk as if they do, especially in popular variants.

POPULAR VARIANTS

According to Kahneman in *Thinking, Fast and Slow* (2011), the distinctions between the two systems explain a range of findings, including: why people see lines as differing in length, even if they know they are looking at the Müller-Lyer illusion (27), why hungry judges deny more applications for parole (44), how priming works, why people are more likely to believe statements in bold print (63), why people seek to believe before they question (81), why the state of "flow" works and fails, Zajonc's exposure effect (66), the inappropriate application of causal principles as opposed to using appropriate statistical thinking (77), like ignoring sample size, a.k.a. "the law of small numbers" (112), why a question like "how happy are you with your life?" is typically transformed into "what is my mood right now?" (98), why people confuse plausibility with probability (159), and so on and so forth. The list is quite extensive.

S1 is an associative "machine" and the two systems conveniently explain the centuries-old philosophical conflict between associationism and rationalism. In S1 "ideas that have been evoked trigger many other ideas, in a spread of cascading activity in your brain" (51), though contra Hume, this happens all at once. System 2 is lazy, busy, depleted, and so slow it creates cognitive "strain." Are these taken to be actual properties of phenomena, predicates of phenomena, or simply metaphors? It is not clear. The evidence for "strain" follows from the notion that S2 requires self-control and cognitive effort, and these demand work as they draw on a limited pool of "mental energy" (41). Again, it is not clear what exactly mental energy is.

Kahneman draws on Roy Baumeister et al.'s (2011) finding that S2 consumes more glucose due to the finding that those subjects offered glucose drinks after an S2 task tend to feel less depleted—technically, one doesn't actually follow from the other: Glucose can decrease the sense of depletion without being the cause of that sense of depletion! Daniel Levitan's (2014) popular psychology tract, *The Organized Mind,* offers a similar theme: Because S2 work requires more metabolic activity, make sure to organize everything in advance or one will be stuck having to rely on S1. In this case, this is not a good thing. For other authors, this would be a good thing (e.g., Gladwell, Girenzenger). With S1, one is at ease, more trusting, comfortable, and intuitive based—one "flows." With S2 one is vigilant yet less creative.

There is also the question of how a mind "knows" which system to use. Kahneman argues that assessments are carried out automatically by S1. Otherwise, he explains, one would have created a real homunculus—an S1 that has to decide among systems. But again, there is a bit of confusing logic in Kahneman's formulations. First, making a process "automatic" does not solve the homunculus problem. It just assigns human properties to automata. And second, S2 obviously cannot monitor S1 to determine those problems that require the intervention of slow thinking because the latter is unconscious and inaccessible to S2. Thus S1 must monitor itself. But if S1 is so error prone, how does it correctly determine the problems that must be rethought by S2?

In other work in this genre, these systems are distinguished by characteristics like intuitive versus reflective systems; conditional versus probabilistic; parallel versus serial; inaccessible and automatic yet universal versus malleable, controlled, yet variable; associative versus rule governed; and/or unconscious versus conscious. In academic psychology, as we shall see, studies are offered that make the case for all different versions of this dichotomy and try to offer lists of what belongs to system 1 or 2 in order to explain them. Lists of attributes, however, are not substitutes for theory.

The basic idea of two systems has found its way into many forms of popular psychology. This is a major theme in Antonio Damasio's (1999) mega-bestseller *The Feeling of What Happens*. Here he argues that much emotional activity and its corresponding biological machinery do not rely on consciousness. In other variants, this distinction is used to explain certain misperceptions of risk with respect to issues like climate change or nuclear power. The public is too reliant on system 1, while experts use system 2 (Weber, 2006; Sunstein, 2002). Sometimes the logic is reversed. Experts have perfected S1 while the public relies on the slow and less insightful S2. Sometimes, this is framed as the importance of habit; other times it means modifying habits. In other words, there is a little consistency in pop psychology about which system is to be preferred.

Another very popular recent example is Charles Duhigg's (2012) *The Power of Habit: Why We Do What We Do in Life and Business*. Duhigg draws on neurological research on rats to make the claim that, as behavior becomes habitual and faster, mental activity decreases. This is due to the work of the basal ganglia that operates independently of the "decision-making centers" and "stores habits even while the rest of the brain went to sleep" (15). Duhigg offers bar charts of spiking brain activity before and after tasks have been habituated, showing that the spikes decrease after habituation. As is typical in this type of popular psychology, there is no mention of what "brain activity" actually refers to—perhaps glucose levels? Is this excitatory activity? Inhibitory activity? Nor is there any defense of the presumed relationship between habit and decreased activity other than it makes intuitive sense. But in this case intuitive sense might be a problem. Actually, nineteenth-century thinkers from Herbert Spencer and Alexander Bain to Ivan Pavlov expressed very similar ideas. The truth is, we do not really know whether specific habits map onto specific brain structures, but given the complexity of both, it is doubtful. How do we improve things for ourselves? Intervene in the cue-routine-reward loop, explains Duhigg, by changing the routine. Edward Thorndike would have said exactly the same thing.

Yet another variant on a similar theme is Richard O'Connor's (2014) *Rewire: Change Your Brain to Break Bad Habits, Overcome Addictions, Conquer Self-Destructive Behavior*, but this time he sees two brains in conflict with each other, and given his clinical focus, borrows some Freudian language to explain this. Self-destructive behavior comes from the unconscious, automatic self, argues O'Connor, and unfortunately the conscious self is not strong enough to prevent this. The solution: One must train the automatic self to make better decisions, withstand temptation, see the world better, and interrupt reflexive responses (3). Sounds good. How is this accomplished? "Neuroscientists have shown that if one simply practices good habits, their brains will grow and change in response, with the result that these good habits become easier and easier" (8).

Neuroscience aside, this basic insight was one of the bases for the classical curriculum in the Greco-Roman world and the method of repetition was defended by Aristotle, Hobbes, Locke, and virtually every other pre-Rousseau-ian philosopher of education. Rousseau's valuation of autonomy led him to reject habit training, which he saw as creating dependency, as has every "progressive" educator since. O'Connor refers to Donald Hebb's often-cited phrase "neurons that fire together, wire together"—who didn't mean it quite so literally—and insists there is a one-to-one relationship between behavior and brain structure. This is about as much neuroscience as one gets in this work of popular psychology, as the rest reads more like a self-help book focusing various "autodestruct" patterns and what they reveal about unconscious assumptions (e.g., "mistrust and abuse" follows from the unconscious thought "I'm bad" [25]). In O'Connor's vision, as was often the case with Freud, the unconscious self seems awfully similar to the conscious self.

In terms of popular psychology, dominating the genre are Malcolm Gladwell and Leonard Mlodinow. Gladwell's (2005) bestselling *Blink* and Mlodinow's (2012) more recent *Subliminal* are still more examples of the new importance given to the unconscious. Mlodinow is a theoretical physicist who also publishes popular science writing. His first bestseller, *The Drunkards Walk* (2008), was more in the behavioral economics tradition, and focused on the underestimation of patterns in randomness in everyday life. *Subliminal* lays out a now-common narrative, where the "hot" unconscious of Freud, filled with repressed memories and sexual fantasies, has been replaced by the new "cool" unconscious of cognitive science, this time a superfast intuitive data-processing mechanism. The only residual idea of Freud's, at least as Mlodinow tells it, is that conscious processes are very much in the minority as compared to unconscious ones. These range from combining disparate sources of "input" into the experience of consciousness to categorizing those inputs for quick decision-making, sometimes leading to error.

In Gladwell's version, a key unconscious ability is "thin slicing," or the capacity to gauge what is really important out of limited experiences. Too much information, argues Gladwell, can lead to information overload, an assumption he derives from the psychology of implicit cognition. In fact, Gladwell's book reviews most of the findings we will shortly discuss, though draws far broader conclusions. He also never presents any of the criticism coming from within the discipline itself. His favorite findings seem to relate to the phenomenon of priming and the IAT (Implicit Association Test). He also presents anecdotal evidence from advertising, medicine, and pop music. This kind of intuitive judgment can be developed through training and experience, yet can also go horribly wrong, suggests Gladwell, as is evidenced by the case of Amadou Diallo, where four New York City police officers shot an innocent man forty-one times. While wildly successful, critics were less convinced by Gladwell's disparate sources of evidence as is suggested by a *Daily Telegraph* review claiming, "rarely have such bold claims been advanced on the basis of such flimsy evidence" (2/6/2005). Even Kahneman, speaking on the talk show *Charlie Rose*, criticized Gladwell for conveying the impression that intuition was magical.

The advice to follow your subliminal or unconscious mind has a long history in popular psychology writing going back to the mind cures of the nineteenth century. One of the most influential examples is Joseph Murray's

The Power of Your Subconscious Mind, first published in 1961 but recently reissued. Not surprisingly, Murray's portrait of the mind is not so different from that drawn by recent psychology. There is consciousness, the reasoning component, and a subconscious, a part that "accepts what is impressed upon it" (21). It is associative, automatic, and outside of awareness. It is also highly affected by suggestion. The good news, explains Murray, is that a "disciplined imagination" via autosuggestion, rather than "willpower," can harness the power of the subconscious to one's advantage. Prayer works, too. Reading like a synthesis of Christian theology, Dale Carnegie, Norman Vincent Peale, and Napoleon Hill, Murray's writing is certainly more reminiscent of Gigerenzer's optimism about intuition than Kahneman's pessimism.

Some psychologists have sought to extend these notions to new arenas. One of the original psychologists in the heuristics and biases program, Richard Nisbett, has sought to expand the distinction between fast and slow systems into a cross-cultural one as well. In one study, he forced his subjects to choose between formal and intuitive reasoning (Norenzayan et al., 2002). By asking a question like "is the pope a bachelor"—perhaps technically true, but intuitively and experientially wrong—Nisbett argued that his subjects revealed a reasoning style preference. He found that European-Americans tended to rely on the formal approach (S2) while Chinese and Korean subjects, when encouraged to attend to all properties of the categories, thereby exacerbating the conflict, relied on an intuitive one (S1).

This reflects a broader distinction, argues Nisbett, between Eastern and Western forms of thinking, the first holistic, dialectic, and context-dependent, and the latter analytic, intolerant of contradiction, and context-independent. Ironically, anthropologists made similar distinctions in the nineteenth century, but unlike Nisbett, they tended to privilege the so-called Western version. Today the pendulum has shifted and "Eastern" forms of reasoning are considered the superior ones, or at least equal. Either way the basic nineteenth-century dichotomy is left in place with Nisbett arguing in essence that Easterners are S1-dominant and Westerners S2-dominant. Of course, if the subjects are answering a different question than Nisbett assumes they are, say responding to conversational rather than experimental norms, then Nisbett's generalizations are unfounded. We might know this if Nisbett tried to replicate the findings with various modifications, but unfortunately, he does not.

As opposed to the case in his academic papers, in Nisbett's quasi-popular psychology book, *The Geography of Thought* (2003), he is less careful and is willing to link these distinctions to different ways of life, which sometimes makes for interesting points, despite sketchy evidence. For example, claims Nisbett, the Chinese lived in villages where they were linked into a network of relationships thus more likely to see the world as continuous, while the Greeks were less likely to see the world in this way because they were more involved in trading (35–36). This makes sense unless one takes Plato as an example of the Greek view. Nisbett naturally chooses to focus on the more "analytic" Aristotle. Plato was, in fact, quite "holistic." Nisbett also collapses any distinction between people from China, Korea, and Japan, and conveniently ignores the hundreds of different ethnic groups that compose these populations. Leaving these obvious problems aside, Nisbett never explains the equally compelling studies that find no differences between similar populations (Kutieleh and Egege, 2008). Most importantly, he ignores the context of the studies themselves and alternative interpretations of his findings. While Nisbett is trying to get at some broad differences in the way people from more "individualist" societies think as opposed to ones from more "collectivist" ones—a useful correction to Western-centered models of cognition—it is just not clear that Nisbett's methods are the vehicle to demonstrate this.

Kahneman (2011) is careful and describes the two systems as useful fictions. He warns that even though he is not supposed to, he will invest them with human-like qualities. These are not systems in the standard sense of entities with interacting aspects or parts, he tells his readers (what other types of "systems" are there?). But he finds the concepts are more easily understood if they describe what agents do, than if they describe what things are or what properties they have (28–29). Kahneman's admission aside, the problem with describing them as agents is not simply that he is not "supposed" to. His language simply covers the fact that he has little idea how these systems might actually work. Psychologists have long been guilty of investing various homunculi with the properties of organisms to cover over gaps in understanding (Ausch, 2015).

The postwar "functionalist" approach of cognitive psychology that established the heuristics and biases tradition in the first place happily assigned the mind the capacity to process, compute, store, retrieve, organize, and receive information, but they, too, had little idea of how these processes actually worked other than by depending on the computer analogy. Nor did they have any idea if they had any relationship to specific physiological mechanisms. While such an approach is useful to a point, in the end, these are capacities of humans, not minds, and certainly not, as has been characterized recently, brains. The computer metaphor made these assignments appear more legitimate than they were; after all, computers process, retrieve, store, receive input, and so on, so perhaps minds do as well? Perhaps the new unconscious is just another homunculus? Is it just a metaphor? Or perhaps a placeholder for what we do not understand?

ACADEMIC SOURCES

The contrast between S1 and S2 while appealing to common sense—after all, we all have the experience of being impulsive or careful and considered—might not be all that relevant when it comes to thinking. The distinction between primitive and advanced systems of thought as well as unconscious and conscious ones has obvious resonance with Freud's id and ego, and was a fairly accepted notion in nineteenth-century thought. It can be traced back to the classical tension between appetite and reason or the animal-like elements of the soul versus the uniquely human ones. As evolutionary thought spread in the nineteenth century, the distinction between the two was blurred, but also turned into a historic one. For example, the influential notion of a psychic reflex described a process that, at various levels of complexity, could be found in animals and humans. Furthermore, the notion of a psychic reflex prepared the way for a behavioral psychology that viewed all human behavior as more or less direct responses to environmental stimuli (Ausch, 2015). Cognitive psychology challenged this. But we now have a paradigm in psychology that seems to suggest both schools were correct all along but only didn't realize they were addressing different systems.

For much of the nineteenth century the notion that the mind was composed of distinct innate and biological faculties, most fully expressed by Franz Joseph Gall, competed with the notion that the mind was an associative mechanism, as described by David Hartley and Alexander Bain. Evolutionary naturalism incorporated both views: The mind was associative yet operated with inherited faculties. The most influential version of the synthesis was that of Herbert Spencer who described a developmental trajectory from instincts and reflexes to associations and finally reason. This model and variants of it influenced all major thinkers interested in child development for much of the next century. In other words, the notion of a struggle between an S1-like system and an S2 one was already well accepted by the time psychology broke with philosophy at the close of the nineteenth century, a struggle that was muted in the United States by the triumph of behaviorism.

But these ideas go back further still. Christian writers have long noted that parts of the mind are unavailable for introspection. "I cannot grasp all that I am," decried Augustine in *The Confessions*, struggling with the limits of consciousness. Notions of unconscious thought surfaced in the eighteenth century as a reaction against Descartes's attempt to reduce the mind to consciousness, which went on to influence British Associationism. For them, the contents of the mind were easily available for introspection. The German philosopher Gottfried Leibniz distinguished between minute perceptions and apperception. The former existed outside awareness, could influence consciousness, and were responsible for maintaining a sense of identity. German Romanticism took up this distinction, but viewed unconscious thought as linked with mystical energies in the universe and a guide for creativity and inspiration. Goethe claimed to have written his *Die Leiden des jungen Werthers* (*The Sorrows of the Young Werther*) while practically unconscious. A few decades later, Schopenhauer linked the notion of unconscious thought with "primitive" thought, creating a link widely accepted in the nineteenth century and helped to frame the unconscious as a reservoir of instinctual energies as we see with Freud.

In yet another influential line of nineteenth-century thought, the French philosopher Maine de Biran described unconscious thought as automatic and habitual in the early nineteenth century. Although critical of the metaphysical assumptions in notions of an unconscious, William James described a similar process, yet used the term "habit" later in the century. T. H. Huxley went as far as arguing that most organismic activity was automatic and that consciousness was simply epiphenomenal. This jibed with the notion that the mind was composed of, or at least began as, mind-less psychic reflexes, the foundation of the new psychologies of Herbert Spencer, Conway Lloyd Morgan, Edward Thorndike, and Ivan Pavlov. It was easy to make the transition from conceiving thought as automatic and habitual to conceiving behavior as automatic and habitual. In other words, these ideas have long shaped views in experimental psychology. Many of the current notions of automatic and non-conscious thought are not new at all, but reflect a kind of return to the nineteenth century.

Influenced by Maine de Biran, Pierre Janet developed similar ideas in his studies of the "automatic" writing of his patients, though referred to the source of these types of phenomena as the "subconscious" to distance his ideas from romanticism. These ideas went on to influence Freud where his "unconscious," termed such to distance his ideas from Janet's, was described as primitive, associative, inaccessible to consciousness, and a source of illness. This is more similar to Kahneman's S1 than he acknowledges, with the exception that S1 processes cause "bias" and not "illness." A bigger distinction between the new unconscious and the Freudian unconscious is that the notion of repression has been replaced with the idea that unconscious processes are simply evolutionarily distinct reasoning processes and influence behavior directly rather than through symptoms. Evans and Stanovich (2013) describe these similarities as "superficial" but that is debatable and might simply be a vestige of experimental psychology's long disdain for all things Freudian.

Still another nineteenth-century precursor of these ideas was the controversial notion of "imageless" thought developed by the Wurzburg School, an idea that Wundt strenuously objected to. What made the idea that there could be thought without awareness so controversial was that it called into question whether Wundt's method of the introspection of consciousness was a viable one. Such questions were dropped with rise of behaviorism, though retrospectively, Evans and Stanovich (2013) describe the work of Wurzburg as an S1 psychology. This seems correct. S1 psychology, or the "new" psychology of unconscious cognitive processes, does appear to be the heir of nineteenth-century S-R (stimulus-response) psychology. In fact, the distinction between S1 and S2 seems a convenient way to settle the post-Cartesian question of whether the mind is simply consciousness following distinct laws of reason and all that means, or yet another object obeying natural law and operating along mechanical principles. What the distinction misses, however, is that terms like "volitional" and "automatic" might not describe opposite things. Awareness or lack of it might not be as central a question as it is made out to be. We will turn to these questions later in this chapter.

The precursors of the new cognitive unconscious began to appear in mid-twentieth-century psychology. Early versions included distinctions between implicit and explicit learning developed during the 1960s as well as that between automatic and controlled processes in social cognition developed during the 1970s (Reber, 1967; Schneider and Shriffin, 1977). Although not necessarily an explicit area of research in the early years of cognitive psychology, as consciousness was identified with attention and short-term memory, there was a covert acceptance that certain forms of long-term memory and pre-attentive perceptual processes were outside of consciousness (Schneider and Shriffin, 1977). Yet there was still not much room for explicit notions of unconscious processes in information-processing models (Kihlstrom, 1987).

A related notion that appears to be resurgent in both academic and popular psychology writing and has historical roots is that of subliminal processing. One can consider the early focus on just-noticeable differences in sensation on the part of nineteenth-century psychophysics the beginnings of research into subliminal perception. Unlike cognitive approaches in general, psychophysics survived the rise of behaviorism. The notion of subliminal processing came to the attention of the public in the 1950s when a marketing researcher superimposed some unnoticeable verbal messages (e.g., "Eat Popcorn") on a movie screen in Fort Lee, New Jersey, increasing popcorn sales by 58 percent. Although never replicated or even confirmed, news of this ignited a panic over the danger of subliminal messaging (Loftus and Klinger, 1992). But by the 1960s, the consensus was that there was no methodologically sound ways to study subliminal perception, and research in this area in psychology dried up until the 1970s, when the new information-processing approach highlighted related non-conscious cognitive processes like filtering and executive processes (Loftus and Klinger, 1992).

Around the same time, Jerome Bruner (1957) began to study non-conscious perception, focusing on how expectations shape what people see. In one study, taboo words were found to be more difficult to perceive than neutral words. A few years later Reber (1967) distinguished what he termed implicit learning from explicit learning in part as a way to talk about non-conscious perceptual processes. By the mid-1980s, the idea of unconscious mental processes was used to explain automatic mental processes usually triggered by specific stimuli that did not involve awareness. These were distinguished from controlled ones that did involve awareness. Some of these unconscious processes were thought to be inherently automatic while others were once conscious but repeated so often they became routinized. They were a part of what was now termed "procedural" knowledge and distinguished from "propositional" knowledge. Thus, unconscious thought became synonymous with automatic, uncontrolled thought. It was knowable only through inference. A similar distinction was made in social psychology to explain the distinction between the attitudes people claimed to possess and their actual behavior (Frankish and Evans, 2009).

Another domain where similar ideas became influential was with the notion of implicit memory, that is, where there was an observed change in thinking or behavior as a result of a prior event, though the event was not remembered (Schacter, 1987). There had long been an unexplored presumption of unconscious activity in traditional memory research as items stored in long-term memory but not in immediate awareness were clearly "not" conscious. Notions of implicit memory led to a focus on the phenomenon of "priming," a phenomenon central to recent thought about unconscious processing. Priming is simply an effect where one task influences another. In one version of priming research, subjects are exposed to a task with content identical to a prior exposure and, although the new task is different, the results of performance are influenced, or "primed," by the prior one (Ferguson et al., 2005). Priming is almost always mentioned in pop psychology variants of these ideas.

Finally, yet one more area where the notion of unconscious processing has resurfaced is in neuroscience. The research of Benjamin Libet (Libet et al., 1982) in the 1960s demonstrated that electrical activity in the brain involved with action appears before people become aware of wanting to perform that action. In addition, work with various types of brain-injured patients has suggested that elements of consciousness seem to be split off from each other. The notion of distinct "advanced" and "primitive" brains, developed by Paul MacLean in the 1960s, describes the human brain as including "reptilian" and "mammalian" components. One could easily describe the "reptilian" brain as the source of unconscious processes. Further, the recent work of Eric Kandel, Antonio Damasio, and others focuses on several neuropsychological processes that take place outside of awareness.

Some in the field have seen this as a vindication of Freud. Drew Westin (1998) for example argues that Freud was essentially correct about five presuppositions: the importance of childhood in personality development, mental representations guiding relationships, mental processes operate simultaneously thus conflicts between them can be resolved without conscious awareness; development involves emotional regulation and a move from dependency to interdependency, and that much of mental life is unconscious. Westin is generous here: Most of these ideas well preceded Freud. Westin draws from much of the literature we have discussed to support the last claim and makes the case that psychoanalytically derived therapies have a much richer evidentiary base than competing ones including cognitive-behavioral approaches.

He also argues that terms like "the" unconscious are misleading as his reading of the evidence suggests that different unconscious processes serve different functions and likely have distinct neurological foundations. It would be similar to lumping all cognitive activity together and calling it "the" cognitive. Furthermore he argues, psychology, like psychoanalysis, must adopt a functional approach to the notion of the unconscious, defining it by what it does rather than what it is, an approach consistent with much contemporary cognitive psychology. Freud did not do this, argues Westin, because he was too caught up in the nineteenth-century notion that the unconscious was the repository of animal-like instincts, itself a vestige of the religious notion that humans have sin already inside them. This led to an unfortunate linking of unconscious processes with primitive ones, adding an unnecessary moral dimension.

Westin draws contemporary ideas closer to Freud by focusing on findings that Freud prefigured. One example is that of the kind of associative memory demonstrated by the phenomenon of priming. Freud clearly accepted the idea of an unconscious network of associations, which explained the rationale for the technique of free association. He also attended to the conditions that activate particular associative networks, as has recent research. Another example offered is from the neuroscience of pathology, where different types of injury effect patient's explicit memories but not their emotional responses (Gazzaniga, 1985; Damasio, 1999; Ledoux, 1996). Westin brings together an array of evidence ranging from the notion from social psychology that people overestimate their abilities (e.g., defense mechanisms and narcissism) to the finding that people can express unpleasant emotions physiologically (e.g., hysteria) as well as John Bargh's (1997) finding that motives often become automated and similar behavior is repeated without explicit awareness (e.g., the repetition compulsion).

One final example Westin offers, one we will discuss in more detail later, is that of unconscious attitudes. One widely circulated study found that black and white students matched on SAT scores performed about the same on difficult SAT problems, unless they were told this was a measure of intelligence (Steele, 1997). In that case, black students performed considerably worse. Even if students were simply asked to fill out a demographic questionnaire in which students checked off their racial identification, black student performance declined. Steele termed this "stereotype threat" and argued that it was due to implicit attitudes around test performance among black students. Westin views it as yet another source of evidence of the power of unconscious processes.

Still, Westin's synthesis of research is not without its problems. Unlike many of the other authors in this field, Westin does not distance his ideas from Freud's, yet it is still not clear why all of these cases represent examples of the same phenomena, other than the fact that they vindicate Freud's view. He wisely argues for a functional approach to unconscious processes, but is not willing to go as far as Freud in attempting to explain how they work or why describing them as "unconscious" is appropriate. Is the fact that they all occur without a person's awareness important enough to qualify them as a distinct type of process? Is the lack of awareness in these cases all a consequence of the same mechanism? There are not simple answers to these questions.

Since the line between conscious and unconscious processes is not always evident, it is not surprising that in the field itself there has been a debate about how broadly the notion of such processes should be defined. This debate played out in the pages of *American Psychologist* in the early 1990s. One influential voice in the field, Anthony Greenwald (1992) argued for a fairly constrained notion including only fairly simple and automatic cognitive processes like priming. Matthew Erderlyi (1992), on the other hand, argued for a broader conception, as a narrow approach limited the reliability and significance of such processes. Likewise, Debner and Jacoby (1994) found that the task-dissociation paradigm most commonly used to study unconscious perception—eliminating conscious perception in a first task and then assigning effects on a second task to unconscious sources—significantly overestimates the effects of conscious perception and argue that the category should include the broader class of phenomena possessing automaticity. Similarly, John Kihlstrom (1987) made this case and defended a broader conception of unconscious cognitive processes and this has certainly reflected the way the field has gone in the past twenty-five years.

Nearly three decades later these ideas have only grown more influential and Huxley's notion of an epiphenomenal consciousness seems more and more acceptable to psychologists in this tradition. By the early 2000s, there were three influential dual-processing theories of reasoning in cognitive science. The first by Evans and Over (1996) describes two types of reasoning: personal (S2) and sub-personal (S1), a second by Sloman (1996) describes a distinction between associative (S1) and rule-governed (S2) processes, and finally, Stanovich and West's (2000) version characterizes the distinction as that between automatic (S1) and controlled (S2) cognitive processes. Kahneman's model actually combines all three approaches without much attention to the distinctions.

Sloman's (1996) version, for example, recognizes a tension in cognitive psychology between a mind that is associative, parallel and distributed—like the brain—and a mind that is a processor of symbols, serial and sequential—like a computer. He also distinguishes between intuitive and rational models of thought. Each of these distinctions appears to incorporate elements of prior distinctions between primary and secondary processes (e.g., Freud), autistic and realistic thinking (e.g., Bleuler), intuition and analytic thinking (e.g., Bruner) as well as creative and rigid thought (e.g., Maslow).

The use of the term "system" is worth taking note of. In cognitive psychology, systems are typically distinguished by the kinds of information they work with, the rules by which they process that information, and ideally distinct neural substrates (Schacter and Tulving, 1994). The analogy is typically to a computer. Thus two systems imply two types of computers that compose the mind, handle different "inputs," and transform them in different ways, based in distinct neural structures. They are, to stick with this metaphor, two distinct general processors. They are mostly functionally discrete, but also have some distinct relationship to brain structures. This is opposed to the traditional view of mind, expressed more clearly by Piaget in this century, as a single formal-operational processor operating much like Kahneman's S2.

It also conflicts with another idea that has made its way in popular psychology via authors like Steven Pinker, the modularity of the mind or the idea that mind involves many independent processors that are products of evolution and functionally specific (e.g., language, memory). The question is whether the metaphor of "system" connotes a kind of organization and coherence with respect to disparate phenomena, which, in this case, may or may not be related. In other terms, what makes all associative cognitive processes part of a singular system? The same question applies to so-called reason-based ones? Why not focus on the functional relationship between organisms and the different environments they operate in order to generate notions of distinct systems? Why remain so dependent on this nineteenth-century dichotomy?

CRITICISM OF ACADEMIC SOURCES (I)

Over the years, the defenders of the "two system" approach have modified their views considerably. Keith Frankish (2009), for example, tries to address some of the problems we reviewed and argues that the "dualism" is better conceived as levels or distinct processes rather than systems. Further, this distinction is also better conceived as that between person-level reasoning (S2) and sub-person-level reasoning, that is, the kind done by neural networks and sensorimotor activity. It is an interesting attempt to respond to the homunculus fallacy and makes S2 more varied than in other cases. Also, argues Frankish, S2 is not a neural system but a "virtual" or holistic one, constituted by the whole organism, thus not a homunculus, though remains dependent on S1 for inputs and initiation (10). S2 is evolutionarily recent and it likely reflects the coming together of distinct parts as a function of cultural change. Thus it is both general and modular.

There is great value in Frankish's newer ideas, especially the idea that cultural-historical processes play a role in the shaping of thought. But it still leaves the fundamental question unaddressed: Why describe S1 as a distinct level or set of processes? Perhaps, this is a consequence of Frankish's evolutionary-assumptions that hold to a hard distinction between primitive and advanced processes? There is nothing that prevents "older" processes from being utilized by organisms in alternative ways to make them "advanced." The key question is why excluding so-called S2 processes from sub-person-level activity and vice versa? Why not make both differing "person acting in a context" level processes? In other words, what are the theoretical implications involved with such a distinction?

Other authors are not willing to go quite as far as Frankish. Stanovich (2009), for example, has modified his views to include two types of system 2 processes, algorithmic and reflective, the latter a higher order set containing beliefs and values but also thinking dispositions like open-mindedness and impulsiveness. In their most recent formulations, Evans and Stanovich (2013) have gone even further and argue that the term "S1" is misleading as it groups together diverse and autonomous cognitive processes, perhaps a concession to modularity theories, and they now prefer to use the term "TASS" (The Autonomous Set of Systems) and refer to type 1 and type 2 thinking. They also refer to the idea that type 1 thinking is always responsible for bias and type 2 for correct thinking, or that type 1 is fast and type 2 is slow as a "misnomer" (ibid., p. 226).

Yet these are points that Kahneman makes over and over again, as is evident in the very title of his bestselling pop psychology book. Most of those influenced by him continue to argue that a dual processing approach best explains why human thinking sometimes diverges from normative models but the differences between the "systems" has become so muddled it's hard to see why. For them, the key element of S1 is its autonomy and that it does not place a heavy load on cognitive resources, making it very much in line with recent notions of the modularity of thought (Evans and Stanovich, 2013, p. 236).

Critics rightly argue that the distinction between the systems is slippery and self-serving. For one, they don't seem to correspond to distinct neurological systems, as for example, the idea of a visual system does (Keren and Schul, 2009). Some critics see differences of degree rather than kind and prefer to describe S1 and S2 as a continuum rather than dichotomy (Newstead, 2000; Cleermans and Jimenez, 2002). Others argue that a distinction between automatic and controlled processes cannot be derived from empirical research but is assumed a priori. Still another issue is that supposed S1 or S2 capacities are not always correlated with each other (Keren and Schul, 2009). For instance, Moshman (2000) argues that authors in this tradition tend to assume a linkage between implicit reasoning and heuristic reasoning as well as between explicit reasoning and analytic reasoning, though one can make the case for the opposite relationships from some of the research as well.

The dual system approach arose as a way to explain seeming conflict among mental processes and uses differential responses to stimuli as a principal source of evidence. Yet it is just as easy to explain the findings using a single system approach, as Piaget, for example, did as he made the distinction a developmental one. At best, differential responses reflect dual sources of variance, though it is really difficult to know what those sources actually are. Such an approach is not really necessary. After all, Kahneman's original findings were widely accepted in the 1970s without any two-system interpretation (Keren and Schul, 2009, p. 31). Others in the field propose alternate models that are more aligned with current understandings of neurological mechanisms. For instance, Cleeremans and Jimenez (2002) describe a system where a dynamic consciousness moves back and forth across a continuum of graded processes dependent on subjective experience linked to each other and only enter awareness given certain conditions are met.

The point is that the two-system model is by no means universally accepted in the field. Many academic versions of a two-system approach have moved far away from Kahneman's dichotomous one, even though *Thinking, Fast and Slow* was published well after most of these criticisms were articulated. There is clearly something intuitively appealing about this distinction and therefore it is not surprising that versions of similar divisions go back a long way in psychology. It appears to provide a simple and practical classificatory scheme that makes sense of complex phenomena as well as a ground for compelling narratives about a conflicted human nature. The metaphor of system has both a computational and a biological resonance. Grounding this heuristic and biases work in biological and evolutionary themes, which the S1/S2 distinction seeks to do, appear to provide Kahneman's work with further legitimacy. Moreover, Kahneman's S1 reflects a broader acceptance of the idea of non-conscious thought in psychology, a real change from when such an idea was seen as a contradiction in terms.

METHODOLOGICAL PROBLEMS IN ACADEMIC SOURCES (I)

The term "unconscious" is extremely flexible. As we see, it can be a type of process, a state of consciousness, a description of a kind of entity or a place in mind. It also brings with it a range of metaphors that seem to make intuitive sense (e.g., hidden, primitive, and automatic). But the distinctions between habitual/automatic and volitional are not self-evident. Nor is that between awareness and lack of awareness. Very different types of phenomena and experience can be described using these terms. Problems like these are related to operationalism. How precisely are unconscious or intuitive processes and systems to be defined? What is their real-world referent? On what basis can we say that these authors are all talking about the same thing?

Just a cursory glance at what various authors mean by unconscious cognitive processes is interesting. Historically, there have been two broad conceptions of unconscious, the first as a hidden source of motivation and the second as simply outside of awareness. Although as Greenwald (1992) notes, the latter can refer to simple non-awareness or a more active failure of introspection. In the nineteenth century, unconscious processes described responses to hypnotic suggestion as evidenced by unintended behavior, ideas present in mind but outside awareness, this time evidenced by the unity of thought, as well as non-conscious instinctual responses to stimulation. Later came the traditionally Freudian view of the unconscious as a motivational system and a source of repressed impulses. Here the unconscious is uncivilized and perhaps even immoral.

Again, "operationally" it involved inferences drawn from performance, this time patients' talk about symptoms, dreams, childhood, and so on. The lack of awareness was not on triggering stimuli, as in the subliminal perception paradigm, nor on the effects of stimuli as in the social cognition program, nor on the cause of seemingly irrational judgments, as in the heuristics and biases programs, but on unintended behavior where the motivation behind the behavior was unknown (Bargh, 2005). Yet, the Freudian program and the social cognition program of someone like Bargh share a focus on motivation. For example, both might focus on unconscious motivation but where social psychologists see an adaptive response to increase bonding, Freudians see a defense against anxiety.

Bargh prefers to distinguish between the focus on preconscious analysis of stimuli, that is, stimuli that have not yet been presented to consciousness, and skill acquisition research on the processes by which behaviors that require attention become automatic. Importantly, the latter process is intentional for subjects and involves awareness, as they are trying to get better at a skill, while the former does not. Both these paradigms require very different operational definitions of unconscious processes. Both involve inferences drawn from performance: the former, on responses to weak stimuli, and the latter, improved skill on a task, inferences that, as Bargh notes, radically expand its scope.

Today's approaches tend to lean toward inferences drawn from certain assigned tasks. In the traditional heuristics and biases program, the unconscious is inferred from distortions in judgment as evidenced by incorrect responses to problem-solving tasks. In Gigerenzer's (2000) adaptive toolbox program, it is inferred from sophisticated "gut" responses to problem-solving tasks as well as seemingly innate priorities in terms of what to attend to. We can distinguish, in a broader sense, between new notions of complex cognitive processes in social and cognitive psychology like judgment, processing information, decisions without awareness, and older notions of perception without awareness in perceptual psychology, like those termed subliminal.

The preponderance of theories of the latter for a long time led Elizabeth Loftus (Loftus and Klinger, 1992) to describe the unconscious as "dumb," while defenders of the former view like John Bargh (Bargh and Morsella, 2008, p. 73) describe the unconscious as complex, flexible, and deliberate, at least as much as consciousness, as well as composed of several distinct motivational, perceptual, and evaluative systems. But again, are we then talking about many distinct things as opposed to various properties of the same thing? To answer this, we need to look at bit closer at how these theoretical terms are translated into observables.

In social psychology, one very popular tool for identifying and measuring unconscious processes is Anthony Greenwald's IAT, or Implicit Association Test. The IAT was developed to replace less reliable self-report measures used in social cognition research. The IAT is a computer-based categorization task that measures the relative strength of associations in memory. According to Greenwald it is easy to use, highly reliable, and generates large effect sizes (Greenwald and Nosek, 2001). It was originally designed to measure implicit attitudes but is currently used to measure all sorts of implicit aspects of phenomena including stereotypes, self-esteem, egoism, partisanship, and self-concept. The IAT procedure has its subjects quickly map items from four categories using two responses. A category exemplar appears on a screen and a respondent tries to categorize it as quickly as possible. The easier or harder it is to assign the same response to different categories is taken as a measure of the strength of the association between them in memory (Perkins et al., 2008; Greenwald and Farnham, 2000).

For instance, attitudes toward self and other might be assessed along with the attributes of pleasant and unpleasant as subjects categorize stimuli using these four options by selecting a specific key on their computer that corresponds with two of these options (e.g., self/pleasant and key 1; other/unpleasant and key 2). The categories and corresponding keys are then shuffled. The IAT is scored as a function of the average difference in response speed between the pre-shuffled and post-shuffled selections with the implication that speed is a reflection of the strength of associations (e.g., an association between self and pleasant). The more compatible the association between the two, the theory behind the method goes, the less the speed of associations will degrade between the pre- and post-shuffled selections. This is termed the "IAT Effect." Responses are then judged by whether the attitudes are "slight," "moderate," or "strong," again depending on the mean differences between the two selections.

Not surprisingly, there is little defense of these theoretical assumptions and instead the focus is mostly on internal validity, construct validity, reliability, and how to increase effect size. The one exception that Greenwald does cite is one claim in support of the "theory" is that priming seems to change the strength of associations—for example, showing an image of a strong woman reduces the association between men and strength (Greenwald and Farnham, 2000). In an actual study, the results of the IAT were compared with self-report measures and found that the fastest responses involved associations between self and pleasant items although correlations between explicit and implicit "self-esteem" were weak. The conclusion, implicit and explicit self-esteem are independent constructs but only weakly correlated.

Developers of the IAT have found many different nonacademic uses for the task as well. College students are sometimes presented with the IAT to demonstrate the existence of hidden attitudes. It has even been used in sensitivity training programs. In 1998, a website funded by the NSF was set up that invited the general public to unearth their implicit attitudinal preferences in order to discover if they had any unconscious associations that could lead to discriminatory behavior. What had been an obscure academic measure was actually made public through federal funding and this, no doubt, helped to further spread its popularity. Turns out, according to the site, about 75 percent of IAT online respondents discovered they had implicit preferences for whites over blacks and about 43 percent had a "strong" preference. Similarly, the young were preferred to the elderly (Nosek et al., 2002).

There was also evidence of implicit stereotypes about men and women. The site explained that these findings were either due to the fact that people are unwilling to admit the prejudiced attitudes they possess or that they are not even aware of them in the first place. It offered a very mild disclaimer about the validity of the results followed by a link to articles about the validity of the IAT. There have been websites that claim to use the IAT to fight hate and promote tolerance (e.g., tolerance.org/hiddenbias and understandingprejudice.org) by encouraging people to "learn what might be lingering in your psyche." By 2003, the IAT had been used on these sites over a million times and was mentioned in stories on bias on the Discovery Channel and the Associated Press (Greenwald et al., 2003).

Given all this support, it might be surprising to find out that there are some serious methodological and conceptual problems with the IAT and its measurement of implicit cognition, although these weaknesses are well hidden. For instance, one might question whether the distinction between a "weak" preference and a "moderate" preference is a valid one. Can this really be measured? The solution, convert the seemingly arbitrary (and ordinal) measure into an obviously measurable (and interval) one. In this case equate preference with time (Blantan and Jacard, 2006). Roughly, a change in speed from 400 to 800 milliseconds implies a comparable increase in preferential attitude. This is actually fairly common in experimental psychology as units of time are clearly measurable. Yet, there is little defense of the assumption that speed of response is a measure of implicitness, nor how the ratio structure of time maps onto the ordinal structure of preference. The obvious assumption is that the supported attitude is more available to consciousness, thus speeding up associations. But could one not make the opposite case? Perhaps discordant attitudes translate into faster associations. Maybe those respondents differ in processing time, which expresses itself differently in the pre-shuffled and post-shuffled tasks, and is due to the influence of a not yet accounted for variable?

The other measurement assumption is that the zero-point on the scale has meaning. In other words, the two ends—"strong preference" and "strong lack of preference"—are assumed to be polar opposites with the midpoint being a neutral state (Blantan and Jacard, 2006). Again, no explanation or evidence for this is offered. Developers of the IAT might at least have offered a theory about how this works so that it could be tested against some concrete predictions. Finally, as is typical in the field, the IAT is scored by converting individual scores across multiple trials into a standardized score. This gives the appearance that the score is not arbitrary, but there is no attempt made to link differences in standardized scores to observable expressions of preference. This would at least give the IAT a link to the outside world, however tenuous. Although IAT scores have high across-subjects variability, a plus for finding statistical significance who is to say whether the actual range of preferences is quite narrow? There is no way to know without asking these questions extensively. These are quite common measurement issues in psychology and we will return to them in more detail in a later chapter when we address these issues directly.

All of this is meant to indicate just how tenuous the evidence for the existence of implicit cognition really is. Now one might argue that the doctrine of operationalism permits a level of arbitrariness. To paraphrase E. G. Boring, unconscious cognition is simply what tests of unconscious cognition measure. Yet, unlike the case with other variables like intelligence that are defined by performance measures, there does not seem to be an extensive literature that either links this to other criteria or makes predictions based in the results of these tests. Moreover, Greenwald's language suggests he is no operationalist. He is a realist. He treats unconscious cognition as a force that exists in the world that causes certain responses on the IAT. Operational entities do not have this type of causal power nor, and this is key, can they be generalized across different measures. How exactly does unconscious cognition cause measured changes in the IAT? This is never addressed at all.

Similarly, when others use different measures of unconscious cognition they are either operationalists and are therefore referring to distinct entities, which is unlikely, or they, too, are realists, far more likely. But as realists they must explain how phenomena-in-the-world cause changes in the scores derived from their instruments and this almost never happens. In one study, for example, Evans et al. (2003) looked at implicit judgment in laboratory tasks designed as analogues of real-work judgment tasks. Participants were asked to predict the suitability of fictional candidates for a job given "ability" tests. The complexity of the task changed as experimenters varied the specific ability tests introduced for making the judgment ranging from relevant to irrelevant. Each test contributed a constant value used to determine the complexity of the task given how relevant they were.

Participants began in a learning phase where they were given corrective feedback followed by a period of no feedback. After this was completed, subjects were asked to rate the relevance of each test on a scale of 1 to 7. Implicit knowledge was assessed by calculating subject's revealed beta weights from test judgments and comparing it to "explicit" knowledge calculated through a measure of the difference between ratings given to relevant and irrelevant cues. Evans et al. found dissociation between the two types of knowledge. In other words, implicit knowledge seemed to have more impact on judgments than explicit knowledge.

Sympathetic critics questioned whether the complexity of the task itself forced subjects to rely more on implicit knowledge. They also asked whether waiting until the end of so many corrective and noncorrective tasks to have subjects rate the tests suggests that the judgments were not immediate but reflective, typically a characteristic of conscious judgments and not implicit ones (Newell, 2014). Thus the generalization about the prevalence of implicit judgment could simply have been an artifact of the conditions of the study itself. One can also question whether subject's beta scores are a measure of implicit judgment and whether the values assigned to the different tests in terms of complexity appropriately map on to meaningful differences in relevance. It is not clear that the participants did not have access to the kinds of cognitive processes typically used to make these judgments (Newell, 2014). In other words, this could just as easily be read as an example of the prevalence of explicit knowledge.

Evans and Stanovich (2013) have responded to these critics by arguing they are putting an unfair burden of proof on designating phenomena unconscious in contrast to that required to describe it as conscious. They argue that the S1/S2 distinction should not be confused with the vague unconscious/

conscious one because S1 can include elements of both. Either way, there is still the question of whether Greenwald's implicit attitudes task and Evan's implicit judgments task reflect the results of similar types of S1 processes. Again, from an operational perspective, this is a meaningless question as the procedures involved in measuring the phenomena at hand are clearly so different. From a realist perspective, we need to understand how these S1 processes cause differences in the variability of scores for both of these distinct tasks. While Evans argues that the cause of all this is the brain and the distinct neural processes associated with the two systems, that is not much of an explanation as Evans is not manipulating molecular activity in the brain.

In just a sampling of other studies, evidence for implicit cognitive processes include: attitudes following distraction (Dijksterhuis, 2004), use of advantageous strategies in the IGT or Iowa Gambling Task (Dunn et al., 2006), changes in skin conductivity responses, a measure of arousal (Bechara et al., 1996), responses to primed stimuli (Hassin et al., 2007), reports of the relationship between electroencephalographic activity and perception of judgment (Libet, 1985) and evidence of animal discrimination. Debates in the field range from whether implicit judgments are evidenced by deviation from expert norms or from average person norms (Thagard, 1982) as well as whether it is meaningful to link differential responses to broader cognitive abilities like intelligence (Stanovich and West, 2000). Looking at neuroscience, the inability to verbally reflect on a process seems to qualify it as unconscious as does discordance between affect and behavior. This is just a brief sampling. Thus we have quite few different procedures that claim to detect the same phenomena.

When turn back to popular psychology versions of this, the "procedures" multiply exponentially. In Mlodinow's *Subliminal*, for example, the unconscious is the cause of both, the fact that people with "blindsight" can still navigate hallways because of residual sensory information as well as unfair racial, gender, and ethnic stereotypes. It is also the cause of the seeming fact that certain typeface improves the ratings of recipes, people fill in gaps in memory in arbitrary ways, and that people seem to be highly sensitive to nonverbal social cues or prefer people categorized as "in-group" members. Impressively in terms of range, the latter finding, a classic one in social psychology following Sherif's famous summer-camp studies, is now refigured as a finding about the social unconscious. There are so many findings here, the book reads like a history of well-known psychological findings retold through the unconscious/conscious distinction.

Mlodinow frames all this as a lesson about the importance of context, which is an important point, but not exactly the obvious lesson of the disparate "findings" he presents. It is hard to describe these as "operational" definitions exactly since they are mostly expressed as anecdotes even if anecdotes about experiments. The book is divided into a common division between the "two-tiered mind" or "cognitive" unconscious processes on one hand, and "social" unconscious process on the other, perhaps simply an organization tool, but might also be a sign of the difficulties of bringing together these very different academic traditions, all operating under terms like implicit, subliminal, unconscious, non-conscious, subconscious—of which distinctions can seem slippery and vague.

A REVIEW OF THE METHODOLOGICAL ISSUES AT STAKE: OPERATIONALISM

How do these methodological issues relate to problem of operationalism in psychology? Answering this question requires a more thorough understanding of the role of operationalism in the first place. Operationalism, as we shall see, arose as a result of a problem. It was a poor solution to that problem and recognized as such but was quickly transformed into a methodological precept. Although conceptually incoherent, it still influences most types of psychological research, especially experimental research. To begin with, there seem to be two different definitions of what it means to generate an operational definition of a phenomenon in psychology, a "soft" one and a "hard" one. The soft one goes something like this: An operational definition is the identification of a specific and observable event or condition so that any other researcher can independently measure or test for it.

In a typical psychology textbook for undergraduates, for instance, it is usually explained simply as a description of the variables employed and the means by which one measures them. In more advanced texts, there is an acknowledgment that these "measurements" can require alignment with other measures, a kind of triangulation. These definitions are pragmatic but also realist. There is a phenomenon out there in the world and the operational definition is a pragmatic tool employed so that findings can be generated, replicated and eventually extended. We will term this the "soft" or realist approach. In this soft version, operationalization is typically presented as a requirement for experimental manipulation.

Not always made explicit, but important in the "advanced" variant of soft operationalism is that the existence of that phenomenon is indicated by other agreed-upon phenomena. It is a part of a network of definitions and procedures. This supplies a kind of ontological support to phenomena. Their place in this network gives support to their existence. This allows one to remain agnostic on the question of realism versus anti-realism, a question that would take the psychologist beyond the boundaries of science. Something like this was termed "construct validity" by Lee Cronbach in the 1950s.

The "less advanced" or basic version presents this as a requirement of all phenomena in psychology, in fact, in science in general, while some "advanced" versions recognize that something in the nature of the phenomenon itself, its "fuzziness" or "unobservable-ness" and the like require that the extent and limits of the conception of such phenomena be defined. Thus, while there still is a recognized phenomenon in the world, the conception of it has a certain arbitrary quality and operationalism will help to bridge the gap between theory and empirical findings. This sort of "deductive" operationalism is employed by most experimental psychologists as it reflects a kind of vague middle ground between soft and hard versions. In other words, one is not required to parse out what is arbitrary and what is real even though both are accepted as true.

In contrast, the "hard" version, which was how P. W. Bridgman's (1927) work was first interpreted in psychology, says the procedures of measurement *are* the phenomenon being studied. Here there is no knowable phenomenon out there in the world but there is only the one realized in this study and other ones employing the same procedures. This is not so far from saying, in contemporary vernacular, that the phenomenon is "socially" constructed. Despite the logical incoherence of this position—how can a symbol (e.g., the concept) and a set of procedures "be" the same thing—this was the position of many behavioral psychologists in the middle of the twentieth century influenced by Bridgman and logical positivism. Psychologists often gloss over the distinction between these types of operationalism but the differences between them are fairly important.

For example, with the respect to the unconscious, is it an artifact of measurement? A convenient surrogate for what cannot be understood scientifically? Or is it a phenomenon in the world that resists a precise definition? Is the uncertainty around the unconscious a problem of the limitations of human understanding or inherent in the phenomenon itself? Either way, is it a thing, a type of thing, or a property of things? Is it a noun, a verb, or an adjective? The softer version of operationalism views the imprecision as a function of the intersection of methodological limitations and a phenomenon that resists simple definition. The harder version simply sees that diverse phenomena have been improperly identified by the same symbol. It therefore views what is being studied as sometimes a thing, sometimes a process and sometimes a predicate of a thing or process. There is no contradiction there. This threat of endless conceptions of similar things was one of the most persistent dangers of Bridgman's ideas—although he did not see this as a problem—and this area of study seems to present a realization of this danger. Luckily, psychologists as a general lot do not seem perturbed by the epistemological and metaphysical confusion operationalism brings (Fodor and Charles, 1965; Lakatos, 1970).

Ironically, the original purpose of the operationalist doctrine was to get rid of fuzzy or subjective concepts in psychology, not use measurement as a way to legitimize them, which is exactly what has happened (Green, 1992). The ideas were laid out by Bridgman, and then adopted for psychology by the psychophysicist S. S. Stevens. But as Green (1992) notes, Bridgman's operationalism was a response to the revolution in physics earlier in the century. The collapse of Newtonian certainty convinced philosophers and scientists that they had been lax in ridding science of its metaphysical presuppositions. If Newtonianism could involve so many extra-empirical assumptions, then scientists must work harder to rid the work altogether of any assumptions that had no empirical basis. Bridgman, a soon-to-be Nobel Prize–winning physicist, developed the notion of an "operational analysis"—incidentally his preferred term as opposed to "operationalism" or "operationalization"—in order to guard against such errors.

By arguing that a concept is synonymous with a set of operations, there would be no residual abstract concepts that could disguise metaphysical speculation. All concepts were tied to physical operations similar to the way theory was tied to observational statements in logical positivist philosophy. This meant that there could be as many concepts as there were procedures for measuring them, especially since different procedures often yielded different results. This was recognized by physicists as the core problem with Bridgman's ideas almost from the very beginning. Such operations were to replace metaphysical concepts. Concepts not amenable to operational analysis were nonsense.

Notably, Bridgman's ideas were not embraced by physicists, who tended to lean toward realism, but did become influential with psychologists, who were also drawn to the "physicalism" of logical positivism (Green, 1992). Bridgman himself struggled to follow through with the "hard" version of operationalism, suggesting at times that there were better and worse operations and gradually modified his position in response to critics (Bridgman, 1954). He eventually took more care in noting that operational analysis was a necessary but not a sufficient condition for meaning and that his was not a method of "definition" as much as analysis (Koch, 1999, p. 372). In other words, operational analysis was a method for fleshing out concepts and guiding analysts toward meaning, not a method of bringing concepts into existence. Bridgman was not especially sympathetic to the behaviorist readings of his work and objected to the notion that "introspectional" terms should be tossed out of psychology because they could not be properly operationalized (Bridgman, 1959). He also came to gradually understand that operations are performed by individuals, and therefore, intimately connected to first-person experience (Koch, 1999). Focus on what you do with concepts, argued Bridgman, not just what you say about them, a fairly important point.

Many logical positivists dismissed the early variants of operationalism as too simple a solution to the problem of meaning and objected that the closed nature of operational definitions inhibited creativity in science (Green, 1992). Even as operationalism was rejected and modified by its founders, its doctrines were broadly accepted by psychologists, particularly behaviorists. The great Harvard historian of psychology E. G. Boring, in a 1923 *New Republic* article, had argued famously that intelligence was what tests of intelligence measure, reminding us that one of the central questions psychologists faced in the 1920s was the question of what it was that intelligence tests measured. His student, S. S. Stevens, was the first to describe operationalism to psychologists in a 1935 article in *Psychological Review*, as did Edward Tolman in 1936. Stevens then made a more thorough case for operationalism in the essay "Psychology and the Science of Science" published in 1939, still one of the most sophisticated treatments on the subject.

Edward Tolman, however, was the first to invert Bridgman's meaning and turn operationalism into a process of measuring metaphysical concepts and attaching them to physical referents rather than replacing them (Green, 1992). In essence, operational definitions involved the rejection of abstract concepts for their behavioral expressions. While Tolman's softer operationalism solved the problem of the endless proliferation of concepts as disparate procedures were regarded as different measures of the same phenomena, it reintroduced Bridgman's original problem of metaphysical speculation. Tolman and his followers continued to accept unobservable and fuzzy concepts themselves but settled on operational definitions as a way to study them. Thus psychologists could study drives, motives, and volition as long as they remained operationally defined (Green, 1992). Stevens, on the other hand, was more sophisticated in his understanding of Bridgman and tried to fuse operationalism with logical positivism (Stevens, 1939).

Tolman's soft operationalism proved to be more influential in the long run after the most prominent neo-behaviorist of the 1940s, Clark Hull, embraced his position in 1943. No matter that philosophers of science and physicists had rejected it, the spread of operationalism proved impossible to impede in psychology. It became synonymous with doing psychology scientifically, as Green (1992) notes in an analysis of leading psychology textbooks. Historian of psychology Thomas Leahey (1980), describes operationalism as a myth "that commands the allegiance of most psychologists" and seems to offer a security that "deludes psychologists about the nature of science" (141).

Yet the myth persists. In fact, one psychologist responded to Leahey's critique by accusing him of being obsessed with philosophy, which he saw as irrelevant, and blinding him to the pragmatic value of operational definitions (Kendler, 1981), a criticism that conveniently forgets that all research has philosophical presuppositions. In the end, as we see clearly in the literature on implicit cognition, psychologists often devote themselves to criticizing the operational definitions of their peers rather than questioning the idea of operationalism itself or the nature of the underlying concepts they study (Rozenwald, 1986).

According to Rogers (1991) one of the reasons operationalism was so successful in psychology so quickly was because many were simply looking to justify existing practices. It seemed to provide a philosophically acceptable defense of why psychologists were not able to precisely define what they were measuring, specifically argues Rogers, intelligence. In fact, intelligence tests adopted a "measurement without definition" approach, meaning measure first even if one is not sure what is being measured, wholly consistent with hard operationalism. This had been an issue for many psychologists for decades. Fredrick Lyman Wells already made this point in 1913, complaining that "we have been apt to develop handy psychological methods and then try to make them mean something, rather than to start from the things that are important to know, and trying to develop methods for determining them" (cited in Rogers, 1991, p. 222).

After the fact, empirical testing essentially allowed statistical analysis, especially correlations, the power to determine the meaning of terms studied. As we shall see in a later chapter on measurement, one effect of this was to reduce notions of validity to a "validity coefficient," defined as the degree to which a test correlated with a criterion (Newton and Shaw, 2014) as opposed to the traditional definition of measuring what it's supposed to measure. Essentially criterion measures became operational definitions. Critics termed this "validity by definition" (Mosier, 1947). Intelligence tests became a battleground over operationalism because it seemed an area where psychologists, in their rush to prove their work practical, had built an entire testing apparatus on a vague and perhaps even meaningless construct (Rogers, 1995).

By the 1950s, operationalism was in deep trouble in psychology and there were several attempts to save it. One such was Campbell's distinction between definitional and multiple operationalism, the latter recognizing that definition in science is the convergence of multiple procedures and sources of measurement rather than a single one. This became known as convergent operationalism or methodological "triangulation" and is often embraced by psychologists critical of the idea that there is a one-to-one correspondence between entities in the world and the procedures used to measure them. It is realist in the sense that these entities exist and pragmatic in the sense that it recognizes a limited capacity to capture them using procedures and measurement. In this approach, validity sits in the convergence of multiple measures of the same entity but also the distinction between measures of different entities.

A more influential attempt to save operationalisn was Cronbach and Meehl's (1955) notion of construct validity. The original construct validity theory held that valid interpretations of scores on psychological tests linked to a network of other theoretical terms and observations, termed a nomological network, required that nomological networks were supported by empirical evidence. Construct validity appealed to the positivist notion that theoretical terms need be grounded in observational statements. It thus permitted a fuller range of theoretical constructs as long as they remained connected to a network of other concepts, all ultimately linked to observable referents and supported by evidence. Thus, psychological terms were given meaning by the role they played in broader networks of laws, concepts, and findings. Critics of Cronbach sought to retain an operationalist notion of validity arguing that construct validity was irrelevant as the measures themselves, especially in the case of testing, provided the best source of validity (Ebel, 1961). Cronbach, on the other hand, viewed construct validity as a way to find validity outside of the measures and procedures themselves and by the 1970s his approach was widely accepted in the field.

The real problem with construct validity was that in psychology one could not find the kinds of detailed nomological networks as one finds in other sciences. The term "nomological network" comes from the writings of logical positivists and requires a precise series of relationships between theoretical and observable statements and the laws that relate them (Suppe, 1974). Setting aside whether it is possible to distinguish theoretical and observational statements, in general, psychological theories are just not that well developed (Borsboom et al., 2009). Cronbach and Meehl (1955) even admitted that psychological networks were "vague" (293–294). But as Borsboom et al. notes, nomonological networks in psychology, at least as defined by positivists, are not just vague but completely nonexistent (137). Thus construct validity in its original form is impossible. The fact that the term is still used suggests that psychologists have come to conflate nomological networks with a limited set of theories linked to some disparate findings. As we shall see in a later chapter, the doctrine survives in a more trivialized form where validity involves interpretation of scores and is a property of test score interpretation rather than tests themselves as well as a function of the evidence brought to bear on those interpretations (Boorsboom et al., 2009, p. 138).

With respect to operationalism, construct validity is confusing because the term "construct" tends to be used to describe both the theoretical term and the properties of a phenomenon in the world that will be captured by changes in measurement instruments. To introduce a theme we will explore later, measurement in psychology requires a theory of causality. It explains how the existence of a phenomenon or changes in a phenomenon cause changes in an instrument. Just as the use of a thermometer presupposes an understanding that heat causes levels of mercury to vary, so, too, the use of an intelligence tests presupposes a theory of how some constellation of phenomena in the world cause measured levels of intelligence to vary. While this makes sense when the term construct refers to things-in-the-world, it doesn't make much sense when the term construct refers only to a theoretical term, as one cannot measure a theoretical term nor attribute causes to it (Borsboom et al.). Theoretical terms are symbols for reality not reality itself. Data are manifestations of phenomena in the world, not manifestations of constructs (Loevinger, 1957).

In other terms, while the notion of construct validity implies that a broader network of theory and findings gives a concept reality, a non-realist position, the forms of measurement used by the researchers as evidence require phenomena with causal power, a highly realist position. The first sense of construct is conventional, pragmatic, and unfalsifiable while the second is technically falsifiable, measurable, and can be correlated with other phenomena. What we have here is a compromise that hides its contradictions, allowing a confusion of the way theoretical terms function with the way phenomena in the world function. Psychologists get to be operationalists when it comes to theory, thus work with any ideas they like, and realists when it comes to measurement, giving the illusion of precision. In the end, this allows the proliferation of shallow theoretical entities without a need to defend them conceptually. As we have seen, this is exactly what has happened with current notions of the unconscious.

Typically, psychologists are operationalists when it's convenient. In one study, Eduord Machery (2007) found that although conceptual definitions change in psychology, operational ones don't always follow. This is surprising given the widely accepted notion of "construct" validity requiring that the operationalization of a construct correspond to the theoretical understanding of that construct. Take the example of concepts. Today a concept is conceived as something like knowledge of a particular category that is used to guide action. In the view of pre-behavioral "introspective" psychology, concepts were understood as entities in consciousness, an abstraction created from encountering category members. During the heyday of behaviorism concepts were simply dispositions to associate category members with a given behavior. Finally, with the more computational approach of the 1960s, concepts became a form of knowledge about a class of objects things belong to. Yet, despite these fairly important conceptual changes, Machery found that conceptual understanding was operationalized as the results of fairly similar categorization tasks using similar "concept learning" experimental designs. Given that, according to the common understanding of the operationalist view, objects of study are the procedures taken to measure them, one would expect different conceptualizations of phenomena to translate into different methodological procedures, yet this is not the case at all. This suggests that although theories change with shifting zeitgeists, the ways in which phenomena are studied doesn't always change as a result.

METHODOLOGICAL ISSUES IN ACADEMIC SOURCES (II)

One of the most troubling long-term consequences of operationism in psychology has been the neglect of substantive theory. This is evident in much of the new psychology of the unconscious. In one key text summarizing recent work on the cognitive unconscious, *The New Unconscious* (Hassin et al., 2005), with contributions by leading authors in the field, one looks in vain for a coherent theoretical understanding of the unconscious but it is not to be found. More often than not, the unconscious is defined by what it is not: conscious, aware, voluntary, volitional, thoughtful, and so on. The other consistent theme in the volume is that this is *not* the Freudian version. This is mentioned over and over again without any careful analysis of Freud's actual writings. Again, this seems mostly an opportunity to describe what the new unconscious is not: hot, drive-filled, motivated, conflicted, and so on (Uleman, 2005, p. 7). Positive definitions describe unconscious processes as intuitive, associative, and automatic. But even this is neither self-evident nor defended.

Why is the automatic necessarily unconscious? The same is true of the intuitive and the associative. The answer to this question, however, requires an elaboration of the concept of unconscious in an extensive way, something few of these authors seem interested in. In other words, convention in psychology allows these authors to point to the effects of unconscious processes in experimental situations without having to lay out precisely what the concept involves other than through one word seemingly straightforward descriptions like "automatic" or "intuitive." Such a form of "explication" could only be acceptable in a field still shaped by an operationalist/positivist bias against substantive theory.

As Daniel Wegner (2005), one of the writers in this volume realizes, the new psychology of the unconscious must struggle with a very old problem in psychology, that of the homunculus fallacy. Yet, his attempt to diffuse it only makes it clear just how much of a problem it is. Who is the controller of controlled processes? asks Wegner. Wegner seems to think that the notion that more and more of mind activity is the result of automatic processes no longer requires a "little person inside the head" to manage mental processes. This controller, argues Wegner, is an illusion as he elaborated in his previously published full treatment of the subject, 2002's *The Illusion of Conscious Will.*

What people experience as agency or what has historically been called "will" is "a cognitive feeling, like confusion or the feeling of knowing (2005,

p. 31). It allows us to keep track of our activity and organize it into a coherent whole. It is not, however, the source of that activity. Our actions, at base, are caused by a "complicated set of mechanisms" (33) synthesized in an illusion so that "it seems we have selves. It seems we have minds. It seems we are agents. It seems we cause what we do" (Wegner, 2002, p. 342). It's hard not to see the resonances with the Freudian project when the ultimate ramifications of this work are spelled out so clearly.

However, the homunculus fallacy extends beyond simply describing minds as if they had little people inside them. It involves assigning properties that operate at higher levels of activity to lower ones as a way to avoid explaining them. It is a way to cover over gaps in theory. And one can find many of such gaps in the new unconscious, just as they once existed in the old unconscious. The old unconscious, or at least the Freudian one, as there have been quite a few, assigned the unconscious the power to desire, to motivate, to hide, and to distort. The new cognitive unconscious assigns other properties once assigned to consciousness to the unconscious: It judges, feels, attends, analyzes, and evaluates.

The new associative unconscious tries to get around this by turning the unconscious into a machine and assigning "evolution" the job of building that machine. Yet it still invests unconscious functions with those same powers—not to mention it also invests evolution, a way of talking about, at bottom, a passive filter, with human powers. The confusion here is that these functions—judging, feeling, evaluating, thinking, processing, knowing, forgetting, and so on—are properties of organisms not parts of organisms. There is a basic category error here. The mind, unlike the brain, for instance, is not a distinct entity nor is it a distinct set of functions but it is a convenient way of talking about the products of human activity. But neither is it is not something that can be willed away by characterizing it as epiphenomenal and a product of neurological activity.

The new cognitivists, it seems, have returned to complete the project of behaviorism in another form. It is no longer the mind that is the illusion, the "ghost in the machine," but a particular conception of the mind. Published the same year as Wegner's *The Illusion of Conscious Will*, Timothy Wilson's (2002) *Strangers to Ourselves* offers a popular psychology version of this thesis. While not quite willing to say consciousness is epiphenomenal in the way Wegner is, Wilson argues that much of everyday mental activity—judgments, feelings, motives—occurs outside of awareness. Freud was correct about this, argues Wilson, but his mistake was that he thought this was a consequence of repression and did not recognize that it was actually a result of adaptation. Wilson's message is similar to Gigerenzer's (2000) notion of an adaptive toolbox. The list of phenomena that follow, insists Wilson, has long been studied by psychology: lower order mental process occurring outside of awareness, divided attention, automaticity of thought, non-conscious prejudice, lack of awareness of feelings, pattern detection, selective attention, and so on. The definition of unconscious processes is simply those processes that influence behavior, judgment, and feeling, yet occur outside of awareness (Wilson, 2002, p. 23). Automaticity and lack of awareness seem to reflect what all processes in the new unconscious share.

But you don't have to accept the idea of unconscious processes to accept that much of what people do is outside of awareness. Shakespeare recognized it over and over again, as did Sophocles. An organism behaves as it does, argued the arch-behaviorist Skinner (1974), because of its current structure, but most of this is out of reach of introspection. Even Skinner understood something that many psychologists today do not. Behaviors often follow certain structures—whether anatomical, intellectual, or environmental. Skinner simply neglected that behaviors also create certain structures. It works both ways. This has nothing to do with consciousness or the lack of it. That is a separate question.

Wegner's critique of consciousness as agent might very well apply to the way people use mental talk in everyday life, but at base, he is setting up a straw position only to tear it down. Who could possibly deny that important activity—physiological, cognitive, affective, linguistic, and behavioral—take place outside of awareness? Freud's value was not simply making this point but developing an elaborate conceptual framework to explain how and why this works, whether it was ultimately correct or not. Other than terming unconscious processes "adaptive," this work leaves us little sense of the connection between the nature of the unconscious and the observable phenomena studied by researchers other than via vague descriptions like "automatic" and "fast."

In fact, a quick read of Skinner's (1971) anti-humanist polemic *Beyond Freedom and Dignity*, which challenges the notion that agency equals freedom, reads an awful lot like Wegner, Wilson, and others seeking to unseat consciousness. This, by the way, was part of what Freud sought to accomplish as well, what he described as his own "Copernican" revolution following in the footsteps of Copernicus and Darwin. Some of the evidence used to make the case that there are unconscious processes today, was used by proto-behaviorists in mid-nineteenth-century psychology to make the case that mental activity was simply complex reflex activity. Stimuli elicit responses without any internal mediation, they concluded. While the language of the cognitive unconscious is slightly different, the basic model is that of S-R psychology. The same is true of much cognitive psychology focused on inputs and outputs, IVs and DVs. And yet it is not clear what the term "unconscious" adds to the analysis. The "associative" model of mind here would have certainly been very familiar to nineteenth-century thinkers. Even if not always identical with nineteenth-century concerns, the new cognitive unconscious seems to borrow much of the basic frame.

Defenders of the new unconscious are not operationalists; they are realists. Still, they seem to have inherited certain operationalist biases against theory. There are undoubtedly some sophisticated conceptions of mind in some of this work intermixed with relatively naive ones. The basic issue is to describe these processes without relying on homunculi. Thought is a product of organism level activity. Thus, assigning various cognitive properties to mental systems creates needless confusion. Also, the distinction between the associative/automatic and rational, which is, in a certain sense, just another variant of the Cartesian split between a mechanical body and an introspective mind, is probably not best understood as a dichotomy. Even the notion of a continuum is misleading as, more often than not, they are not poles of a spectrum but moments of more complex processes taking place across multiple levels of biological, psychological, and social activities. The fact that, sometimes, complex mental activity can become habitual and automatic over time need not mean that "higher" processes are no longer involved.

If one conceives of the mind functionally, as most psychologists do, then it is reasonable to expect many functions to be complex enough to incorporate elements of both the associative and the rational. All of this thinking takes place in a context, and Gigerenzer is correct to call attention to the adaptive logic of certain kinds of thought. Though there is a danger of taking this perspective too far as well and turning the dual consciousness hypothesis into a distinction between evolutionarily primitive and more recently acquired forms of thought. This, too, is a difficult dichotomy to uphold, as it requires divorcing elements of thought from the rest of biological change as well as imposing a fairly anthropocentric scale in order to characterize the primitive.

If one conceives mind as a functional system, meaning that its properties are not static or independent but emerge through interrelationships between various functions, properties, and mechanisms operating at different levels of organismic activity—the neurological, behavioral, psychological, interpersonal, cultural, experiential—then we are left with trying to understand something that has no parallel in the natural world. The mind is neither a complex reflex nor a sophisticated computer, though it can sometimes function in ways similar to these.

Returning to where we began, where does this leave Kahneman's model of the mind? If his point is that certain activities of the mind occur outside of awareness, one doesn't need Kahneman to say this. If his point is that hidden elements of the mind consistently generate problems for humans in their quest to solve problems, then such findings can be useful, but quite frankly, it has been said by others in much more thoughtful ways. Either way, such a position must begin with an understanding of the mind appropriate to the twenty-first century.

Notions of the unconscious probably bring with them too much conceptual baggage. Why continue to fight the battles of Cartesianism and Freudianism? In the end, perhaps they focus too much on awareness or lack of it, as opposed to all the interacting components, organs, functions, mechanisms, and contexts required for various human-mind activities to happen. Moreover, the real issue with psychology as a science—contra Skinner—is not its unobservable referents, but its lack of shared referents. If the "unconscious" was truly a single phenomenon, there might be some hope as to explaining it. Imagine the state of the natural sciences if there was not widespread agreement as to the basic nature of its fundamental concepts like those of gravity or radioactivity. But psychology has never been anything like a natural science. Theories tend to be cyclical, knowledge is rarely cumulative, and similar concepts are renamed over and over again. This makes the doctrine of operationism a much more difficult issue than is generally regarded.

Chapter Four

Happiness Psychology and Uncertainty

What makes people happy? Can we find ways to increase happiness? These are just some of the questions asked in one of the more successful fields of popular psychology, and yet another area where Kahneman's imprint is felt, the relatively newish sub-discipline of "positive" psychology. On the website of the Positive Psychology Center at the University of Pennsylvania, it is described as the scientific study of "the strengths that enable individuals and communities to survive." While originally described as simply "the scientific study of happiness," it has become clear to most working in the area that, as with the unconscious, happiness is notoriously difficult to define. Early critics objected that happiness was defined too "hedonistically" and recent research has focused on pursuit of the "good life."

This particular definition is associated with one of the sub-field's founders, Martin Seligman. Other leading academic figures in the field include Daniel Gilbert, Mihaly Csikszentmihalyi, Jonathon Haidt, Sonja Lyubomirsky, and Christopher Peterson. All of them have produced works of popular psychology intended to spread the findings of happiness psychology more broadly. Still more findings from the field have been disseminated by a diverse range of writers in the genre including Dan Ariely, Malcolm Gladwell, and Gretchen Rubin, former Supreme Court law clerk and the author of one of 2009's mega-bestsellers, *The Happiness Project*.

In fact, it is probably fair to say that, in recent years, a consensus has developed in the field that the simple pursuit of happiness doesn't work. This is explained by the popular concept of hedonic adaptation, a "biologically" framed way of conveying a bit of the wisdom of ancient Stoicism: External things do not bring happiness. Just as humans adapt to their environment in general, so too does their level of happiness—a sort of evolution-ish response. It is probably also fair to say that happiness research often recycles long-held bits of wisdom from other religious and cultural traditions, especially Greco-Roman Stoicism, Christianity, and Buddhism, but uses more technical-sounding terms to describe them.

In terms of academic research, a great many studies of happiness psychology employ experimental designs. They have long been and continue to be regarded as the gold standard in the field. In the first two chapters we identified some of the possible problems with experimental designs related to context and operationalism. Because the context is so specific, generalization requires extensive variation in sample, condition, design, and stimulus. This is the purpose of replication and it is fairly standard in the natural sciences. It also requires one to develop substantive theory explaining the nature of the object of study and how it might vary in relation to other entities. These cautions should not lead us to reject the value of experimentalism. In certain cases, perhaps far fewer than psychologists would prefer to admit, control over possible confounds can yield suggestive findings about causal relationships. But this doesn't fully resolve the problem of induction.

There are two basic issues here. The first is related to explaining variation. When groups are compared, average scores will vary. Yet we do not know how much of that variability is caused by the phenomenon of interest and how much is simply random or error in measurement. The second issue relates to inference. How to generalize from sample to population? How much confidence should we have in the robustness of the findings? The current solution to these problems in psychology involves using statistics to distinguish between acceptable and unacceptable levels of uncertainty. Thus findings are conceived in probable terms. Yet, if Kahneman is correct about the fact that people struggle with relations of uncertainty, as we suspect he is, we can be fairly certain that stochastic processes will be treated as deterministic ones or at the very least, that they will be mischaracterized. As we shall see, this is exactly the case with significance testing in psychology, tests designed to express findings in probable terms, and this will be our focus in this chapter.

When one group is exposed to a treatment and another a control and means are compared, psychologists are interested in determining if they are still part of the same population, the so-called null-hypothesis, or if they are now part of different populations, meaning the treatment worked. This is the point of Null Hypothesis Statistical Testing, or NHST, and is expressed in probabilistic terms using *p*-values. The point of group means is to swamp measurement error without repeated measurement. The use of mean differences between groups is in contrast with much of the natural sciences, which instead focuses on extensive replication of findings under differing conditions. This method was first developed by Ronald Fisher as he fused experimentalism and statistics in the 1910s and 1920s and became dominant in psychology by the 1930s, though still competed with the "Galtonian" correlational approach we will review in the next chapter.

By focusing on the likelihood that data were generated by chance, NHST attempts to answer the question: How much "confidence" should we have in particular findings? One possible approach is to use significance testing to choose between competing hypotheses. Though it is a popular procedure in other fields, it is rarely used in psychology. Instead, in much psychology, one looks to reject the hypothesis that there are no "statistically significant" differences between the two groups, the so-called null hypothesis, meaning the differences were due to chance. Again, another way of saying this is that the researcher is trying to reject the idea that both samples are from the same population as the idea is, the treatment created a new population. If we can reject the null because it is too unlikely we would have found the differences we did due to chance or error, convention tells us, we have identified a possible cause of the change in the dependent variable.

Since the 1930s, NHST/comparing group means has been at the heart of the dominant methodological approach in all of experimental psychology. The psychology of happiness simply provides us with an illustration of this setup, perhaps an especially problem-filled one, but also allows us to understand the basic problems with null hypothesis significance testing in general. As we will discover, this approach was already well criticized by the 1950s, but as with operationalism, the criticisms tended to have little effect on practice. We begin with the happiness psychology paradigm itself, where it is not so easy to distinguish between "popular" and "academic" variants, and then turn more explicitly to issues of method.

POPULAR AND ACADEMIC VARIANTS (I)

The architect of positive psychology and still the most well-known figure in the field is Martin Seligman. Seligman began the research that eventually described the phenomenon of "learned helplessness" in the 1960s in an attempt to understand depression. He was influenced by the cognitive therapy of fellow University of Pennsylvania faculty member Aaron Beck. Seligman's controversial research with dogs, administering electrical shocks at random intervals until they became helpless, led him to conclude that Skinnerian conditioning was "false," as the dogs did not seek to modify their behavior even though they could. Instead they became paralyzed. Seligman (1970; 1975) extended this finding to depressives, who, he argued, had a perceived lack of control over situations in their lives. Later, notions of differential attributions were introduced to explain why some people generalized this helplessness to other situations.

During the 1980s, he turned from the study of helplessness to learned optimism. In 1998, Seligman chose positive psychology as the theme for his presidency of the APA, arguing that psychology was too focused on treating mental illness rather than promoting mental health. The term was borrowed from Abraham Maslow's *Motivation and Personality* (1954) and reflected Seligman's desire to find empirical support for the humanist themes of Maslow, Eric Fromm, and Carl Rogers. Since then, hundreds of mostly approving articles on it have appeared in the popular media, including a six-part series on the BBC as well as well over a thousand in peer-reviewed journals (Azar, 2011). Even the United States Army has begun to use insights derived from positive psychology in their soldier fitness program. In March of 2006, the *Boston Globe* reported that a course in positive psychology had become the single most popular course at Harvard.

Seligman and Mihaly Csikszentmihalyi (2000) first defined positive psychology as "the scientific study of positive human functioning and flourishing on multiple levels that include the biological, personal, relational, institutional, cultural and global dimensions of life." The IPPA (International Positive Psychology Association) was established in 2007 to promote research in and the application of positive psychology. Disturbed by the "negative" focus of the DSM, in 2004, Seligman decided to develop a "positive" counterpart, which he published with Christopher Peterson as *Character Strengths and Virtues*. Recently Seligman (2011) has advocated "PERMA" as the path to the good life. It refers to <u>P</u>ositive emotions, <u>E</u>ngagement, <u>R</u>elationships, <u>M</u>eaning, and <u>A</u>chievement. It's hard to miss the resonance with Abraham Maslow here, and Seligman readily acknowledges this influence along with other members of the Human Potential Movement of the 1960s, ancient stoicism, and Buddhism. Still, some have argued that there are key differences between humanist and positive psychology including that the former used qualitative methods, was less scientific, and was less interested in discovering an unchanging human nature (Waterman, 2013).

One of Seligman's key sources of evidence in terms of the importance of optimism is his prior research into "learned helplessness," which is associated with a pessimistic explanatory style (2006, p. 15). These "styles," by which one explains events to oneself, are habits of thought developed in childhood (44). For Seligman, a key characteristic possessed by optimists is persistence (2006, p. 101). While optimists persist, pessimists give up. Seligman (2006, pp. 150–152) cites a Princeton-Penn Longitudinal Study where subjects assessed as optimists by the ASQ (Attributional Style Questionnaire) before going to college did much better than pessimists by the end of their first semester compared to what one would have expected given past grades and SAT scores. In other words, optimists exceeded expectations more than pessimists. In general, Seligman's (2006; 2007) "self-help" pop psychology writings make two basic points. First, "authentic" happiness, to be distinguished from the pursuit of pleasure, is achieved by developing positive personality traits reflecting "signature" strengths. Second, such happiness is achieved by developing an optimistic attitude toward self and events. Happiness is defined as "positive" feelings about the past and present (e.g., satisfaction, serenity, hope, etc.) in the context of activities that generate those feelings (2007, p. 267).

Two assumptions in Seligman's pop psychology stand out. People have some level of conscious control over their personality traits, attitudes, and even on some level feelings, as well as that people's attitudes can be characterized as "positive" or "negative." These assumptions are not ones that can be tested via research, as they preexist it, and offer critics easy targets. For instance, in *The Positive Power of Negative Thinking*, Julie Norem (2001) makes the fairly obvious point that pessimists can be happy and successful as well, but to be fair to Seligman, even he acknowledges that "mild pessimism has its uses" (2007, p. 7). The problem, Seligman explains, is the kind of habitual pessimism that says misfortune is always one's fault. Yet another typical line of criticism concerns the implicit value judgments in terms like "positive" and "pessimist." Attitudes like these are better understood as relational, both to other people and to other elements of self (Goldie, 2002). Jonathan Haidt has acknowledged many of these criticisms (Gable and Haidt, 2005), but the basic orientation of positive psychology has changed little as a result, which is not surprising given its success.

It is worth noting that Seligman's basic assumption about consciously shifting one's attitude seems very much out-of-sync with the implicit cognition research we reviewed earlier whose point was that many traits, attitudes, feelings, and the like, operate outside awareness. Moreover, the faith in a positive attitude seems to go against the very basic sensibilities of the biases of tradition, much more pessimistic about what humans are capable of. Although these two distinct traditions often borrow each other's findings, they seem to have very different ideas about human nature.

At times, Seligman seems to suggest that learned helplessness is associated with depression, while at other times he suggests learned helplessness is depression. There is similar lexical ambiguity with pessimism, which is sometimes associated with learned helplessness and depression, while at other times Seligman uses all three terms interchangeably. Despite this confusion, some of this certainly seems plausible. Even classically trained Freudians would likely accept that depressives have overly pessimistic evaluations of self and world, except that they would view this as a symptom rather than cause. In his popular psychology bestseller, *Learned Optimism*, Seligman goes a step further and offers example after example where various interventions have trained people to think optimistically. They tend to have a cognitive-therapy feel to them, evidence of Beck's influence. Seligman himself is very optimistic about the power to change attitudes saying, "One of the most significant findings in psychology over the last twenty years is that individuals can choose the way they think" (2006, p. 8). There are no cited studies here so it is not clear what findings he is referring to. It is certainly one of the foundational assumptions of CBT. It also resonates with nineteenth-century mind-cure therapies. Yet when Seligman makes claims like "optimists catch fewer infectious diseases than pessimists" (14), it's not hard to see why some don't take him seriously.

One of the means to change attitude offered by positive psychology involves expressing one's signature strengths in absorbing activities—what has also been termed "flow." Seligman (2007) has identified twenty-four signature strengths and has grouped them into six core virtues: wisdom, courage, humanity, justice, temperance, and transcendence. He views these as universal and argues that they appear across various philosophical and religious traditions. Jonathan Haidt (2006) goes as far as saying that these traditional values have found new life in Seligman. Expressing these in daily life, argues Seligman, will generate more happiness. He even suggests employers should reconfigure work in these terms to generate more productivity (2007). Haidt advises people to give up on trying to change themselves by sheer will and work to one's strengths (2006, p. 169).

Seligman's "strengths" are fairly vague, highly value-laden, and divorced from any context. Moreover, Seligman's traits, attitudes, and behaviors are already linked in tight semantic networks so it's no surprise that they are correlated with each other. This does not mean that these correlations are meaningful. Applied psychology has long been in the virtue business anyway—intelligence, personality, mental "health"—these are all virtuous things to have in spades. Perhaps the most striking thing about the literature on the "positive" traits of positive psychology is just how culturally naive it is. It is one thing to value virtues that promote individualism, autonomy, and person-centered models of happiness in a culture that shares those values; it quite another thing to argue, as Seligman and others do, that these are universal (Christopher and Hickinbottom, 2008). Such problems are fairly typical in psychology, especially those subfields concerned with mental well-being, which tend to blur the distinction between the descriptive and the prescriptive, but they seem especially pronounced in the psychology of happiness because it does purport to mine other cultural traditions for virtue, yet it does so in a particularly ethnocentric way. And there is no question that positive psychology is prescriptive, yet the supposed ground in empirical research helps to disguise this (Christopher and Hickinbottom, 2008).

POPULAR AND ACADEMIC VARIANTS (II)

Americans have a long tradition of both advocating optimistic thinking as well as ridiculing it. Some of the great advocates of optimism include the members of the nineteenth-century mind-cure movement, Mary Baker Eddy, Ralph Waldo Emerson, William James, and Norman Vincent Peale, while the great ridiculers include Mark Twain, H. L. Mencken, and Sinclair Lewis. A recent example of ridicule is Barbara Ehrenreich's (2009) bestselling *Bright-Sided*. She presents this approach as Pollyanna-ish and absurd, even describing an awkward interview with Seligman himself at one point, but then seems to adopt the overly simplistic attitude she rejects. Seligman himself acknowledges the value of "measured" optimism for some, calling it mild pessimism, which he suggests might be characteristic of prudent and measured persons (112) as well as lead to a more realistic attitude (111).

Unfortunately, Ehrenreich is not interested in this kind of subtlety. For her, American optimism is a reaction against the pessimism of early Puritanism, though, as she well points out, it retains some of its key themes: harsh judgmentalism and the constant monitoring of inner life. She also notes the interesting fact that some in positive psychology seem to have taken a politically conservative turn, arguing that religion and Republicanism make people happier. She also highlights the conflict of interest between Seligman's professed desire to promote happiness and his corporate consulting work seeking to create eager and productive workers (2009, p. 149). There is also Seligman's recent "rejection" of his earlier focus on happiness, which he claims is scientifically unwieldy, and turn to the study of "virtue," which according to Ehrenreich, only confuses his students who are trying to further develop his ideas.

On the other hand, Mitch Horowitz's (2014) *One Simple Idea: How Positive Thinking Reshaped Modern Life* reads like the anti-Ehrenreich. While they focus on the same history, Horowitz, a self-described writer on "alternative spirituality," is much more sympathetic to various advocates of positivity. Horowitz reminds us that nineteenth-century mind-curers, New Thinkers, and Emmanuelists all saw themselves as advancing ideas that were part of the new scientific worldview. For instance, they incorporated a notion of natural law into their ideas, specifically a principle known as the "law of attraction"—recently made popular again by the bestseller *The Secret*. The idea was that mind is constantly attracting things and through proper control of one's thought, the law of attraction could be used for one's benefit. Dale Carnegie had his own version of this: the law of accumulation. William James was sympathetic to New Thought, and it influenced his notion of the religion of the healthy-minded in *The Varieties of Religious Experience*. It also helped to shape the philosophy of Alcoholics Anonymous, which may or may not be effective depending on the research one examines, yet is certainly accepted by mainstream medicine and psychiatry. Horowitz also argues that there are several variants of positive thinking, from the "magical thinking" of the law of attraction to other variants that focus on reconditioning, conversion, and the more existentialist "meaning-making" program. It is simply not a singular phenomenon.

Critic of positive psychology Barbara Held, author of *Stop Smiling and Start Kvetching*, claims that the underlying message of the field is that all one needs to do is change one's attitude and happiness follows. Julie Norem, author of *The Positive Power of Negative Thinking* (2001), agrees that optimism helps but insists most of it is dispositional and thus not modifiable by positive psychologists. Another critic, James Coyne (2013), has argued that the field has moved far beyond what it can substantiate through evidence, especially in its practical applications as companies like FedEx and IBM hire happiness coaches for their employees. He is critical of the army program, which ignores differences between people and promotes the idea that people only need become more optimistic in order to be healthier, wealthier, and wiser.

Coyne also points to distinctions in the field, like that between hedonic happiness and eudaimonic happiness. According to Barbara Fredrickson in an *Atlantic Monthly* article, these are related to "distinct genetic regulatory programs"—which are so highly correlated with each other as measured even by Fredrickson as to render her findings meaningless. He also gives examples of where the field borders on absurdity, as again evidenced by a claim of Fredrickson's (2005) that, using differential equations from fluid dynamics, a balance of 2.9013 of positive to negative feelings was necessary to flourish! Finally, because economically privileged white people tend to do better on measures of the attributes valued by positive psychology anyway, Coyne argues that the message of the field for minorities and the poor is clear: Be more like rich white folks!

Ironically, positive doesn't always mean positive as positive psychologist Jordan Peterson (2011) shows when he borrows the Buddhist notion that "all life is suffering" to argue that optimists accept reality on its own terms. The point is, optimists just seem to be able to do everything right. An almost slightly critical evaluation of it even appeared in a July 2006 *New York* magazine story whose author, Jennifer Senior, tells of receiving a 2.8 score on an Authentic Happiness Inventory at the Positive Psychology Center at the University of Pennsylvania. Her response to being told that the happiest people live in the Bible belt and the least happy in New York City was to ask whether New Yorkers even want to be happy in these terms? Her conclusion, they don't. Unlike the case with the heuristics and biases program, criticisms of the happiness program are quite mainstream.

Fellow happiness pop psychology writer, Jonathan Haidt, comes directly out of the positive psychology tradition developed by Seligman though he is currently appointed at the New York University School of Business and was named a top global thinker by the magazine *Foreign Policy*, suggesting less of a clinical focus and more of a business one. Haidt's original research in positive psychology focused on the psychology of positive moral emotions. He has two *New York Times* bestsellers, *The Happiness Hypothesis: Finding Modern Truth in Ancient Wisdom* (2006) and more recently, *The Righteous Mind: Why Good People Are Divided by Politics and Religion* (2012). The *Happiness Hypothesis* introduced the dual consciousness model we discussed previously, describing the mind as containing a small rider—rational and conscious—on a very large elephant—intuitive and automatic. Haidt views moral emotions and judgment as belonging mostly to the intuitive and automatic elements of mind rather than the rational ones. He argues that people only later attempt to rationalize those judgments in one of his most widely cited papers, "The Emotional Dog and Its Rational Tail" (2001). More recently, he has developed the idea that there are six categories of moral intuition: care/harm, fairness/cheating, liberty/oppression, loyalty/betrayal, authority/subversion, and sanctity/degradation. He uses these categories to explain cultural differences in morality—they develop moral traditions around different categories—as well as conflict between liberals and conservatives.

Daniel Gilbert, unlike Seligman and Haidt, is more directly a product of Kahneman's psychology of biases research and is known for his research on affective forecasting. His mega-bestseller, *Stumbling on Happiness* (2006), points to three biases in affective forecasting related to happiness: the tendency to fill in details to create coherent narratives about the future, the tendency to see imagined futures as very different from the present, and the tendency to fail to recognize that negative future events will not feel as bad, or positive ones as good for that matter, as predicted. American college students in particular, argues Gilbert, are not very good at prospection. They tend to think they will live longer, stay married longer, and travel to Europe more often than average. They also believe they are more likely to have a gifted child, own their own home, appear in a newspaper, and less likely to have a venereal disease, drinking problem, or an auto accident (19). While people in other parts of the world are not quite as optimistic as Americans, they too imagine their futures will be brighter than their peers'.

While the finding that everyone seems to think they are better than average makes for a fun talking point, as does ridiculing American college students, interpreting this is not quite as straightforward as Gilbert makes it sound. Like many of the "errors" in judgment identified by Kahneman, the biases Gilbert focuses on tend to be removed from any context and the conditions under which they were created are ignored. For instance, the finding about college students comes from a 1980 study by Neil Weinstein in which 120 female students in an interdisciplinary class in a small Northeastern college were asked to compare the likelihood that an event would happen to them as opposed to their classmates at that specific college. The "optimistic bias" was a function of finding that they were more likely to see positive events as happening to them and negative events as less likely to happen to them, as compared to their classmates.

Yet, it is not clear how the students interpreted the question. They were given response options like "80 percent more likely" and "40 percent less likely" but most people do not compare themselves to others using percentage categories in everyday life, nor is it clear whether the bias was a result of the comparison itself or what the comparison might mean about something else. For instance, is this a "self-esteem" rating or a "luckiness" rating? While events listed like "having gum problems" or "having a drinking problem" (Weinstein, 1980, p. 810) can be described as "negative," a judgment about their likelihood can also be a reflection of personal experience, family history, or the way the question is interpreted. For instance, a participant might be confused about whether to base responses on rates of phenomena in population or whether they currently deal with these issues. These are also college students in a particular type of school at the start of their adult lives. It is unlikely that this generalizes to people in general, as Gilbert assumes. The effect size seems fairly large, but the choices presented are also fairly stark, which typically ensures large effects, especially given the small sample size. These are many of the same methodological issues we identified in the biases program.

Despite all this, Gilbert interprets these findings as due to a human need for control, so much so that humans act as though they can control the uncontrollable (2006, p. 23). For instance, people feel more certain they will win the lottery if they can control the numbers on the ticket. Gilbert's logic is so tight it's hard to see his rhetorical and logical leaps. This is great pop psychology writing. Start with a vivid anecdote, then take a very specific finding, link it with other specific findings, ideally divorced from any context, and relate it to phenomena that most readers will identify with and use that to generalize even further. Thus questionable interpretations are glossed over. Does the survey of college students accurately reflect beliefs about the future? Is the cause of the response in Weinstein's study the same as that which causes the increased certainty among lottery players? Is all this caused by a universal need for control? Taken independently, the findings are plausible enough, but strung together in a tight narrative, the argument becomes too seamless to reject.

The problem with prospection, argues Gilbert, is threefold. There is the tendency to assign value by comparing one thing to another—a variant of Kahmenan's "anchoring." Yet there are many comparisons to choose from; some lead to higher and some to lower valuations of the same thing (158). The comparisons people make today are not the ones they will make in the future. This is the error of "presentism": using a current standard of comparison rather than a future one. Humans have a kind of psychological immune system where we make the best of whatever circumstances we find ourselves in; thus we end up making the better comparison. Yet how much of this phenomenon is a function of how the research frames the judgment is difficult to say.

Christopher Peterson's recent *Pursuing the Good Life* (2012) attempts a more restrained pop psychology version of positive psychology. Peterson tries to summarize the findings of positive psychology, including references to specific studies, but present them as bits of advice. At the start of the book, Peterson provides a helpful summary of the basic findings of the field. They include the findings that people in general are happy, happiness is the cause of good things in life, happiness is a buffer against disappointments, other people matter, religion matters, work matters if it provides purpose, money can only buy happiness if spent on other people, eudemonia trumps hedonism, the heart matters more than the head, good days involve autonomy, competence, and connections to others, and happiness can be taught (5). It's not quite clear that these are findings as opposed to presuppositions, but Peterson goes out to defend many of these claims via research while also criticizing interpretations of findings he thinks go too far. Happiness, he argues, has become a human right and the effectiveness of positive psychology interventions makes unhappiness treatable.

One of Peterson's goals in the volume is to tone down the exaggerated claims of some positive psychology writers—he calls them the "stupid ones" (27). He correctly explains that predictors in psychology are probabilistic and that the relationship between them and outcomes is a complex one given that there is a lot of variation in psychological phenomena, a qualification one does not ordinarily see in popular psychology writing but a very important one. He also recognizes that positive psychologists have tended to speak to Dionysian values and have neglected Apollonian ones like moderation and self-restraint. Among his concrete recommendations: Enjoy one's shower, savor the small things—they bring more happiness and unhappiness—optimism is beneficial—but not Panglossian variants—and live in "heart" cities like El Paso or Omaha as opposed to "head" ones like San Francisco. In the former, residents have greater "emotional and interpersonal strengths" and report more "positive emotions and a greater sense of meaning" (107). My guess is that residents of San Francisco would beg to differ.

Sonja Lyubomirsky's (2013) *The Myths of Happiness* seems firmly in the "self-help" popular psychology tradition and is a good example of the sum of excesses in the field Peterson criticizes. Lyubomirsky covers a lot of ground, from Gilbert's studies on prospection, to Kahneman's S1 and S2 distinction—she advises relying more on S2 than S1—but mostly offers advice like "consider the opposite of whatever your gut instinct is telling you to do" (11), "appreciating" your spouse, spicing your marriage with "variety" so hedonic adaptation does not set in (18, 27), and being thrifty so one is happy with what one has (149). She describes these as "evidence-backed practical suggestions" (11) and says things like "empirical evidence suggests that being happy with less is not a fallacy" (149), though she does not cite a study but refers to "ancient wisdom."

She uses the word "scientific" a lot to describe her interests and work. Gone is Peterson's restraint, only to be replaced by vague suggestions typical of self-help psychology. Like many popular psychology writers, she describes her own research but then generalizes the findings into almost law-like claims. One example, to be discussed later, is her claim that happy people are less affected by the opinions of others than unhappy people, a finding that also seems to come straight out of "ancient wisdom," but made its way into her first book, *The How of Happiness: A Scientific Approach to Getting the Life You Want*. In the end, though, the difference between Lyubomirsky and Peterson is one of degree rather than kind.

CRITICISM OF ACADEMIC SOURCES (I)

Academic happiness psychology researchers have developed some of their own, unique methodological setups to study the phenomenon of happiness. One example involves the comparison of findings from Csikszentmihalyi's method of "experience sampling" (ES) (Csikszentmihalyi and Larson, 1987) to Kahneman's "Day Reconstruction Method" (DRM) (Kahneman and Krueger, 2006). It seeks to explain the divergence between how people evaluate their experiences at different time frames. When subjects are told to record their experiences every time a beeper sounds throughout the day (ES), as well as appraise the previous day the following morning (DRM), it turns out the appraisals of the some of the same experiences change. For instance, while the longer-term appraisals reflect that parents enjoy their children, the shorter-term experience sampling suggests that parents do not enjoy caring for them as compared to other activities (e.g., housecleaning). In other terms, people are not always very good at appraising what makes them happy on a moment-to-moment basis.

In a paper published in the *Journal of Economic Perspectives*, Kahneman and Krueger (2006) provide evidence that ES and the DRM typically reveal similar patterns (11), thus their divergence around certain activities like child care is notable. Despite the reconstructive and unreliable nature of memory, Kahneman argues that the less taxing and less costly DRM can replace ES. Kahneman (2011) explains these findings by distinguishing between an "experiencing self" as compared to a "remembering self." However, there is not a lot of theory here. There is the fairly obvious point, memory is unreliable, but other than this, what does it mean that people have these two selves? How are they constructed? How are they related to each other?

Kahneman relates this to a memory bias in the remembering self that he terms the "peak-end" affect wherein people focus on dramatic elements and the final moments of experience when evaluating it as opposed to the entire experience. He found, for example, that when colonoscopy patients are asked to evaluate a procedure after sixty seconds was added to the end of the procedure with no activity, they evaluate it as more pleasant as compared to those who are asked to evaluate it immediately, Thus, the lack of discomfort in the final minute changes the evaluation of the entire procedure. This explains, according to Kahneman, part of why people are so bad at affective forecasting. It would have been interesting if Kahneman had varied the treatment to determine what kinds of contexts elicit this effect, but Kahneman is interested in a universal process and not a study of how minds work.

Kahneman (2011) uses his DRM to quantify the time individuals spend in an unpleasant state/emotional pain, calling it a U-index (e.g., four hours of unpleasantness within a sixteen-hour period has a U-index of 25 percent). Kahneman notes that the distribution of emotional pain is highly uneven; some have it for most of the day, others not at all. Kahneman then compares the U-index across some everyday activities. For one thousand women from a Midwestern city, the U-index was 29 percent for their morning commute, 27 percent for work, 24 percent for child care, 18 percent for housework, 12 percent for both watching TV and socializing, and a nice 5 percent for sex (394). The U-index was higher on weekdays than weekends. It was also a bit higher for American women than French women with respect to child care, probably because French women do less of it, suggests Kahneman (394). Kahneman then leads the reader through the implications of these findings: Spend more time doing the things you like as, contra Seligman, "few individuals can will themselves to have a sunnier disposition" (395).

Unlike Seligman, Kahneman seems to be more focused on "negative" psychology. In fact, he argues explicitly that rather than focusing on the more nebulous goal of increasing happiness, policy makers should try to reduce misery, thus it makes sense to study it. But there is a larger methodological project here for Kahneman, as well, and that is to improve measures of subjective well-being (Kahneman and Krueger, 2006). For instance, economists often criticize happiness researchers for relying on self-report data instead of behavioral data that counts up what people actually do. Yet, the problem with behavioral data according to someone like Kahneman is that it works under the assumption that people do what makes them happy and part of the goal of his research is to question this. The DRM and corresponding U-index seem like a compromise, self-report transformed into measurement. It's clever to be sure, but what do the numbers really mean? Kahneman seems to take a fairly ambiguous finding—his Midwestern subjects are miserable for 24 percent of the time they spend doing child care but only 18 percent of the time they spend cleaning—and turns it into something fairly provocative.

Clearly, one can imagine very different interpretations of the similar U-index ratings for housekeeping and child care, if one accepts that it has any meaning in the first place. Do people spend the entire 29 percent of their commute in equal levels of misery? Commuting can be frustrating, no doubt, but is that the same as "unhappiness"? Do people only engage in one activity at a time? (Kahneman acknowledges this and allows for more than twenty-four hours in a day to measure them separately). Can I have a happy experience talking on my cell phone or listening to music while my U-index is elevated during commuting because of the traffic? Do people even evaluate their experiences in this way as they are having them? Still, it is not hard to see why Kahneman is held in the esteem he is. He has an incredible talent for describing complex phenomena in very accessible ways, yet retaining a scientific feel through quantification and using terms like "index." But assigning numbers when they reflect little about the actual nature or structure of a phenomenon is not good science, even if it is common practice in psychology.

Happiness psychology also looks to found correlations in large-scale data sets for findings, for example, the much-researched relationship between happiness and wealth. One well-known finding, the "Easterlin Paradox," named after economist Richard Easterlin, is also reported in Gilbert's *Stumbling on Happiness.* Gilbert describes Easterlin's finding that for people in poverty, money does indeed correlate with happiness. This relationship exists up to a certain point—one study proposes 75K a year in the United States (Ankin et al., 2009)—when the effects of wealth greatly diminish. Enjoying work, however, increases happiness more than spending money does. Gilbert thus recommends that people who are not in poverty, presumably the audience of the book, find jobs they enjoy.

And yet, other published studies came to the opposite conclusion. Notably, the correlation between increasing GDP on a national level and increasing levels of happiness continues well past the achievement of middle class levels (Stevenson and Wolfers, 2008). What can this mean? Turns out, it depends on which data you include and how you analyze it. These methodological questions have turned into symbols for underlying political positions—liberal economists/psychologists support Easterlin, thus argue that governments must do more to support happiness, while conservatives and free marketers argue that focusing economic growth is enough, as happiness will follow. Studies in this area have produced a range of findings, often contradictory, and few seem to recognize this is probably due to chance and sampling more than anything else, especially since large data sets can lead to interpretations that make too much out of small yet statistically significant effects.

According to various happiness studies, there are a whole bunch of things that are supposed to bring happiness but don't: education, IQ, parenting, liberalism. Then there are the things that do: marriage, extraversion, strong relationships, attractiveness, moderate alcohol consumption, weather, religion, spirituality, and the country you live in. Because happiness is relative, being a slum dweller in Kolkata is better than being homeless in Fresno. The consensus is that happiness returns to a kind of baseline that, according to Sonia Lyubomirsky (2007), is partially set by genetics. Genes explain 30–40 percent of the variance between individuals, she claims. Exactly how she comes to this claim is unclear. How then does one become happy? Move to the slums of Kolkata? Spend more or drink less? Gene therapy? Medication?

These, of course, are the wrong questions. The better question is, what exactly are these researchers studying? Can one really compare the same measures across such different contexts/samples? Does the term "happiness" or similar ones mean the same thing when translated into different languages? Once again, we cannot easily separate the context of measuring happiness from the outcomes of those measurements. Nor can we treat the various approaches to operationalizing happiness as if they describe the identical phenomena, especially given the range of happiness indicators, including results from large-scale surveys, results from experience sampling, self-report ratings, Kahneman's day reconstruction method, brain imaging, and hormone sampling. Surveys are notoriously "blunt" instruments for capturing these type of phenomena, given they require that the participant set the questions into a context so they can be meaningful. Since not much of a context is provided, participants typically choose one for themselves.

Another important issue is the fundamental difference between a variable like income, which can theoretically rise forever, and a variable like happiness, which presumably cannot. In fact, the focus on correlations with recognizable variables allows happiness researchers to gloss over the fact that there is little theory of happiness here and there is little understanding of what an increase in a measured level of happiness actually means, or how that increase goes on to cause an alteration in a particular instrument for that matter. This ambiguity is why, we suspect, if it were not for the expense, some happiness psychologists would much prefer to find physiological correlates of happiness like levels of serotonin or oxytocin. That would eliminate the need to consider a theory of happiness psychology entirely.

METHODOLOGICAL PROBLEMS WITH ACADEMIC SOURCES (I)

There are still some basic questions about what is being assessed here and what generalizations can be made. For one, it's hard to believe that anyone would accept that the complex of factors that result in a behavior—variegated traits, dispositions, meanings, situations, choices, historical and cultural contexts, physiology—can be reduced to a single term like "optimism," or that all the behaviors, attitudes, judgments, circumstances, luck, and so on, that go into college success can be treated as a single outcome variable or simply attributed to perseverance. It's not hard to see why critics describe positive psychology as offering "pat" answers. Furthermore, as we discussed in a prior chapter, the context of assessing optimism cannot simply be treated as irrelevant. If the interpretation of psychophysical phenomena differs across subjects and contexts, as we have already seen, you can be sure the interpretation of the ASQ and similar assessments will differ across subjects and contexts. Yet, these are fairly accepted practices in much of the experimental research published in the field itself, so we turn to additional problems.

Other instruments and experimental conditions present similar problems. For instance, in an online-based, controlled, randomized study designed to test the efficacy of several happiness improvement programs, Seligman and his student Tracy Steen (Seligman et al., 2005) developed the "SHI," or "Steen Happiness Inventory," based on Aaron Beck's widely used Beck's Depression Inventory. The SHI consists of twenty items that require subjects to read a list of five statements and select the one that best describes them at the current time (e.g., from "Most of the time I am bored" to "Most of the time I am fascinated by what I am doing"). Seligman et al. describe the SHI as sensitive to week-to-week upward changes in happiness levels, better suited to measure the effects of interventions. This is a consequence of the decision to include a wider range of positive response options, as opposed to negative ones, to offset the fact that people tend to rate themselves as happy. It also seeks to distinguish between three types of happiness: the "pleasant" life, the "engaged" life, and the "meaningful" life. The SHI is also highly correlated with other established measures of happiness (Seligman et al., 2005).

In the study, subjects were recruited from Seligman's website and randomly assigned to one of five happiness exercise groups or a placebo. They were tested for happiness levels before the exercises and again immediately after, as well as at one week, one month, three months, and six months afterward. The study began with 577 participants and 411 completed the entire program—a fairly high 29 percent attrition rate, especially since the sample was already a motivated one given that they chose to participate—

though this is never discussed and one is left to assume the authors make the assumption that this attrition is random. Seligman and his colleagues found that two out of the five exercises continued to increase happiness and reduce depression for over six months. The findings reflect "significant" differences on average happiness scores between the two successful treatments and the control group over the various intervals.

According to Seligman et al.'s published data, the scores of all groups were elevated immediately after the task, though they do not attempt to interpret this, but the placebo group returned to their baselines after a week, while some in the intervention groups, especially those that continued the exercises, remained at elevated levels of happiness for months to follow. Thus, the specific interventions increase happiness, claim Seligman et al. Because there are no real controls here, this is a bold interpretation, to say the least. Looking at the graphic representations of the data, it is clear that in some of the treatment groups, mean happiness levels dropped over time, more so than was the case with the control group. Does this mean the treatments decreased happiness? Seligman et al. neither mention this nor seem to view the drop as caused by the intervention.

There is the obvious problem of the convenience sample as well. Although Seligman views this as a strength, as the sample is "tilted toward those that want to become happier" (415)—this means that the sample is drawn from a very specific population, those who are open to and familiar with these types of interventions. This leads to the question of whether the "placebo" control is really much of a placebo given that many of these subjects probably know what happiness exercises look like. Regardless, the more serious methodological issues relate to the effect sizes and the power of the statistical tests, and we will return to them later.

A REVIEW OF THE METHODOLOGICAL ISSUES AT STAKE (I): INFERENCE AND PROBABILITY

Statistics emerged in the nineteenth century at the confluence of the study of probability in gambling, the concern with error in observations in astronomy, and the collection of population data by governments. Over its development, statistics went from explorations of data—often discursive/nonmathematical—to a branch of mathematics, and finally, to a useful technology. Statistics developed to account for uncertainty. It recognizes a basic fact about probability: While individual events are uncertain, sometimes a collection of events is less so. Probability was first introduced into psychology by Gustav Fechner to deal with the problem of variability in measurement. In psychophysics, variation in response had been described as "the personal equation," but it was gradually reconceived as "error" (Stigler, 1986). For Fechner, this was a way to line up a variable stimulus with a standard one, allowing them to be treated as subjectively equal, and therefore develop more precise measures of psychological magnitude (Hornstein, 1988). Variability was viewed as a source of the distortion of a true value.

For much of the nineteenth century, the language of probability was also a way to talk about regularities in social phenomena, without necessarily understanding such phenomena at the individual level (Porter, 1986). Given his grounding in Darwinism, for Galton, variation was no longer regarded as error, but became the phenomenon of interest in itself. Galton turned Quetelet's method of identifying the "average" man given error, into a method devoted entirely to variation. He was interested in the extremes, or the tail end of the bell curve, not the peak, as had traditionally been the case (Porter, 2003, p. 243). The statistical techniques developed to explain uncertainty allowed Galton to find order on the level of the group even given the variation at the level of the individual. He accomplished this by focusing on relative standing in a group rather than any absolute measurement of characteristics (Hornstein, 1988, p. 9). This was soon recognized as a benefit of studying groups/aggregates as opposed to individuals (Danziger, 1987). It was a solution to the problem of induction. Yet, what prior theories of probability made clear was that key to working with statistical phenomena were large populations where Gaussian and other distributions were easily applied.

The small samples of experimentalism posed a problem. For one, the issue became not only one of error but also the inferences researchers needed to make from sample to population in a context where the "law of large numbers" did not apply. The solution, NHST, a fusion of experimentalism and statistical inference, was developed by Ronald Fisher and later integrated with the work of his critics, Jerzy Neyman and Egon Pearson. It came to dominate experimental psychology by the third decade of the twentieth century, and despite over a half century of extensive criticisms, it continues to do so. As we shall see, its problems call into question the meaningfulness of a great many findings in psychology, especially those with the kinds of small effects one typically finds in the field. Lack of meaningfulness, in this case, implies that the likelihood of consistent replication is too uncertain to ground broader inferences about relationships between phenomena.

How does NHST work? We begin by reviewing what is well known to most researchers in psychology before turning to its problems. It requires that a researcher define a null hypothesis of no effect. This posits that there are no mean differences between the groups compared. The researcher then determines the chance of finding at least the observed differences *given that the null hypothesis is true.* As we shall soon see, it is the tendency to ignore this last part that gives psychologists the most trouble with NHST. If the chance of finding at least these differences is lower than a predetermined threshold or p value, usually .05 percent, the result is said to be "significant." As convention has it, this gives the researcher the right to say that the observed differences between the groups are "reliable" enough to be meaningful and not simply due to chance. This allows researchers to claim that their theory behind the cause of those effects is provisionally correct.

In psychology, a finding of statistical significance is generally taken to be confirmation of a theory, and such cases constitute the great bulk of published studies in the field. Estimates are that for papers published in psychology using NHST, around 96–97 percent of them contain positive findings where nulls are rejected at $p < .05$ or less (Sterling, 1959; Sterling et al., 1995). What makes this surprising, as we shall see, is that given the small effect sizes in much psychological research, effects even more difficult to detect given the small samples typically used and high variability in those sample, studies are often "underpowered" (Cohen, 1990). This means that they are not sensitive enough to detect these types of effects in the first place. Thus, if published papers were remotely representative of the research being done by psychologists, there should be a lot more "negative" findings. Psychologists are either very lucky or there are other factors at play here that distort the overall number of positive findings in the field, again calling the meaningfulness of positive findings in general into question (Bakker et al., 2012).

For example, at first glance a finding of significance at $p < .05$ might seem like a good bet that the null should be rejected. Such a finding, however, might be less attractive if that study is understood to be in the company of thousands of others of failed unpublished studies—including those that are done in the heads of experienced researchers as they glance at data or select various statistical tests in order to test findings—making it far more likely that the finding is a function of chance than might be recognized. The identified mean differences are still based on the sample, not the population itself. All we can really know after a test of significance is the likelihood that the two sample means are drawn from the same population. Yet, in psychology, convention allows researchers to use a single finding to make generalizations about populations, even if, for example, there was no attempt made to account for how the sample was selected from that population. In more direct terms, the way NHST is employed in psychology encourages a lot of inappropriate inferences about populations.

Just to be clear, there are lots of ways to compare group differences. The most basic and clear involve graphic representations of complete data. Often with large enough effect sizes, as in Kahneman's studies, the differences are easy to see. Means can be helpful, but as is well known, they are not actual data points and tell us nothing about variability. When there is not too much variability in either group and the effect size is large enough, subtracting one mean from another can provide a clear-cut demonstration of an effect. In fact, this works as a straightforward measure of an effect size. NHST obviously allows one to go further as this is based on comparing a measure of variability across groups with a measure of variability within groups, weighted by the number of members within each group.

A finding of statistical significance can mean either the difference between sample means is large, this is the case if the within sample variability is large and the sample size is small. It can also mean the difference between sample means is small, and in this case the within sample variability is small but the sample size is large. The latter makes sense given that the larger the sample, the more likely it represents the population from which it was drawn, and that the less variability there is, the more likely small differences will stand out. But it should also be clear why statistical significance is more difficult to achieve in studies with small effects and small samples, yet this is precisely what has been found to be the case in psychology (Bakan, 1966).

To put it another way, in NHST, a finding of significance means that the treatment sample no longer represents the original population while the control sample continues to do so. Under the null hypothesis, that is, the hypothesis that there are no differences between the treatment and control groups, differences in means between the groups can be expected only as far as sampling fluctuations occur when drawing from the same population (Carver, 1978). Thus these sampling fluctuations are said to be "random" or due to "chance," but what is really meant is that the differences are not caused by the treatment or an unrecognized confound. Again, intuitively, these sampling errors should decrease with larger sample size and less variation. The function of the significance testing is to determine just how often the differences found—in other words, the specific data—would occur as a result of sampling errors. If such differences occur rarely enough, we reject that the null is due exclusively to sampling errors, as error alone cannot explain the differences found. We reject that the groups represent the same population (Carver, 1978). If they don't, at least in experimental contexts with controlled conditions, we can claim to have identified a cause.

This is a really important point that deserves repeating. NHST allows us to draw inferences about a population from a sample. With the null, one uses the *known* variability in the sample groups to estimate the *unknown* variability in the population. The estimated population variability along with known sample size allows a calculation of how often one can expect to find mean differences due to error (Carver, 1978, p. 380). Thus a p value simply represents the proportion of time one can expect to find mean differences as large as or larger than what one gets from sampling the same population if the null were true. In other words, at $p < .05$, when sampling a pair of means from the same population, one should expect the groups to differ by the mean difference or more less than 5 percent of the time. We should expect to find sampling errors of the kind we found in less than 5 out of every 100 pairs taken. Take note, this says nothing conclusive about the likelihood of the null, yet alone the treatment effect.

Assuming the truth of the null hypothesis allows for the calculation of a *p* value, which in turn allows researchers to reject or not reject the truth of the null, at least this is how convention has it. This why one popular interpretation of a *p* value, that it conveys the likelihood that findings are due to chance, is incorrect. We have already assumed the null is correct to calculate the *p* value. The assumption in most psychological research, then, is that sampling errors that occur in less than 5 out of every 100 cases—the 0.05 level of significance—are rare enough that they can be discounted and the null hypothesis can be rejected. When the null turns out to be true and the populations are the same, the researcher will only make the mistake of rejecting it 5 percent of the time (type I error). Here, statistical significance is a measure of rareness (Carver, 1978, p. 381). A finding of a statistically significant difference in means communicates that given certain assumptions—the two groups are random samples from the same population—which does not necessarily mean they are the same—and the properties of the population can be estimated from the properties of the samples—one can expect the mean differences between the groups to be larger than mean differences from other groups sampled from the population, 95 percent of the time.

This does not mean, as is often stated, that the findings will replicate 95 percent of the time. NHST cannot predict the future. In fact, such a replication rate is almost impossible to imagine given future sampling variation. To put it another way, the *p* value is not the probability that a hypothesis is true given the evidence but the probability that the evidence would arise if the null hypothesis is true. Although the first question is understandably the more attractive one to researchers as it tells us the probability that the null hypothesis is correct and that the two groups were sampled from the same population, NHST can only answer the second question: What is the probability of obtaining this finding if the two samples represent the same population?

As we shall see, this leads to yet another common mistake when interpreting the results of significance testing, taking a *p* value as a measure of the strength of the effect. Such an interpretation is one a researcher might seek to make, but it does not follow from a low *p* value, which permits a far more limited set of inferences (Bakan, 1966). In essence, what psychological convention has done is blur the distinction between the likelihood that a theory is correct and the likelihood that findings are correct. It has permitted psychologists to simply report the details of statistical analysis instead of explaining and defending the inductive inferences they are making. How did this state come to be?

The original methodological program of psychology developed by Wundt in the 1870s focused on reports of conscious experience by trained individuals in the laboratory. The idea of "control" referred to control over various sources of psycho-sensory stimulation. Group comparisons were a hallmark of the Galtonian program, which in turn shaped the development of intelligence testing, but did not play much of a role in the early experimental tradition. Yet, by the middle of the twentieth century, all that had changed and psychologists focused almost exclusively on group comparisons. As Kurt Danziger (1990) reports, between 1915 and 1950, the percentage of empirical studies reporting only group data in the *American Journal of Psychology* rose from 25 percent to 80 percent while those reporting only individual data fell from 70 percent to 17 percent. This is the case even though some of the most influential psychologists of the time—Piaget, Kohler, Pavlov, Skinner, Bartlett, just to name a few—did not use group data.

We have detailed some of this history already and in this section we will limit our focus to the question of how certain practices for making inferences from group differences were institutionalized and the role of statistical significance testing in these developments. This history revolves around the influence of the greatest statistician of the twentieth century, Ronald A. Fisher. As to the role of Fisher, Paul Meehl puts it directly:

> Sir Ronald [Fisher] has befuddled us, mesmerized us, and led us down the primrose path. I believe that the almost universal reliance on merely refuting the null hypothesis as the standard method for corroborating substantive theories in the soft areas is a terrible mistake, is basically unsound, poor scientific strategy, and one of the worst things that ever happened in the history of psychology. (1978, p. 817)

The place of Fisher in psychology is related to what Gerd Gigerenzer has called the "inference" or "probabilistic" revolution in psychology. Unlike other sciences like biology and physics, where probabilistic notions transformed the understanding of the objects of study themselves, the influence of the probabilistic revolution in psychology tended to affect methods much more than theory. For psychology, this meant a novel form of inferential statistics based in the ideas of Ronald Fisher with some of the ideas of his critics thrown in, though not always made explicit (Gigerenzer and Murray, 1987). Specific procedures for statistical inference became statistical inference itself. The classic problem of inductive inference, how to generalize from particulars, was afforded an algorithmic solution to be employed in a mechanical way, made even easier today with statistical software (Gigenzenger, 2000, p. 270).

In the early twentieth century, Fisher employed tests of statistical significance as part of the formalization of inductive inference. He had two poles between which ideas about inductive inference had historically been located. The first pole considered inductive inference as a kind of informal cognitive process based in informed judgment, while the alternative viewed inference as a procedure described by a single formal rule, independent of the context (6). The first pole is more similar to the inferences employed by physicists and other natural scientists while the alternative tends to use probability to formalize inductive inference, as was the case with Fisher (Gigenzenger and Murray, 1987).

One of the earliest attempts to formalize inductive inference using probability was that of Pierre-Simon Laplace. In an attempt to answer the question "What is the probability the sun will rise tomorrow?" he proposed a rule of succession, essentially calculating a conditional probability, which he derived from the theorem of the Reverend Thomas Bayes. Bayes's theorem offered a method of calculating the probability of a hypothesis given evidence, also known as posterior probability. This offered a formula for revising the probability of a hypothesis given new data. To put it into this context, NHST in contrast allows for the calculation of a likelihood function or the probability of evidence given the hypothesis. Yet, because posterior probability involves degrees of belief, it is often described as "subjective" probability. Frequentist critics of Bayesianism, which included Fisher, argued that inference must be "objective," which meant based exclusively on the relative frequency of observed events.

Again, this meant for Fisher that one could not talk of the probability of a hypothesis given data, but only the probability of data given a hypothesis. To be fair to Fisher, Darwin offered a more straightforward version of this logic as well, when defending his deductive method in the 1872 edition of *The Origin of Species*:

> It can hardly be supposed that a false theory would explain, in so satisfactory a manner as does the theory of natural selection, the several large classes of facts above specified. It has recently been objected that this is an unsafe method of arguing; but it is a method used in judging of the common events of life, and has often been used by the greatest natural philosophers. (476)

This is the defense of a theory by its explanatory power, certainly a common argument in contemporary science. The key difference between Darwin and Fisher is the uncertainty in the "classes of facts" themselves. Fisher's statistical tests had to provide the grounds to draw valid inferences from the findings of experimentation, or else what was the point? The result was the strange logic of Fisherian statistical inference that has become institutionalized in modern psychology.

Fisher's statistical techniques were based in agronomic research. He transformed the single observations of astronomy into a sampling distribution (Gigerenzer and Murray, 1987, p. 9). His early work discussed issues like the weight of pigs and the effects of manure. While his later work dropped these references, they still focused on a key question important to agronomics: Will intervention X work? There was not much room for subtlety. Fisher used NHST along with his method for the analysis of variance, a technique he used to demonstrate the primary influence of heredity. This kind of partitioning of variance in an experimental context made it very attractive to psychologists interested in multiple explanatory variables (Porter, 1986).

Previously, Karl Pearson had doubted the possibility of identifying causes and was not interested in experiments. He saw large numbers as a better guide. Fisher rejected this approach for small samples. Fisher first used randomization in his agricultural experiments where blocks could be treated as independent since they were assigned to treatment groups at random. If observed differences between yields of fertilizers was unlikely to occur by chance, that is it differed from what might have occurred by chance even if fertilizer was ineffective, as yields regularly varied by chance, it passed a test of significance. He preferred to test many factors at once and therefore developed techniques for the analysis of multiple sources of variance. These were techniques well suited to deal with variation, as opposed to the kind of tight control of factors that was the ideal in physics (Porter, 2003, p. 248). Thus it transferred well into fields like experimental psychology and medicine.

Still, as Gigerenzer et al. (1989) note, as time passed, Fisher became more and more explicit about the fact that in science, as opposed to farming, one experiment can never be conclusive. Yet, all the while, he continued to use language that implied otherwise (96). Interestingly Fisher's major critics, Jerzy Neyman and Egon Pearson came out of industrial research in which they were more interested in a cost-benefit analysis that compared the value of two rival options rather than a straight-up accept or reject. This led them to see statistical testing as choosing between two rival hypotheses rather than trying to reject the null. They therefore introduced the notion of a Type II error, a notion that focuses more directly on the power of tests and one that Fisher rejected. Fisher thought the idea of determining acceptable levels of significance before the test, as Neyman and Pearson recommended and has become standard practice, did not make sense. Instead, studies should publish exact levels of significance after the test, as it should depend on the specific case.

In essence, the phrase "level of significance" came to have three meanings. It can be understood as a standard level determined before the experiment, an exact level determined afterward, or the relative frequency of Type I errors in the long run to be decided in advance based in a cost-benefit analysis (Gigerenzer et al., 1989, p. 272). The first two meanings derive from Fisher, while the third comes from Neyman and Pearson. In the first and second meanings, significance level is a property of the data, while in the third it is a property of the test. Yet, all three are used indiscriminately, argues Gigerenzer, in the hybrid version that has come to dominate psychology. The difference is that the first two meanings attach an epistemic interpretation linked to a particular experiment, while the latter attaches a behavioral interpretation that implies repeated experiments, which was not a realistic option in Fisher's agricultural research. For Neyman and Pearson, the goal is not "disproving" the null, as in Fisher, but a pragmatic course of action. Therefore, Neyman and Pearson viewed hypothesis testing as selecting between two hypotheses as opposed to simply rejecting the null. While not exactly Bayesians, Neyman and Pearson allow room for the informed judgment of the researcher.

Given their interest in industrial production, they were also more concerned with misses (or Type II errors) as they are more costly than false alarms (Type I errors), which you expect anyway. Fisher's epistemic orientation, more concerned with the truth or falsehood of assumptions, led him to focus more on Type I errors. This is implied in the logic of contemporary NHST in general, as low power studies, by definition, are more amenable to Type II errors. Fisher's epistemic orientation, as opposed to Neyman and Pearson's more pragmatic one, easily led to confusion between statistical significance and substantive significance, and again, this has come to be the case today in much psychological research. On a similar note, it became easy to dismiss non-significant findings as worthless even though this inference does not follow.

In the end, the hybrid version of mostly Fisher with a bit of Neyman and Pearson tossed in created by psychology textbook writers in the 1950s ignored the substantial differences between them and their underlying assumptions, creating many opportunities for confusion in the field. The two "advantages," argues Gigerenzer et al., were that editorial decisions were streamlined—there was only one path to acceptable findings—and theory construction, experimental ingenuity, and informed judgment were transformed into a highly mechanical, standardized process that could easily be taught to graduate students (286). Another consequence was a shift away from a focus on the inherent problems with psychological measurement to the creation of new numbers like *F* values, *p* values, and the like.

A REVIEW OF THE METHODOLOGICAL ISSUES AT STAKE (II): NHST AND ITS CRITICS

The inference revolution took hold quite quickly in psychology, although there have been questions as to the value of significance testing since its inception, both the tests themselves as well as the types of inferences drawn from the tests. In the 1930s, fewer than twenty psychological studies used NHST (Rucci and Tweney, 1980). By 1952, NHST was used in nearly 82 percent of studies in four leading journals (Sterling, 1959). NHST was criticized by Joseph Berkson in 1938, just as Fisher's ideas were first spreading in psychology, and then again by many social scientists in the 1960s (Rozeboom, 1960; Bakan, 1966; Meehl, 1967; Lykken, 1968). Many of these criticisms were published together as *The Significance Test Controversy* (Morrison and Henkel, 1970), still one of the best books on the subject.

One of the many criticisms of null hypothesis testing laid out in the book is that it encourages dichotomous thinking. Either the null is accepted, meaning there are no significant differences between control and treatment group and the "theory" is judged incorrect, or it is rejected and the treatment has an effect, meaning the "theory" is judged correct. Even the APA 1974 publication manual uses the terms "not rejecting the null" and "negative" findings interchangeably (Murray and Gigenzenger, 1987, p. 23). Yet, this is really a statement about belief in a proposition, which is never an all-or-nothing affair (Rozenboom, 1960). Beliefs tend to come in degrees. Most scientists do not give up a belief because of the results of one statistical test, but their beliefs might be strengthened or weakened given a result. Certainly no scientist would give up their belief because the findings were significant at $p < .06$ as opposed to $p < .04$.

This leads to fairly narrow research questions. It also, and this is key, discourages the publication of non-significant findings and ultimately discourages replication. It is easy to underestimate the importance of negative findings in science, just as it is easy to overestimate the importance of positive findings in NHST. A significant finding is supposed to suggest that a question is answered and a theory is correct. Given the small effects sizes in psychology, this is, at best, hopelessly naïve. As we have already noted, this is exacerbated by the "replication crisis" in psychology. In fact, the further one goes down the "hierarchy" of sciences, the more the proportion of positive results—about five times more in psychology (91 percent) than space science (70 percent) with the social sciences in general somewhere in the middle of the two (Fanelli, 2010).

Because effect sizes in psychology tend to be fairly small in general, a finding of statistical significance does not necessarily translate into a meaningful finding of difference, especially given that one often deals in ordinal data where the differences between the ratings are already imprecise. NHST allows for the confusion of hypothesis testing with statistical testing. Testing a statistical hypothesis is not the same as testing a theoretical hypothesis, as the former is simply a reflection of whether the observed differences are likely or not to be obtained from two samples drawn from the same population. This does not tell us that the null is false, and it absolutely does not tell us that our original hypothesis is true. Nor, by the way, does failing to reject the null tell us the null is true and a theoretical hypothesis is false. Sometimes small effects can be meaningful, as is the case with difficult-to-manipulate dependent variables as well as minimal independent variable manipulation, but neither are true in the kind of research we are reviewing (Prentice and Miller, 1992).

A more recent battle against NHST in psychology flared up when Jacob Cohen published his 1994 polemic, "The Earth Is Round (p < .05)" in *American Psychologist*, criticizing the wide dependence on NHST in the field, and inspired a range of vigorous defenses. This resulted in an APA task force to study the use of NHST in psychology (Wilkinson and the Task Force on Statistical Inference, 1999). Cohen reminds his readers that NHST substitutes the question psychologists want answered—given these data what is the probability that a null hypothesis is correct—with the less useful—given that the null hypothesis is correct, what is the probability of these data? Again, these are very different questions. The logic of NHST in practice, argues Cohen, goes something like this: If the null hypothesis is correct, then this statistically significant result would *probably* not occur and the result has occurred, thus the null hypothesis is *probably* not true and therefore formally invalid. This is a misapplication of deductive syllogistic reasoning as one is treating the premise as if it was certain and not probable. You cannot, in this case, "confirm" a theory by rejecting the null hypothesis. Cohen calls it the "illusion of attaining improbability" (1994, p. 998). There are numerous reasons to reject a null hypothesis that have little to do with whether a theory is correct or not. This confusion is repeated in published psychological studies again and again, as well as in statistical texts for psychologists alongside the correct interpretation (see also Dawes, 1998). As Cohen notes, they are treated interchangeably.

Cohen describes this as a "Bayesian" interpretation of NHST. Two issues follow. First, power analysis becomes redundant, as there is no longer any need to worry about the probability of obtaining data that will lead to the acceptance of the null hypothesis if it is false, as the analysis already "tells" you directly the probability that the null hypothesis is false (Oakes, 1986, p. 83). Second, one assumes after a successful rejection of the null hypothesis, it is highly probable that when the research is replicated the null hypothesis will be rejected again (Cohen, 1994, p. 999). In other words, the assumption that the randomly drawn sample data is representative of the population leads to the common misinterpretation we identified earlier, that $p < .05$ means that if the study was repeated 100 times the findings would be replicated 95 of those times. Rosenthal (1993) calls this the replication fallacy, even more of a fallacy given the small to medium effect sizes of most psychological studies. This interpretation views the probability of successful replication as $1\text{-}p$ and views significance tests as revealing the likelihood that the null is true given the evidence. In a similar vein, p values are not effect sizes, even though they are often treated that way, a tendency not helped by describing results as "significant," as if one could not imagine any other possible hypotheses. Instead, p values can be used to make decisions—note the p

value does not decide but the researcher decides—about whether to accept or reject the idea that chance caused the results (Carver, 1978).

NHST might be more useful if a null was actually set up to test a real hypothesis, but in psychology, a "straw" hypothesis is set up simply to prove it wrong. The hope is to find a conditional probability. In fact, argues Cohen, with a large enough sample, it's almost impossible for a null hypothesis *not* to be rejected. Cohen quotes Tukey, "It is foolish to ask 'Are the effects of A and B different?' They are always different—for some decimal place" (Tukey, 1991, p. 100). Again, NHST says nothing about the size or nature of those differences. By the time papers are published, statistically significant findings become "significant" findings in general when all one really knows is that the difference between groups is not nothing at all, which is hardly surprising given the conditions of the real world. Other factors contribute to this, including a publication bias toward studies that seem to say something substantive. This is in addition to a bias to publish statistically significant results on the part of researchers and journals in general and has been termed the "file drawer" problem (Rosenthal, 1979). As we already noted, the research that gets published is hardly representative of the research that gets done. In the end, insists Cohen, there is no substitute for the informed judgments of researchers. Mechanically employed Null Hypothesis Statistical Testing cannot substitute for that. Nor is there a substitute for looking at data: Use graphs, advises Cohen (1990) in *What I Learned So Far*.

One of Cohen's points is worth focusing on directly. Studies in psychology are notoriously underpowered. Power is the probability of not making a type II error, that is, failing to reject the null when it is false. In other words, it is inferring that a difference between groups is not statistically significant when in fact it is. It is a way to talk about the sensitivity of a test to an effect. Is there enough data to distinguish phenomena from random variation? The simplest way to increase power is to increase the size of the sample. In Neyman-Pearson theory, power is the long-run frequency of acceptance of the alternative hypothesis, if the alternative hypothesis is true (Sedlmeier and Gigerenzer, 1989). Actually, this is not only a clearer definition of power but also stays true to the origins of the notion of a type II error in Neyman and Pearson. The power of a statistical test depends on the sample size—typically, the larger the sample the more power, but also the selected p value—the smaller the value, the more power—and the effects size—the larger, the more power. Psychological studies, which typically have small samples, high-ish p values and small effect sizes, do not make for much power.

One analysis of leading experimental journals in psychology found a median sample size of 40—suggestive of low powered tests (Marszalek et al., 2011). Other studies have shown an average effect size in psychology of $d = .50$ (see next paragraph), leading to an average power of about .35 in a typical study (Bakker et al., 2012). This is obviously only an estimate, but just to put it in context, with a power of .50 the chance of finding significant results if they are there is about 50/50. This is interesting given the convention of setting alpha at .05, which is also the probability of making a type I error, accepting the null when it is false. Thus most tests are conservative in the sense they are much more concerned with making sure not to accept findings even at the risk of missing them. If a study is not likely to detect an effect even though it might be there, it is obviously not especially useful. Given this, one would expect lots and lots of published studies with findings of non-statistically significant differences, and again that is just not the case.

The responses to Cohen's *American Psychologist* article were varied but the basic premises of his criticisms were generally accepted. Yet not much has changed. Cohen recommends studies report an estimation of the effect size or *d* computed as the difference between means divided by the common standard deviation (Cohen, 1977). In other words, divide the within treatments variability from the between treatments variability. This means the path to increasing effect sizes is simple: Either increase between treatment variability by focusing on meaningful treatments with large effects or decrease within treatment variability, also known as error, with more considered and precise forms of measurement. Unfortunately, there are ways around this, like creating instruments that by their very nature inflate effect sizes or operationalize treatment variables in ways that increase their effects, but are not necessarily characteristic of the phenomenon in general. The latter is one way to explain some of the large effect sizes in the heuristics and biases research, while the former is an issue in some of the happiness psychology we reviewed.

Another more common effect size indicator is *r*2 (the coefficient of determination), which shows the percentage of variance in a dependent variable explained by variance in an independent variable, and as we will see in the next chapter, another notoriously difficult-to-interpret statistic (Rosenthal and Rubin, 1982). Ideally, effect sizes are calculated before the research begins or at least the level of effect size worth further study is decided in advance and are described in meaningful units of measurement, although this is sometimes impossible in cases where the scales used are not meaningful to anyone but those experienced with them and then a standardized effect size makes more sense. One danger is that researchers end up confusing "effect" size with "cause" size, as the former is a function of the latter, but they are not the same (Abelson, 1997).

Much more valuable still, as even the APA has recognized, is to describe the size of the effects reported as well as confidence intervals (CI) around point estimates. The technique was developed by Jerzy Neyman in 1941 in order to provide frequency interpretations to the problem of estimation. Interestingly, psychologists have either objected to these recommendations, arguing they are unrealistic, even illogical (Knapp and Sawilowsky, 2001), or more often, simply ignored them despite arguments to the contrary (Thompson, 1988; Leventhal and Huynh, 1996; Wilkinson, 1999). There is a danger, however, that CIs will become in practice yet another mechanically applied formula and quickly lose its value as well.

A confidence interval is essentially a range of plausible values for the population mean (or other parameter). Thus a CI with a 95 percent confidence level has a 95 percent chance of capturing the true mean of the population. Because they are typically shown in the units of measurement utilized by the researcher, they are fairly concrete and easy to interpret. They also make clear the level of precision in the analysis; for example, a calculation of a 95 percent CI with a wide range is not very precise, or in other terms, there is a lot of uncertainty associated with the estimate. Confidence intervals, like effect sizes, can also allow one to compare many different studies and therefore can be used in a meta-analysis concerned with replication of findings. Technically you could estimate a *p* value from a CI if one is interested in hypothesis testing, but not the other way around, and even predict if the difference between means will differ significantly depending on whether the intervals overlap or not. Typically, a very wide CI suggests either that there is not enough data for more precise estimates or the data is too variable.

Given the amount of confusion in psychology around significance testing, it is not surprising to find a lot of confusion around confidence intervals. Some have incorrectly described CIs as range of plausible values for the sample mean, a range of individual scores (Fidler, 2005), or that a 95 percent CI means that if the experiment were repeated researchers have a 95 percent chance of capturing mean. In fact, the likelihood drops with each repetition (Cumming et al., 2004). CIs are no panacea, especially if they are framed within a NHST framework, which they often are. One study found that when behavioral science researchers were asked via email to interpret findings of two fictional studies of the same phenomena, one with statistically significant results and one without, some presented using NHST and others CI, interpretations were generally poor (Coulson et al., 2010). However, the CI respondents were far more successful in interpreting findings if they did not reference NHST than if they did (95 percent versus 60 percent). Not surprisingly NHST easily creates misinterpretations. Cohen offers his own take on why CIs have not replaced NHST in psychology: Most of the confidence intervals in psychological research are embarrassingly large (1994, p. 1002). A focus on CI would push psychologists toward much larger samples, more precise measurement tools, and more replicable findings (Schmidt, 1996; Maxwell, 2004).

One of the reasons NHST survives in psychology, other than resistance to change, is that psychologists share some profound misunderstandings about what such testing actually can and cannot do. One common misunderstanding is that NHST reveals whether observed differences are "real" or simply due to chance. Unfortunately, no statistical test is capable of this given their frequentist assumptions. This is only possible when the problem is considered from a Bayesian perspective, which a small minority of psychologists are now doing. This allows for the calculation of the probability of a hypothesis, a calculation that can be revised in the light of new evidence.

Again, this misunderstanding involves a reinterpretation of the p value as the probability the research results are due to chance so that, for example, $p < .05$ is interpreted as meaning the findings could have been due to chance less than 5 out of 100 times. But this is not possible given that the p value is calculated by already assuming the null is true and thus the results are due to chance. This means (a) the assumed probability that the results are due to chance is certain or 1.0 as this is *assumed*, and (b) the p value is used to *determine whether to accept or reject the idea that the probability is 1.0 that chance caused the mean differences* (Carver, 1978). It is correct that a p value implies the odds are 1 out of 20 of getting a mean difference of a certain size or larger, *if the two samples represent the same population.* This is a big "if" and there is no way to estimate the odds of this in real-world research without replication.

NHST is often not even capable of this, given how underpowered psychological studies tend to be. If we accept the estimate that the average study in psychology has a power of about .50, meaning about one half of all tests will be non-significant when there actually is a significant difference, NHST will be incorrect about 50 percent of the time. This confusion comes from the convention of describing a non-significant difference as "no" difference, leading non-significant findings to be interpreted as simply due to "chance" (Schmidt and Hunter, 1996). Increasing power appears like a viable solution, yet that would require not only larger samples, but also larger effect sizes. Another widely shared misunderstanding is that scientific hypothesis testing requires significance testing in order to determine whether hypotheses should be accepted or not. This assumption is testament to the influence of Fisher, who brought them together in the first place. Of course physicists and chemists test hypotheses, yet they do not rely on significance testing, as they instead compare data across many studies to determine the verity of hypotheses and rely on something closer to confidence intervals when computing predictions (Hedges, 1987).

There is something eminently practical about NHST that makes it very attractive to researchers. What can be easier than a simple finding of accept or reject? However, no single study contains sufficient enough information to make a final decision of whether to accept or reject a hypothesis. Findings, both significant and non-significant, need be replicated in various forms in order to determine whether they have any meaning. Moreover, the current attitude invariably leads to "data mining" and "p fishing," simply looking for significant enough differences and then developing theories post-hoc about why they exist, no matter how small the effects (Gelman and Loken, 2013). Sometimes this is not even done intentionally, but involve cases where the selection of a specific test or variable yields significant findings while selecting others would not. The researcher naturally chooses to report only or mostly on what works. Sometimes several statistical hypotheses follow from the same scientific one. Sometimes this is the unacknowledged effect of choices in how to organize data. This is exacerbated by the combination of small effect sizes, small samples, large variability, and the large measurement errors typical in psychology. This is also exacerbated by the convention on the part of many journals to publish only, or even mostly, studies with significant findings. Statistics is no substitute for judgment. Inferences are best made from data using judgment, not NHST (Tukey, 1962). Today, factors like sample size and effect size, which end up determining the power of the statistical tests, end up substituting for judgment as well.

METHODOLOGICAL PROBLEMS IN ACADEMIC SOURCES (II)

Nothing we have said here is unique to the psychology of happiness other than especially small effect sizes, which can only be determined through meta-analytic techniques given that effect sizes are not often published. Let's return to Seligman's finding about the effectiveness of three out of the five happiness exercises. Seligman et al.'s (2005) analysis focused on the interaction of time passed and the six different groups (five treatments plus one control). The way the authors present the findings, focusing on those significant at $p < .001$, they imply that these effects are the more important or powerful ones. However, as we have reviewed, some of this can be attributed to variability in the sample. Summarizing the findings, Seligman et al. write, "We found specific interventions that make people lastingly happier" (419), making the leap from statistical significance to theoretical significance that is so typical in psychology. But just "eyeballing" the graphic depictions of the data suggests otherwise.

Seligman et al. use bar charts to represent the difference in means between treatment and control groups at various time frames, a choice that makes the differences appear larger than they actually are. Unfortunately they don't use charts that give readers a sense of the variability in the scores—although this is built into the F value—which would help put the changes in the means into a context and determine the breath and stability of the changes over the subjects. Seligman et al. calculate the effect sizes for some of the significant findings of intervention by time (ranging from r2 = .06–.50). While they range from small to large, they are quite inconsistent (e.g., one treatment has the highest effect size at post-test, another at one week, another at six months). Yet, Seligman et al.'s theory offers no explanation as to why this would be the case. Should one assume that the variable of time frame is so self-evident that there is no need to explain why an intervention would be more effective after a certain amount of time has passed as opposed to a different amount of time? Regardless, a more basic measure of effect size, mean change, in this case a change in 2 or 3 points out of at least a possible 65 as compared to the placebo, is fairly small, even if statistically significant, and much of it might very well be due to sampling variation and chance more than anything else given the sampling biases. This is a great example of confusing effect size with cause size. In the end, though, it is difficult to interpret even mean change, as the measurements have no intrinsic relationship to the phenomenon and the inventory itself seems designed to maximize minimal differences.

The effect size measures used by Seligman are not very helpful because correlational measures are highly dependent on sample size and variability. Small effect sizes are typical of happiness psychology. For instance, one meta-analysis of about 40 studies with a total of over six thousand participants found typical effect sizes in positive psychological intervention strategies research to be fairly low—between standardized mean differences or d = .20 to d = .34 where at least d = .50 is considered moderate. This is the case even though many of the findings had statistically significant differences (Bolier et al., 2013). Effect sizes varied quite considerably between studies, from below 0 (indicating a negative effect) to 2.4 (indicating a high effect). While other meta-analyses by positive psychologists themselves have found higher effect sizes (e.g., Sin and Lyubomirsky, 2009), they also tend to include both high and low quality studies. Bolier et al. (2013) found, not surprisingly, higher effect sizes associated with lower quality studies.

In general Bolier et al. found lots of low quality studies in which randomization procedures were vague and there were high levels of heterogeneity in terms of treatments identified as positive psychology interventions. These points about quality are not intended to be evaluative as much as suggest that the findings of statistically significant differences between treatment and control groups can be a result of a myriad of factors and do not necessarily reflect the effects of the intervention itself. The low effect sizes are tempered further by the fact that studies with non-significant findings are not likely to be published at all. Bolier et al. found higher effects for face-to-face interactions, although most interventions were in a self-help (or non-face-to-face) format. This suggests further questions about Seligman et al.'s online intervention study as it adds yet another confounding variable.

The meta-analysis did find, in line with Seligman et al., that interventions of longer duration increased effect sizes. However, given that the attrition rates in the studies included in the meta-analysis, as well as Seligman et al.'s, were quite high at follow-ups (around 30 percent), even this is difficult to interpret. What is really missing from Seligman et al.'s research is any theory about why the interventions he selected should have an effect on levels of happiness. They are positing a cause-and-effect relationship between a treatment and a score on an inventory, but other than telling us the inventory correlates with similar inventories, they do not explain what mechanisms or processes are affected by the treatment. This is not atypical in psychological research dependent on NHST as the capacity to identify causes while ignoring actual mechanisms is part of what made Fisher's work so attractive to the field in the first place. Seligman's study, ironically, is probably one of the better ones in happiness psychology.

In another study we referred to in a previous section, Lyubomirsky and Ross (1997) sought to test the claim that unhappy people are more sensitive to social comparison information than happy ones. The study was composed of a sample of fifty undergraduate females at Stanford. Based on their mean scores on a questionnaire that asked them to rate their level of happiness on a seven-point scale, they were assigned to a happy group and an unhappy group—there was a group mean of 6.55 for "happys" versus 3.44 for "unhappys," with much more variation in the "unhappys." Individuals in both groups were asked to solve an anagram puzzle alongside another student, who was actually a confederate, where the second student completed the puzzle either very quickly or very slowly. Thus there were four conditions: happy/slow, happy/fast, unhappy/slow, and unhappy/fast. The hypothesis was that those in the unhappy/fast group were mostly likely to be affected by their perceived shortcomings as reflected in a change in a post-treatment puzzle solving and mood self-assessment. Not surprisingly, given that it was published, the study found this to be the case.

For "unhappys" self-assessed ability decreased (-0.42 on average) while for "happys" it increased (+0.79). Effects sizes seem moderate at first glance. But there are serious questions as to the quality of the study. To start with, the instruments seemed designed to maximize effect size. As if to offer insight into quality, Lyubomirsky and Ross go on to perform about twenty more significance tests in different variations of the same question, raising the issue of p fishing as well as increasing the likelihood of finding some patterns even if due to chance (Diaconis, 1985). They found several significant relationships, but it would have almost been impossible not to given the sheer number of tests. Given enough opportunities, chance creates patterns as well. This is a perfect example of the problem of "researcher degrees of freedom" as described by Gelman and Loken (2013). Who knows how they chose these tests out of the hundreds of possible tests. It is unlikely they were all selected before looking at the data.

Regardless of whether Lyubomirky and Ross are correct about "unhappy" people and social comparison, their data do not permit any such claims. One finds generalizations like these quite regularly in positive psychology, especially in its popular versions where the caveats typical of academic research are dropped entirely. In her book, *The How of Happiness* (2008), Lyubormisky describes these results as "dramatic." This might very well be the case given the single condition she uses to operationalize social comparison. Lyubormisky then reports that since the study, she and her students have "conducted many more studies showing essentially the same result"—though she offers no citations or details—and finally concludes with the claim: "The happier the person, the less attention she pays to how others are doing" (118–119). Sounds good and is in line with what most people already believe. What is one to make of the fact that an entire academic sub-discipline is built on such a tenuous foundation? Happiness psychology, more than anything else, is a good lesson on the limits of "scientific" psychology. And yet, confusion around statistical significance and its interpretation is certainly not limited to this work. Conventional talk of *p* values at less than .05 confuse what is a really a continuous category, belief in a hypothesis, with a categorical one—right or wrong. Too often, success in the field requires, as is expressed in this infamous phrase, "torturing the data until it confesses."

Chapter Five

The Effects of Parenting

Correlations and Causes

Americans have a long tradition of giving advice to parents. Though most twentieth-century writers in this genre have been physicians, psychologists have participated in it as well. And even when they have not directly participated in it, their work has certainly influenced it. Important sources of parental advice emerged from the psychological ideas of John Watson, Arnold Gesell, Jean Piaget, Erik Erikson, and of course Sigmund Freud—including many working in the Freudian tradition like John Bowlby, Selma Freiberg, Bruno Bettleheim, Erik Erikson, and Margaret Mahler. With respect to academic research, in the late 1960s, Diana Baumrind introduced the notion of three distinct parenting styles to explain the effects of parenting: authoritarian, authoritative, and permissive. But only one, the authoritative style, led to ideal outcomes. During the same decade, Mary Ainsworth extended John Bowlby's notion of three types of maternal-child attachment relations, again only one of which was ideal. Though the two ideals came from fairly different sources, they slowly became linked with each other as the valuation of nurturance in attachment theory became more central to authoritative parenting. This generated a fairly broad consensus in the field about how children should be raised that, in subtly modified forms, is still accepted nearly fifty years later.

Both approaches offered psychologists a simple typology of parent-child dynamics that, based on a theory and subsequent research, were said to have specific types of effects on children. There was a recipe to be followed: authoritativeness + secure attachment = psychological well-being. It was clearly a story about causes and effects, but told through correlational data. Perhaps most importantly, it was a story that confirmed American middle class parenting values already long in place. Mother-love was at the center of this story, as was fair discipline. By the middle of the twentieth century, it had taken on a therapeutic frame with talk of boundaries, validation, and emotional availability. At the dawn of the twenty-first, it is being rewritten again in the language of the brain.

Baumrind's typology has both inspired a lot of research and made its way into every introductory psychology textbook and many popular psychological works as well. Following Baumrind's approach, the idea of particular parenting "types" has become a topic of popular psychology, and when a new "controversial" one comes along, as they almost always seem to do, they tend to get a lot of media attention and inspire debates about good parenting. "Attachment Parenting" and "Tiger Moms" are two of the most recent examples, and they mark out the two poles preferred parenting styles tend to swing back and forth between, though this dichotomy is clearly too simplistic. Authoritativeness, the superior type of parenting style, is typically described—incorrectly, as we shall see—as the ideal balance between discipline and nurturance, a middle ground between authoritarianism and permissiveness, which tends to stress only one or the other. The importance of "nurturance" in particular is supported by a range of academic findings from attachment theory and, especially in recent years, neuroscience, all making their way into popular psychology. The popular translations of developmental neuroscience tend to simplify complex biological processes, not surprisingly, and suggest we know much more about the development of the brain than we do. Much of this trades in the plasticity of the developing brain and ends up being easily misconstrued as a revival of traditional notions of infants as *tabula rasa*. In development, the relationship between plasticity and specificity or constraints is a subtle one and not easily translated into the oversimplified categories of popular writing.

Baumrind herself has not written much for non-academic audiences—though she did get involved in a public debate where she defended spanking—but many influenced by her ideas have. Her typology, however, is injected into all sorts of contexts. Finally, as we shall see, in the past few decades, critical positions downplaying the role of parents, especially those that stress the importance of genetics and innateness, have also made their way into popular psychology, but there is little to explain to parents what some of the problems with either approach are, other than stale accolades about the "interaction" between nature and nurture.

At their heart, these theories tell a causal story. To put it simply, the key questions answered are a version of these: What are the forces that relate to changes in children as they grow older? What are the forces that determine specific differences in outcomes? Can we utilize those forces to get the outcomes we want? In academic research, we are looking at studies where certain "independent" variables, sometimes characterized as "predictors"—

our focus will be on parent style and practice—are related to changes in certain "dependent" variables—various child-related outcomes.

In psychology, one is generally taught, in the tradition of Ronald Fisher, that the ideal way to answer questions about causes is through experimentation. But this is not always feasible. One can hardly control for all variables and manipulate parenting styles, nor would it be ethical to raise children with "placebos" for successful child-rearing strategies/parenting styles, even if it were possible to transform parental behavior in such a global way. Sometimes causal inferences are based in "intervention studies," where the results of a treatment designed to modify parenting technique is compared to a control, but the samples tend to be preexisting ones and substantive randomization and control is impossible. Instead most of the research we will review utilize various correlational and regression techniques. Sometimes they simply employ basic correlational analysis to highlight a directional relationship between variables, sometimes they attempt to explain variance in one variable through another and sometimes they generate causal/prediction models using regression. As we shall see, the misapplication of these techniques in much of the academic research we review yields all sorts of specious conclusions that then make their way into popular psychology.

POPULAR VARIANTS

Books about the importance of parenting style abound in popular psychology. There is widespread acceptance that experts support "authoritative" parenting. One of Baumrind's most influential students, Laurence Steinberg, has produced a series of popular psychology books, including *Beyond the Classroom: Why School Reform Has Failed and What Parents Need to Do* (1996) and *The 10 Basic Principles of Good Parenting* (2004), that extol the value of authoritative parenting. Both books make the case that raising children in a certain way produces the outcomes that parents want. This is a case, as we shall see later, that simply cannot be made based on the evidence. In general, both books are filled with fairly common-stock US middle-class parenting advice—be involved but not too involved, express affection, be emotionally responsive, set "boundaries" but avoid "harsh" discipline—all described as the findings of science—though specific research sources are not identified. Talk of the importance of parenting style, along with secure attachments and optimism, also find their way into journalist Paul Tough's (2012) recent bestseller *How Children Succeed: Grit, Curiosity and the Hidden Power of Character*. He employs them as part of his case that success relies on character more than cognitive skills.

Another place to find popular psychology about the authoritative parenting is on various parenting blogs. For example, Gwen Dewar, an anthropologist by training, authors a blog called “Mom Stories” on BabyCenter.com, and has her own site established in 2006 called “Parenting Science,” both of which offer parents findings from the latest research. In one April 2013 entry entitled “Kids with Permissive Parents Show Less Self-Control” she describes a study by Jessica Piotrowski and her colleagues (2013) that offered, in Dewar’s words, “strong evidence” that preschoolers with permissive parents had more problems with self-control. The study looked at various risk factors associated with low levels of “self-regulation.” Dewar describes “self-regulation” as a “package of skills” to control impulses, stay focused, and manage moods that is linked to school achievement, behavioral problems, substance abuse, and criminality, though she doesn’t cite any studies that found this link in case readers wanted to question it. Here are the findings as described by Dewar: “When they analyzed the results, there was one risk factor that towered over all others. The most substantial and significant predictor of poor self-regulation skills was having a parent who answers ‘yes’ to questions like ‘I ignore my child’s bad behavior’ and ‘I give in to my child when he/she causes a commotion about something.’”

Dewar acknowledges other risk factors (age, gender, income) and that “authoritarian” parenting was associated with even worse outcomes. She goes on, “So while we have to be cautious about jumping to conclusions—studies like this only tell us about correlations, not causation—we’ve got reason for concern. The data are consistent with the results of other studies and they fit well with our theoretical expectations.” How can one expect self-regulation on the part of a child to improve, she asks, if parents don’t instill it? She then recommends readers click a link to some of her previous blogs—“The authoritative parenting style: A guide for the science-minded parent,” “Unreliable adults may cause kids to be impulsive,” and “Teaching self-control: Evidence-based tips”—where parents are taught how to instill this in their children. When we look more carefully at the study later in this chapter, we will discover that the evidence is not all that “strong” and that the risk associated with a permissive parenting did not “tower” over the others.

Turns out, Dewar’s “evidence-based” blog is one of many, perhaps a reflection of the number of PhDs without full-time university positions. Dewar’s entry fits well into the prototypical science blog entry. It starts with a flashy title and a major problem. The problem is then translated into “academese” and linked to a particular study—often an obscure one—with “towering” results. There is typically one study per post, as these are not literature reviews. The study is followed by the requisite caution—a favorite seems to be that “correlations are not causes” or “these findings still need to be replicated”—ironic given the absence of replication in the field—and then, some research-based solutions are offered. Finally, in the comments section, there is typically the full range of responses: from grateful people struggling with this issue who explain that they finally understand it, to the “haters” who describe the whole topic as ridiculous, to the occasional articulate critique of the entry itself. In this case, one finds mostly parents describing their disciplinary styles and a few "haters."

While not always referring to Baumrind's typology, there has been a proliferation of pop psychology books about "parenting styles" in recent years. We will focus on two: "attachment" and "Chinese" because they seem closest to Baumrind's categories, but the list of well-known ones is quite extensive: helicopter parenting, overparenting, unconditional parenting, positive parenting, French parenting, and so on. Pediatricians William and Martha Sears first coined the term "attachment parenting" in the early 1980s. They view it as an extension of John Bowlby's notion that secure attachments have positive and lasting effects, despite the fact that most university psychologists influenced by Bowlby tend to distance themselves from Sears. Their *The Baby Book* (1993), sometimes known as the bible of attachment parenting, lays out several principles: The first few hours after birth are key to mother-child bonding, parents must immediately learn to interpret and respond to their babies' cries as "you can't spoil a baby," mothers must breastfeed, parents must wear their babies in slings, sleeping in the same bed and frequent overnight breastfeeding are important, parents must be appropriately responsive—not too much, not too little—and never ever sleep-train your baby.

Currently, the two principles that generate the most controversy are that breast-feeding is superior to bottle-feeding and the Sears' position on sleep training, particularly their assertion that the "cry it out" method causes brain damage. The lasting effects of post-birth bonding and continuous wearing also have their share of skeptics, given the consequences for working parents, adopted children, and parents who would like to get a full night of sleep. While the Sears' ideas have been around for over twenty-five years, they became the focus of media attention when their views were aggressively defended by sitcom actress/neuroscientist Mayim Bialik. Bialik revealed that she had breastfed her son until he was four. She also announced she would not vaccinate her children—though this was not a part of the Sears' approach—which led to even more attention, and in some cases, ridicule and anger. One can probably make a few generalizations about the type of people that attachment parenting speaks to: white, middle class, college educated, organic-ish, politically liberal, and "post-feminist." They often view attachment parenting as the "natural" or "instinctual" approach that modern societies have lost touch with.

For some, attachment parenting romanticizes a past that was not especially good for women. Critics like Judith Warner (2006) argue that an ideology of "total motherhood" has created an age of anxious and guilt-ridden mothers. One wonders whether any of the progressive women who adopt attachment parenting are familiar with the Sears' 1997 book, *The Complete Book of*

Christian Parenting and Child Care, where they complain that "mothers choose to go back to their jobs quickly simply because they don't understand . . . [how bad] that is to the well-being of their babies. So many babies in our culture are not cared for in the way God designed, and we as a nation are paying the price." If one can't afford this, Sears' advice: Borrow money. A slightly more-to-the-point critique comes from Village Voice blog writer Jeff Ote (5/14) responding to a *Time* magazine cover story on attachment parenting:

> Babies are assholes. They're demanding, they're utterly self-centered, they have no empathy, and they shriek horrible horrible shrieks when they don't get what they want. And that's okay because they are babies . . . but nobody likes a grown adult who acts like a fucking baby. Hell nobody likes a kid who acts like a fucking baby, either, but that's exactly the kind of kid attachment parenting produces because, by definition, the model requires no adjustment.

His point is that attachment parenting does not allow babies to learn to tolerate disappointment, which turns them into children who cannot tolerate disappointment. This argument might feel correct, but as with parenting styles in general, there really is no way to demonstrate this conclusively and is yet another radical oversimplification. As we will explore in more detail later, the adjudication of these types of claims is simply beyond the purview of science. Still, attachment parenting does introduce some more specific questions that might be more amenable to research. For example, defenders of attachment parenting offer research to defend the breast-feeding claim, the negative effects of early separation (e.g., in day care) claim, as well as some of the others. They typically tend to cite single studies, whereas a review of the literature in general is much more ambiguous. As a general rule, human infants are quite adaptive, and given the variability in parenting practices across the globe, it is fair to say that almost anything can work.

Here are a few examples. The co-sleeping suggestion conflicts with the American Academy of Pediatrics position that co-sleeping is associated with higher rates of SIDS (sudden infant death syndrome), though the AAP does advocate room sharing for the first few months, which is linked with decreases in SIDS. The findings about SIDS has now become part of conventional wisdom and are defended by medical authorities even though the risk of SIDS is extremely low either way—about 60 infants in a year die from SIDS while co-sleeping (there about 2,000 SIDS deaths a years in total)—and is mostly associated with the combination of poverty, maternal exhaustion, drugs, alcohol and cigarette use, and/or infants placed to sleep under pillows or duvet covers. Defenders of attachment parenting often blame the "crib industry" for perpetuating the notion of the danger of co-sleeping. In fact, co-sleeping, along with the other SIDS-associated behavior, prone sleeping, are fairly common around the world. Judith Warner is surely right about how "facts" like these create anxious and guilt-ridden mothers.

Others studies often-cited point to the long-lasting effects of early deprivation. One influential study of "late-placed" Romanian orphans found links between early global deprivation and specific cognitive and behavior deficits. These were also linked to the decreased glucose metabolism in certain areas in the brain, areas typically affected by stress including the orbital frontal gyrus, the infralimbic prefrontal cortex, the medial temporal structures, the lateral temporal cortex, and the brain stem (Chugani et al., 2001). While the small sample size should suggest caution as far as generalization and correlations between deficits and brain structures are very difficult to interpret, it seems reasonable to infer that prolonged institutional care along with parental deprivation affects the brain in adverse ways. This in itself is a fairly robust finding across different types of deprivation. Still, the specific causal pathways are unknown. What it really means is that children require intensive parenting to grow up in the ways that we want them to in modern Western industrialized societies. This should not be very surprising given how much we expect from children as they grow and how culturally and historically specific those expectations are. We might describe this as "goodness of fit" between parenting and society. That being said, one doesn't have to adopt an attachment parenting style to make this happen. For better or worse, the best path for success in modern, Western industrialized societies, at least as we have elected to define it, is growing up in middle and high SES homes with parents with at least college degrees.

Dewar, a defender of attachment parenting as well, lists a few of the commonly cited studies on her parenting science website. One study of British schoolchildren found that those who co-slept with parents or did not attend day care during the first four years of life had lower levels of the stress hormone cortisol after family discord than those who did not co-sleep or did attend day care (Waynforth, 2007). Dewar actually offers several studies with similar findings about the relationship between secure attachment and lower levels of stress in infants. Of course, we will never know how many unpublished studies didn't find this relationship. Nor will anyone bother to study the "negative" effects of decreased cortisol in securely attached infants. Cortisol is not always bad. But it has become "bad" as it becomes associated with things we don't like (e.g., stress, bad parenting, weight gain, anxiety). This reminds us of an important lesson when it comes to making sense of popular psychology, even psychological research in general: Always consider what research questions do not get asked. Maybe our understanding of parenting will become clearer when we start to investigate the positive effects of "bad" parenting or the negative effects of "good" parenting.

Finally, another set of studies often mentioned by other defenders of attachment parenting are those that involve caregiving among the !Kang San people. They live as hunter-gatherers and caregiving includes almost constant physical contact between infant and caregiver, constant carrying in a sling, almost continuous feedings for the first three years of life, and immediate responsiveness to infant distress (Barr, 2013). In other words, they are the ideal version of attachment parenting. They have been used to make the case that Western "separation" parenting is a relatively recent phenomenon and maybe even an unhealthy one. Their infants tend to show less distress behavior (e.g., crying) and shorter responses to stressful or painful experiences. When Western mothers were trained in the "!Kung San" style, similar effects were found. Does this make "attachment" parenting the ideal form of caregiving? No, argues Ronald Barr (2013), as different practices are adaptations to the particular societies they evolve in. While nice for parents, who says an infant that cries less will end up better off than one who doesn't? Infants are remarkably adaptive organisms that easily adjust to a variety of potential caregiving conditions. There is simply no way to make a judgment about the optimal one for a particular infant.

Attachment parenting had its moment in the media spotlight. A few years before the media-provoked debate over attachment parenting, there were media-provoked debates over "helicopter" parenting, followed by ones on "overparenting," and "unconditional" or "positive" parenting, all seeming to lead to the "permissive" end of Baumrind's spectrum. As if to brandish the helicopters, positives, permissives, and unconditionals once and for all, along came Chinese parenting, or "Tiger Mom." The most recent parenting-related media moment belongs to Chinese parenting inspired by Amy Chua's *Battle Hymn of the Tiger Mom*. In a *Wall Street Journal* piece coinciding with the publication of her book, Chua began her battle cry.

> A lot of people wonder how Chinese parents raise such stereotypically successful kids. . . . Well, I can tell them, because I've done it. Here are some of the things my daughters . . . were never allowed to do: attend a sleepover, have a play date, be in a school play, complain about not being in a school play, watch TV or play video games, choose their own extracurricular activities, get any grade less than A, not be the No. 1 student in any subject except gym or drama, play any instrument besides the piano or violin, not play the piano or violin. . . . even when Western parents think they are being strict, they usually don't come close to being Chinese mothers. (1/2011)

Chua's book set off a firestorm in the media and blogosphere: Was she bringing sanity to the current crop of overly permissive American parents obsessed with "nurturing" their children, or was she a narcissistic monster torturing her daughters for her own unmet needs? Was this really about culture: West versus East? Other books joined the fray. Pamela Druckerman's *Bringing Up Bebe* (2012) advocated French parenting where, according to her, children must accept being mostly ignored by their parents as they learn their place and enjoy delicious French food from infancy on. On her blog, attachment parenting advocate Gwen Dewar cites a longitudinal study showing that Tiger Parenting hurts—they are too negative, and "negativity" in parenting is associated with poorer outcomes (Kim and Rohner, 2002). Although Dewar doesn't mention this, Kim's study is difficult to interpret because SES is a major confound. One possible interpretation is that Tiger Parenting is better for middle-class parents who have the time to put in the work like Chua did. Dewar also neglects other studies that found that authoritarian techniques were interpreted differently by whites and Asians (Chao, 1994).

More recently, former "tiger baby," Kim Won Kelter, published *Tiger Babies Strike Back*, her account of growing up with a strict, authoritarian mother. In this case, Tiger Parenting comes across as anything but good parenting. In response to this and similar criticisms, Chua likes to remind her critics that children of Asians are overrepresented in the best high schools and colleges in the country and that those are pretty good outcomes. The problem is, her analysis leaves little ground to separate cause from effect and, as we shall see, this turns out to be the case in the academic research on parenting as well, not to mention that "Asians in the best high schools and colleges" are hardly representative of Asians in general. In the end, as Peter Stearns (2004) notes, these questions about what makes a good parent are both sources of parental anxiety and responses to parental anxiety. Living in a more uncertain world means parents feel more responsible for how their children turn out and the parenting advice literature tends to capitalize on that anxiety as it also tries to treat it. Would it help parents if they understood that it is not possible to ever really know the effects they have on their children?

ACADEMIC VARIANTS

Recipes for good children are, of course, not new to the late twentieth century. As Ann Hulbert (2003) tells it, at least since the nineteenth century when the Second Great Awakening inspired a "theology of feelings," experts have been advising mothers on using their "feminine instincts" to shape innocent souls in their charge. Several elements of Rousseauian romanticism—the innocence of the young, the importance of mother-love, the privileging of the heart over the head—were combined with Victorian notions of true womanhood to create a mother whose very nature was designed to bring forth "men of character" (Hulbert, 2003, p. 25). Similar forms of maternal power appear again and again in the history of parenting psychology in the United States. They seem to counterbalance the "fatherly" forces concerned with discipline and instilling a proper Christian disposition, forces less available anyway as the spheres of home and work were further separated from each other in the age of industrialization. Such important work was simply too daunting to be left to women and their instincts alone, thus a new class of experts arose to guide them.

By the turn of the twentieth century, there was G. Stanley Hall, on one hand, whose child study movement urged mothers to observe their children carefully and respect their "natures," and L. Emmett Holt, on the other, of the newly established field of pediatrics, whose *The Care and Feeding of Children* promised to replace sentimentality with rigor and detachment. Both agreed that modern life and its effects on the psyche and the body had made child-rearing too complex for mothers to handle alone. Middle-class women, argues Hulbert, flocked to this scientific approach. Each of these positions would be repeated again and again in the twentieth century in various incarnations. The defense of sentimentality in its diverse forms would be taken up by Arnold Gesell, Benjamin Spock, and John Bowlby, while criticism of it, especially when it was seen as going too far, would be taken up by John Watson, Bruno Bettleheim, and in a sense, the early work of Diana Baumrind. Over time, Baumrind's notion of an ideal parenting style would combine elements of both positions.

Earlier in the twentieth century, psychologists, influenced by either psychoanalysis or behaviorism, began to look toward parenting behavior to explain certain childhood outcomes. For behaviorists, the key to these outcomes lay in patterns of parental reinforcement, while for psychoanalysts, the conflict between biological drives and societal expectations as expressed, for instance, in a situation like toilet training, resulted in certain types of personality configurations. By the 1950s, some psychologists began to call into question whether specific parenting practices could be mapped onto certain outcome variables and instead looked to broader parental "attitudes" as shapers of outcomes (Schaefer, 1959). The "attitude" was seen as determining not only parental practice, but a whole set of broader behaviors and relationships that gave those practices meaning (Darling and Steinberg, 1993).

Talk of parental attitudes, and later parenting "styles," became a way to describe an emotional climate in which specific parental behaviors were expressed and meaning assigned to them. Certain behaviors were seen as representative of broader attitudes that influenced behavior including granting autonomy, punitiveness, control, use of fear, and patterns of affection. Those influenced by behaviorism used various techniques to link specific behaviors together as part of a parenting style, but viewed the notion of a "style" as a convenient heuristic, while in contrast, those influenced by psychoanalysis tended to regard parenting styles as real, linking parental behavior to childhood emotional processes (Darling and Steinberg, 1993). There remained across the field a tension between a focus on behavior and one on emotional processes, a tension that Baumrind's work sought to resolve. There was agreement, however, on what the ideal outcome was supposed to look like: a child who was socialized, cooperative, friendly, emotionally stable, cheerful, honest, dependable, and a good citizen (ibid., p. 489). Baumrind (1970) later described this type of child as "instrumentally competent." There was also consensus that certain parenting practices contributed to that outcome. Typically those practices were said to include warmth, encouraging autonomy within certain limitations, and explicit communication of guidelines.

One early approach to capturing differing parenting styles was the distinction made in the work of Robert Sears (Sears et al., 1957) between love-oriented and object-oriented parental disciplinary styles; the former used warmth and affection and the latter tangible objects to respond to their children's behavior. The children of love-oriented parents, argued Sears, were more likely to internalize their values and therefore led to better outcomes. There were other theories of parenting styles before Baumrind that involved distinctions between democratic and autocratic (Baldwin, 1948), dominance and submission (Symonds, 1939), as well as control and non-control (Schaefer, 1959). There was a consensus that parents who provided children with nurture/warmth, independence/autonomy, and firm control had children who were both more competent and more socially adept (Spera, 2005).

Baumrind combined all of these approaches. To do this, she reconfigured the notion of parental control, turning it from talk of strictness and punishment toward a strategy used by parents to integrate children into the family and society by requiring behavioral compliance. By the late 1960s, Baumrind saw the notion of parenting style as a means of capturing the relationship between certain beliefs about parental roles and the nature of children with specific affect patterns, values, and practices. Here is her classic description of the authoritative parent:

> She encourages verbal give and take, and shares with the child the reasoning behind her policy. She values both expressive and instrumental attributes, both autonomous self-will and disciplined conformity. Therefore, she exerts firm control at points of parent-child divergence, but does not hem the child in with restrictions. She recognizes her own special rights as an adult, but also the child's individual interests and special ways. The authoritative parent affirms the child's present qualities, but also sets standards for future conduct. She uses reason as well as power to achieve her objectives. She does not base her decisions on group consensus or the individual child's desires; but also does not regard herself as infallible or divinely inspired. (Baumrind, 1968, p. 242)

She distinguished this type of parental control from an authoritarian and permissive type, offering three fully operationalized categories of parenting style in which behavior, values, and attitudes were all linked together into whole and stable patterns. The permissive parent, as described by Baumrind, comes across in a much more unflattering light.

> The permissive parent attempts to behave in a nonpunitive, acceptant and affirmative manner towards the child's impulses, desires and actions. She consults with him about policy decisions and gives explanations for family rules. She makes few demands for household responsibility and orderly behavior. She presents herself to the child as a resource for him to use, as he wishes, not an ideal for him to emulate, nor as an active agent responsible for shaping or altering his ongoing and future behavior. She allows the child to regulate his own activities as much as possible, avoids the exercise of control, and does not encourage him to obey externally defined standards. (1966, p. 889)

She then links permissiveness to psychoanalytic notions of infantile gratification, Benjamin Spock's defense of lenient child-rearing practices, and what she terms extreme child-centered educators like A. S. Neil and Nelson Goodman. It is worth noting that some of these qualities would be considered key to good parenting today, especially the accepting attitude and nonconformity to external standards. Baumrind seems to suggest that some of the parental behaviors valued today—more democratic structure, avoiding control, and ambivalence about making demands—are a problem. Working in Berkeley, California, it is not hard to imagine there were lots of hippies-turned-parents and these were clearly some of Baumrind's original targets, less so with the authoritarian ones.

Baumrind's real target in these early articles is permissiveness, which gets most of her scorn, as well as the child-centered educators who defend it. There is also a notable absence of any mention of affection or nurturance in these descriptions, although her students suggest those were important issues for her from the get-go (Criss and Larzelere, 2013, p. 3). Despite these protests, it does seem that these elements, what eventually becomes described as responsiveness, were not that central to her original formulations but were stressed later as a function of the influence of others. In this early work, Baumrind goes on to apply these principles to several common parenting practices. She defends the value of "mild" punishment from those who use either harsh punishment or seek to replace it with reward withdrawal. She also defends high demands for order from those pseudo-Freudians who see them as leading to obsessive and compulsive characteristics in children as well as firm parental control from those who view it as leading to passivity and dependency. Much of her argument revolves around the value of the right kind of control.

Her findings suggested a link between these styles of control and a range of more or less directly related parenting practices, including communication and expectations for achievement—often termed "maturity demands." For instance, both authoritative and authoritarian parents had high maturity demands, but the latter were unwilling or unable to communicate the reasons for them to their children (Baumrind, 1978). Similarly, both authoritative and permissive parents were moderate to high on responsiveness, yet the latter were low on maturity demands. Only authoritative-styled parents got the balance right for the outcomes they sought. While recognizing that children contribute to their own development in ways that had not been fully understood previously, her framework attempted to separate parent-child relationships into a parent-behavior component and a child-behavior component. While she sought to focus only on the former, she insisted that the parent component could affect the child component, as is the case when authoritative parenting makes children more capable of making better choices on their own (Darling and Steinberg, 1993).

Baumrind's approach combined a broad theoretical view about the role of parents with a simple typology that was easily translated into a research program. Its influence is not surprising. By the 1980s, this model was employed in the great bulk of research into the effects of parents on children. Sympathetic critics Eleanor Maccoby and John Martin (1983) added a fourth "uninvolved" style as well as argued these findings were better captured along two dimensions: responsiveness and demandingness. The ideal authoritative type was high in both demandingness and responsiveness, creating the unique blend of conformity and autonomy that the instrumentally competent child possesses. This change, soon adopted by Baumrind as well, was methodologically advantageous because parenting style could be captured by quantitative differences along two measures.

Two things about this research program were never questioned: (1) that there are better and worse parenting styles, and (2) that each of these styles are associated with specific outcomes. It seemed self-evident that parents who are "virtuous" with respect to their children, at least in terms that made sense to late-twentieth-century America, had children who were "virtuous." Perhaps we have found an instance of Kahneman's representative bias where like goes with like. Clearly, parents who raise children in the right way—loving, communicative, respectful, enforcing discipline firmly but not harshly—raised the right kind of children—reasonably obedient, autonomous, respectful, cheerful, and successful in school, with lots of friends. And even though, over the years, clear-cut evidence for this link has never really been established, in fact, as we shall see, it is probably impossible to establish, it gradually became part of accepted wisdom in psychology. Judith Harris (1998) called this the "nurture assumption" and attributes it to a general interest in socialization on the part of psychologists. But it's probably fair to say that this has been a fairly established belief in the West for a long time. It was certainly shared in some sense by both Locke and Rousseau, two of the most influential thinkers in the West when it comes to laying out the nature of childhood.

PROBLEMS WITH ACADEMIC SOURCES (I)

The consensus in the field today is that the balance between responsiveness and demandingness associated with authoritative parenting consistently leads to optimal outcomes. Some authors have also sought to link the authoritative style with secure parent-child attachments (Morris et al., 2013). Research over the years has focused on identifying the components that make up parenting style, viewing style as part of a broader context. Yet the actual practices associated with authoritativeness are quite diverse and not always consistent across studies. Based on a recent review of findings by Carolyn Henry and Laura Hubbs-Tait (2013), here is just a short list of authoritative practices: warmth, acceptance, support for autonomy, valuing children, lack of intrusion, emotion coaching, scaffolding, developing mentally appropriate demands, firm direct monitoring, behavioral containment, structure, redirection, reasonable hierarchical sequentially applied power assertive strategies, adult-defined limit setting, promoting self-reliance, quality relationship reflecting goals and skills of parents, firm control, and involvement (240–241). In terms of outcomes, over the years, a range of measures have been the focus, including aggressive incidents, delinquency, levels of depression or anxiety, externalizing behaviors, internalizing or mental health issues, cognitive abilities, academic outcomes, social competence, quality of peer relationships, pro-social and popularity ratings by peers, emotional understanding, perspective taking, emotional regulation, self-esteem, self-concept, frequency of sexual and health-risk behaviors, frequency of physical injury/accidents, and obesity.

More importantly, the consensus in the field is that the findings support weak to moderate correlations between parenting and most of these outcomes, though there is little to connect specific elements of parenting to specific outcomes (Maccoby, 2000). As we will review later, the field has generally moved to giving more attention to the complex interrelationships between biology, temperament, parenting style, family system, and a broader cultural context (Henry and Hubbs-Tait, 2013; Morris et al., 2013), though one would not necessarily know this reading popular psychology, as it still focuses on the primary influence of parents. While the findings on authoritativeness had traditionally been interpreted as demonstrating the effects of parents on children, as Eleanor Maccoby, one of the most influential psychologists in the field notes, the relationship can go in the other direction as well: Competent and cooperative children make it easier for parents to be firm yet responsive. According to Maccoby, until the mid-1980s, parenting research showed only weak correlations between parenting styles and child characteristics, though since then, she claims, more robust findings have emerged. She attributes this to improved methods and measures including multiple data sources rather than single measures. When these data are aggregated, argues Maccoby, correlations rise in a meaningful way. She identifies several studies, but when most are examined carefully, it is not clear that they demonstrate a general relationship between parenting style and child outcomes.

For example, quite a few of the notable findings cited by Maccoby as to the effects of parenting style on outcomes come out of research looking specifically at the association between aggressive behavior among disturbed adolescents and parent-child relationship quality. This makes sense given that these are the types of families that seek psychological treatment and thus are more available to participate in such studies. For example, Patterson and Forgach (1995) found relatively high correlations between parental characteristics and children's antisocial behavior, but they did so in the context of treatments for preadolescent children's antisocial behaviors. Part of what makes generalizing from similar studies complicated is that aggressive behavior, or the more generic term "externalizing" behavior, is often defined differently depending on the particular study. Thus, it is unclear exactly what a reduction of these behaviors as a measure of a successful outcome exactly means. Moreover, they tend to point to the effects of bad parenting practices and the changes that can come with modifying them as opposed to the effects of good parenting, where an intervention and a study of its effects would not make sense.

Another study cited by Maccoby is also difficult to interpret. She refers to a study by Conger and Elder (1994), published as part of *Families in Troubled Times*. The particular study Maccoby references is one of many out of a decade-plus longitudinal study of 451 rural Iowan families that focused on the effects of the farm crisis. The authors developed a "Family Stress Model," wherein families in economic difficulties enter a downward spiral that affects, among many other things, parenting behavior. The authors describe a path analysis that identified a causal relationship between economic hardship, increased emotional distress in parents, and increases in negative parenting practice (e.g., yelling, withdrawal). These in turn led to adolescent depressed moods. Over time, the young people whose families were hit worse financially fared worse on social, academic, and psychological outcomes, though this was mitigated by adaptive responses by some of the adolescents studied (Conger and Conger, 2002).

Although the study presents a vivid portrait of the effects of economic crises on rural families, it is difficult to make generalizations about the effects of parenting given how specific these conditions are. Even if one could make these generalizations, despite the authors' claim, it is likely that the relationship between parenting practice and adolescent outcomes is not one of direct cause-effect, but one that involves multiple sources of mediating processes and relationships. The problem is that these types of longitudinal studies are expensive, rare, and usually issue specific. Further, as Maccoby herself admits, predictive relationships derived from longitudinal studies are, not surprisingly, often weaker than concurrent ones, and findings tend to depend on the way variables are measured and other variables controlled.

Maccoby describes a few other studies that address the link between parenting behavior and outcome a bit more directly. In one study Kochanska (1997) found a small but significant correlation between parenting practice and children's self-regulation assessed a year later. Another study found even weaker predictive relations between parenting and academic performance (Petit et al., 1997), but a bit stronger ones with antisocial behavior (Loeber and Dishion, 1983). Still others found stronger predictive relationships between certain dynamics of the parent-child interaction (e.g., mutual responsivity, shared positive affect) and outcomes (Kochanska and Thompson, 1997). Specifically, the Kochanska and Thompson study found that firm parental control was ideal for temperamentally aggressive children but not temperamentally fearful ones. The authors interpret this as evidence that there might not be a singular ideal parenting style, but instead good parenting involves a fit between a particular parent and a particular child. This seems to make a fair amount of sense.

Similarly, Petit et al. (1997) focused on specific components of authoritative parenting and found that certain ones are associated with better outcomes as opposed to others. This led them to call into question Baumrind's and the field's holistic "parenting style" approach. Certain parenting practices did appear to correlate with outcomes: For example, parental monitoring of adolescents living in high-crime neighborhoods was correlated with lower levels of delinquency, but the same relationship did not extend to low-crime neighborhoods. In other words, successful parenting is not only child-specific but is also specific to the broader context. Again, all this makes sense and it calls into question whether the notion of an ideal parenting style makes any sense.

One general question about these findings over the years is the extent to which they describe the dynamics of white, middle class families and universalize them. Some have argued that one sees better outcomes with authoritarian parenting when looking at minority families (Baumrind, 1972; Chao, 1994), while others have made the case that authoritative parenting also produces the better outcomes in minority families, even though it is rarer (Steinberg et al., 1992). Some view the values described in this tradition as more suited to individualist as opposed to collectivist cultures, while others simply see that the same authoritarian practices in different cultures are interpreted differently (Sorkhabi and Mandara, 2013).

Maccoby acknowledges these problems and sees them reflected in the methodological changes over the years (2000, pp. 6–7). For one, recent studies no longer rely on first-order correlations between parenting variables and outcomes, but instead, multivariate analyses are used to look at different types of effects, with different children at different time points in different circumstances. This is key to ensuring that effects do not "wash out" in a more general analysis. Yet, despite Maccoby's claims, it is really difficult to generalize from these studies, especially since, given their size and cost, they are almost impossible to replicate. Even in the case of indirect relationships acquired via regression and other correlational-based techniques, common practices in psychology that we will review shortly, the variance explained in the findings are often as much about sample and variable specification as they are about parenting.

More importantly, argues Maccoby, there has been recognition in the field that small correlations are not necessarily indicative of small real-world effects, another important question that we will pick up shortly. Furthermore, not all elements of parent-child relationships can be measured. Summarizing this, Maccoby explains,

> When [small correlations are] translated into the number of children who are at risk, for example, for failing in school or becoming delinquent or seriously depressed, predictive coefficients of this magnitude can be seen as by no means trivial. From the standpoint of social policy, the issue becomes one of how much importance a society attaches to social/behavioral outcomes. . . . this is obviously a matter of values not statistics. (2000, p. 7)

This makes sense despite the fact that "small correlations" cannot be translated into a "number of children." Recent meta-analyses have confirmed most of Maccoby's criticisms—though it is rare to find a published meta-analysis today that looks exclusively at parenting effects on outcomes, as the associations tend to be small, indirect, and the consensus in the field is that one must include variables related to heredity and temperament. For example, one meta-analysis of 161 studies looking at the relationship between parenting practice and delinquency found that specific practices like parental monitoring, psychological control, and negative support like rejection or hostility were associated with delinquency, yet the actual correlation means ranged from 0.12 to 0.23 (Hoeve et al., 2009). Interestingly, the effect sizes were higher for "negative" parental practices as opposed to "positive" ones (.30 versus .17).

One needs to be careful of over-interpretation, but it might just be that bad parenting affects children more than good parenting does in the case of "delinquents." The authors also found slightly higher effects when accounting for parent and children's gender or delinquency type, though still quite small. They interpret this, as Maccoby did with the other studies reviewed, as an indication that parenting might have greater effects with specific subgroups or situations. Yet there are other, simpler ways to interpret the fact that looking for multiple correlations with different variables and subgroups yields "significant" relationships related to the very nature of statistical significance. Another recent meta-analysis found even smaller effects for parenting styles (McLeod et al., 2006) and the few that do find larger effects—e.g., between parenting and academic achievement (Kordi and Baharudin, 2010)—tend to include fewer, lower-quality studies focused on very specific populations.

To summarize: There are some basic conceptual problems with this research program. To start with, the assumption of monolithic parenting styles or even consistent parenting practices is probably unwarranted. Most parents with more than one child would likely acknowledge that one's nurturing and disciplinary attitudes and behaviors are often child-specific and context-specific. Different children need different things from parents and different contexts tend to trigger more or less nurturance and discipline. On the other hand, these shifts probably occur within certain ranges. Certain parents will never be all that loving with their children. Perhaps they are not especially nurturing in any relationship. Either way, the role of specific children is central, whether one elects to describe this as an effect of a reciprocal relationship or as a response to a child's temperament or genetics. But it also suggests that parenting style is not simply a choice parents make but might be related to parent's own unique combination of temperament, history, and habit.

Moreover, how does one decide what elements of a parent-child relationship are to be included in the variable parenting? Is "parenting" limited to moments when parents are focused on responding to a specific child's behavior and needs, or does it include all that plays into a relationship between parents and their children? Is making dinner together parenting? Is buying a house in a certain neighborhood parenting? Is fighting with your spouse around your children parenting? Typically, "parenting" is operationalized using measures of select variables related to discipline, nurturance, etc., but that seems to leave much out.

In the end, it is probably impossible to establish any generalizations about how parents affect children, impossible to isolate the effects of parents from everything else that is going on, and impossible to make predictions about how children will turn out given their parents. There is simply too much that is unpredictable. Yet, it is also understandable why both psychologists and parents would wish this were not the case. This does seem to get to the heart of what psychologists are supposed to be able to do in our society: help to create better people, even though "better" is always culturally and historically variable. Thus it is not surprising that these themes make for good popular psychology. The real issue is whether the correlation- and regression-based methods that psychologists employ can reliably identify a directional relationship between parenting and childhood outcomes at all. This is the question we take up in the next section.

A REVIEW OF THE METHODOLOGICAL ISSUES AT STAKE: CORRELATION AND REGRESSION

There are two basic rules of thumb about correlations in psychology that are worth making explicit. First, correlation is not causation—except for sometimes, and second, most everything in psychology is correlated with everything else. Given a large enough sample, correlations are not all that difficult to find. In an unpublished study by Paul Meehl and David Lykken in which fifteen selected variables (e.g., parents' education, birth order, future plans, religious preference) were cross-tabulated for a sample of 57,000 Minnesotans, they found that all of them turned out to be statistically significant—96 percent of them at $p < 0.000001$. Reflecting on the study, Meehl (1990) concluded that the "null" hypothesis that the correlation between arbitrarily paired variables is close to zero and that one is therefore justified in attaching importance to statistically significant correlational findings is almost certainly wrong. As we shall see, correlations vary with variable selection because this changes the population studied. Despite the wish to the contrary, correlations can hardly be a path to causal relations if the latter operates on single instances and the former on populations whose members vary (Cohen, 1994, p. 1001). The real advantage of correlations is that they make it easier to avoid thinking about what exactly is being measured (Scheines et al., 1998; Mcdonald, 1997). The danger is to forget that "uncorrelated" simply means not related in a very specific way, not that variables are unrelated.

Correlations were the first widely used statistic employed by psychologists. They were derived from the original Galtonian program of linking talent and heredity. Galton's interest in how one set of properties about groups was related to another led him to discover that when one quality was plotted on a graph in relation to another, then the slope of the best-fit line offered a way to describe a relationship that appeared free of human judgment and simply a product of the data (Pearl, 2000). While Galton's original formulations treated "reversion to the mean," or regression, as a biological law—the tendency of future generations to revert to an ancestral mean—he gradually recognized that the linear regression model he identified was a special case of correlations in general (Porter, 1986). For him, the identification of a correlational relationship was indication of a common cause. It allowed him to explain the cause of the stability of natural variation (290). Galton's real innovation was not so much the depiction of this linear relationship, but that variation could be distinguished into classes, that were explained by the correlated variable and the rest, which could be attributed to error (293). This capacity to partition variation is what made the technique of correlation so revolutionary, especially given that Darwinist thinking was pushing psychologists to deal with variation more directly.

Through the work of Galton's student, Karl Pearson, correlational techniques were developed so that mathematical analysis could be extended into many fields, including psychology. Like many in his generation, Pearson was initially skeptical of such statistical techniques as they seemed to undermine the "exactness" of science, but ultimately described himself as liberated by Galton from the assumption that mathematics could only be applied to natural phenomena under the category of causation (Stigler, 1986, p. 305). This allowed uncertainty to extend deeper into science. It was no longer simply a means for accounting for error so that constants could be identified, as it was for Fechner, but it actually established the ground for the definition of the very quantities psychologists were interested in making inferences about (360). For example, correlations became the basis for Spearman's argument that intelligence was a single attribute and it quickly became an essential ingredient in the toolkit of IQ testers and educational reformers interested in the characteristics of large populations, not causal process in individual minds (Danziger, 1987, p. 40).

Unlike the case with the classical Wundtian experimental model where there was disparity between variables—one was clearly dependent on another and this was established via controlling conditions—in the correlational model, variables were symmetrical and no controls were possible (Danziger, 1987). From a purely Wundtian perspective this was a weakness, yet in the case of American psychologists looking to move into more applied settings where such controls were impossible anyway, this was actually an advantage. As we reviewed in a prior chapter, for those interested in identifying causes more directly, the notion of comparing "treatment" and "control" groups sustained the focus on variability in a population, yet permitted inferences about causes. Yet even this was not necessary with the further development of regression techniques. Pearson's student, George Yule, went further than Pearson and conceived the linear regression line as a surrogate for a causal relationship (Stigler, 1986).

Given this, it is clear why early psychologists found them so attractive. They appeared to offer a path to causality in the sense that the closer a correlation between two variables is to 1.0—that is, the distance from the mean for one variable corresponds with the distance from the mean of another—the more likely one can be said to be the cause of the other. What made them still more attractive was that the relationship could be represented graphically and used to predict future data. Here, prediction acted as a stand-in for causality without having to explain any actual mechanisms. Moreover, because they indicated the strength and direction of a relationship, they could also be used to compare the strength of different variables that do not share the same units of measurement.

Yet, there are basic problems with comparing correlations, correlation coefficients, or anything from this entire family of data across groups. Naturally, correlations can differ because of the strength of a relationship, but they can also differ if the variances in the samples are different. Thus, when one changes the sample, the variance changes and therefore the correlation changes (Achen, 1977). In other words, when comparing samples, a stronger correlation is no guarantee that the relationship is necessarily stronger. The reason this is the case is due to the fact that correlations are computed by relating the way two variables vary together in relation to how they vary separately. It is a measure of the relationship between specific locations in one variable's distribution as compared with another's. Change the distribution and you change the correlation. This gives a lot of influence to outliers in the data and also is easily distorted when one's data are limited to a restrictive range (e.g., due to intentional or unintentional sampling or design issues).

An area where correlational research has thrived yet is especially misleading is in neuroscience, from where findings often make their way into psychology. The problem has been one of inflated correlations or what critics have termed "voodoo" correlations (Fiedler, 2011). Researchers often forget that while correlations are measures of the relationship between two variables, their limits are determined by the reliability of measures. For instance, one study focused on correlations between brain measures and behavioral criteria across some high-profile findings in social neuroscience. They found that certain measurement points were selected to maximize the strength of correlational relationships (Vul et al., 2009).

The specific correlations criticized were those between blood oxygenation level–related activity in the brain and various behavioral measures of individual differences, personality, and social relationships. Measuring changes in blood oxygenation using FMRI scans to indicate activity is fairly typical of neuroscience research. The assumption is that the increased oxygenation implies increased activity. Thus the point was to correlate certain behavioral measures with brain activity. But as Vul et al. explains, some of the correlations they found in their survey of recent findings were unusually large, some up to $r = 0.88$, which is typically the case only if one is correlating measures of the same variable—in the real world there is always measurement error. The idea that specific brain areas are that closely associated with specific behavioral measures of empathy or distress seemed unrealistic at best (275).

At the very least, the high correlations suggest the variables are not independent of each other. Yet, they certainly seem to be at first glance, at least until one looks at the measures themselves. Typically, a full brain analysis involves the measurement of about 100,000 points or voxels, and only those voxels with the highest correlations were included in the analyses. In other words, the researchers were using data from the dependent measure—the behavioral variable—to construct the independent variable—brain activity.

By selecting measurements already correlated with the criteria, even if these correlations were derived from previous research, the authors are guilty of circular inferences, or "double-dipping," meaning the conclusions are used to interpret the evidence (Fiedler, 2011, p. 163). This is exacerbated by the low power of correlations in general but especially given the small sample sizes in FMRI research, which makes it likely correlations will be inflated anyway (Yarkoni, 2009). This suggests the authors are missing a lot of stable correlations and perhaps focusing mostly on outlier ones.

But this problem goes well beyond neuropsychology. Fiedler describes this as the problem of non-independence. At base, the problem identified by Vul et al. is one of sampling. The problem is the failure to treat various forms of stimuli/independent variables and measures/dependent variables as one treats random factors. In other words, they are carefully chosen because of the effect they have on the outcome variable. We took note of this in the previous chapters as we suggested that Lybomirsky's specific puzzle-solving task used to make the case that happy people are affected less by social comparison than unhappy people might be the source of some of the found differences as was the case with the way Kahneman framed his biases problems. There is obviously no way to know without varying the task. This is even more of a problem in correlational research, where it is easy to generate a variety of ways to define variables, thus making it easy to focus on those with the largest effects. Often this is done intuitively and is simply a result of the fact that researchers are skilled at variable construction that lead to publishable outcomes. In correlational research, independence is easily lost given certain sampling decisions, research questions, and operationalization of variables (Fiedler, 2011, p. 164). Fiedler offers the example of the relationship between TV consumption and aggression. Even if one does finds a correlation there, because no one bothers to study the relationship between TV and pro-social behavior, the found correlation easily leads to misleading inferences about the effects of television. Again, change the measure, the correlation changes.

There is also the example from the previous chapter of the IAT used to measure unconscious inference. We have already identified several problems with this instrument, but there is another related to the current discussion. In order to set up the procedure, researchers will select specific terms that are thought to stand in for broader categories. For example, in a typical study on implicit racial attitudes, the researchers might use "Michael Jordan" as an exemplar of the category "black" and "jail" as an exemplar for the category "unpleasant." If findings demonstrate a link between the category black and the category unpleasant, an implicit racist attitude is said to exist. Yet, it is not clear whether the findings are effects of the categories or specific stimuli.

In fact, one study interested in these questions looked at several findings on racial biases using the IAT and discovered that the exemplars for whites tended to be well-liked figures, while exemplars for blacks tended to be disliked ones (Mitchell et al., 2003). Another study found that when stimuli are altered, but not categories, results change (Bluemke and Friese, 2005). In other words, experimenters can select stimuli so that they yield the largest effects. One can make the same case for much of the research in positive psychology as well. After all, it is the researcher who constructs both the "stimulus" (e.g., happiness statements) and the "outcome" (e.g., happiness inventory). The only way to know this is to vary stimuli during successive replications. With correlations, these choices are even harder to detect, especially if the measures are themselves unreliable.

Misunderstanding the nature of correlational findings easily leads to confusion around which ones are meaningful. Typically, psychologists have a tendency to overestimate the degree of the estimated relationship. For instance, when presented with a correlation of 0.5, thirty psychologists described it as a "strong" one, but when faced with unknown data without actual correlations, they interpreted the same relationship as a "weak" one (Oakes, 1986, p. 91). Correlations can also lead to underestimation of relationships. In a well-known paper, Rosenthal and Rubin (1979) offer a fictional case where 100 patients are assigned to one medical treatment and 100 to another. After one year, 70 percent of patients in the first group are dead and 30 percent of patients in the second group are dead. A researcher is interested in measuring how much better the second treatment is than the first. The Pearson Product Moment Correlation between surviving and receiving treatment is $r = .40$, medium to large by psychology standards but the coefficient of determination or $r2 = .16$, typically interpreted as 16 percent of the variance in survival is explained by the variance in treatment, looks like a fairly small finding. Yet, there is no question the second group is the superior one in terms of reduction of the death rate if one understands that theoretically, though it makes no practical sense, for every 1 standard deviation increase in treatment, one can expect a .40 standard deviation increase in survival.

The confusion comes from the fact that neither r nor $r2$ are necessarily related in a straightforward way to the extent of the effect sizes that determine their impact in the world (Ozer, 1985). In this particular case, if the problem is expressed in meaningful units of measurement and the two groups compared, any test of the difference in means between the two groups would yield significant results. The point is, variables can account for only a small percent of the variance in a dependent variable, yet can have very important effects. Correlations can easily mislead researchers into confirming theories that are not justified by data or finding more stability in certain psychological activities than actually exists (Oakes, 1986; Clark, 1973).

There are similar misinterpretations of $r2$ or the very over-used coefficient of determination. Typically it is described as the percentage of the variance in the dependent variable explained by the variance in the independent variable (or, in regression, as a measure of the goodness-of-fit of a specific model). It is sometimes used as a measure of effect size as it can describe the amount of variance in outcome explained by a treatment, though this is highly misleading. It is important to understand where these interpretations come from in order to fully understand their limitations. In simple terms, *r*2 is equal to 1 minus the unexplained variation in the dependent variable divided by total variation in the dependent variable. It is a way of characterizing the amount of accounted for variation as compared with the total variation.

But the term "explained" in this case is a statistical concept and not a real-world one. Unexplained variation in statistical terms refers to the total sum of squares in excess of the point predicted by the regression line. It is a summary of the data. It is only one's interpretation that gives it meaning. The researcher selects the IV and DV depending on a credible theory. The data do not determine this. This can be more informative than a simple correlation as it provides more information than simply how two variables vary in relation to each other. The problem is, the cost of this additional information is the fairly restrictive assumption that one variable is dependent on another. A more accurate description of *r*2 is the measure of a spread of points around a regression line, says Gary King, and it is often a poor measure of that (1986, p. 675). This is because very differently distributed data points can have the same result. It shares the other problems of the correlation coefficient in general: *r*2 measures the strength of the relationship in such a way that it is dependent on the sample variance. It is difficult to use it to make inferences about populations. This is why replication is so important.

Because of the vagueness of its meaning, *r*2 is easily used to hint at a causal relationship in non-experimental contexts. In other words, the statement "X explains 50 percent of the variance in Y" trades on the slide from "explain" as a statistical relationship—meaning one value can be used to predict another—to "explain" as a real-world causal one. Often researchers get caught up in trying to increase *r*2 to demonstrate a stronger relationship, but again, this is deceptive. There are some simple ways to inflate *r*2 that have little to do with the strength of a relationship: use similar independent and dependent variables and add/delete variables or observations to increase variance in the independent variable (King, 1986, p. 677). Turns out, we can find examples of all of these strategies, though again perhaps not intentionally, in psychology, especially in the academic sources of popular psychology.

Regression is one of the most powerful of the correlation-derived tools, but also the most easily misused. All models are wrong, wrote the statistician George Box (1976, p. 792) but later added that some are still useful. Regression is an excellent technique for data description, an okay technique for data prediction, and a downright lousy one for causal analysis (Berk, 2004). A basic definition of regression is that it looks at how a conditional response varies across subpopulations determined by the value of predictors (12). An even more basic definition is a linear summary of data. Identities like "predictor" and "outcome" are not specified by the data itself (21). Often variables in conditional responses are described as being "held constant." This is true in the limited sense that the value is fixed but *not* in the experimental sense of control. By including multiple variables, associations between them change as the values of different ones are fixed. The choice of which ones to hold constant is also not a product of the data itself. In fact, if one moves beyond the study of specific conditional distributions, one requires information excessive of that produced by the data. Here is where problems can enter the picture.

Like the correlation coefficient, regression slopes are easily swayed by a few extreme values in data, meaning they tend to generate problems when one is looking to make inferences about populations. This makes it likely that new samples will bring different results, especially given the constrained samples of psychologists that tend not to represent populations. Using regressions to generate predictions, especially when one is drawing inferences from samples to populations, requires samples representative of that population in terms of variance. Clearly, this presents a problem for small samples. It also requires one stay within the range of values covered by the original data, a problem with constrained samples. Causal inferences require information excessive of the data. Using regression this way obscures the distinction between the real-world manipulation of variables and the statistical manipulation of variables. In the case of the former, the manipulation has actually happened; yet in the case of the latter, one is characterizing what would happen if such a manipulation would occur (Berk, 2004, p. 83).

Identifying causal effects always requires a comparison. In the case of the experiment, the comparison is the control and this is achieved by manipulating a single variable. In the case of regression, these comparisons are hypothetical. Comparisons are achieved by holding confounding variables constant. But if these possible confounding variables are not independent of each other, meaning no such individual manipulation is possible in the real world, then the results do not make any sense. As Richard Berk puts it, such inferences require a very cooperative real world that provides "interventions" separately (116). Despite this, the draw of multiple regression techniques in psychology is not hard to fathom. Especially in the age of computers, one can regress multiple independent variables on a single outcome variable and end up with a hierarchical list of "causes" that better explain the outcome. In multiple regression analysis, the estimated regression coefficients are now interpreted as partial slopes. They answer the question: When IV#1 changes by one unit and the other IVs are held constant—in a statistical sense, nothing is actually being controlled—how much change can we expect in the outcome?

While there is a temptation to interpret the different regression coefficients associated with different independent variables as an indication of the "strength" of the relationship, this is not possible unless they are standardized, as they reflect different units of measurement. Even then, one must tread carefully as regression coefficient differences are also a function of the variance in the specific variables. Interpretation of variables and their relationships requires a theory about what is happening. What typically happens is that certain conventionalized variables in a subfield are included in a stepwise regression—gender, age, race, ethnicity, income, family size, geography, parental education are some of typical ones of the parenting research we have been describing—and the outcome is parsed out along these variables. Adding variables increases the likelihood of a finding of statistical significance as $r2$ will almost always increase. This can then always be explained post-hoc.

One serious limitation of multiple regression techniques is that as they attempt to account for the variance in the "DV" by various "IVs," they exclude estimates of the associations between IVs. This is the problem of multicollinearity. It also tends to inflate $r2$ as well as makes it difficult to assess the independent contribution of any variable to the outcome. In stepwise regression, the program will start with the variable with the most statistical explanatory power, but this will end up distorting the value of other variables if they are highly correlated, which they almost always are in this type of psychology. Had the computer first regressed on a different variable, the results would have been different. Thus, the variables included—or specification—and their order in multiple regression analysis should always depend on theory, ideally developed before the analysis. In most areas of psychology, variables are highly correlated—in parenting research one should expect that obvious variables like race, ethnicity, income, and parental education are highly correlated, thus "accounting" for the same variance, but so are less obvious ones like specific attitudes, practices, values, politics, experiences, etc.

Similarly, across various psychological scales and measures, items are not independent of each other. This is exacerbated by the tendency in psychology to privilege statistical significance over real-world significance. Multicollinearity weakens the inferences one can draw from the data as it limits the variation required to calculate independent effects. Statistical significance tests disguise this by allowing small effects to count. Some of the crude measurements employed in psychology, to be discussed further in the next chapter, only end up making findings even more difficult to interpret. A partial solution to all this is straightforward: replication with different data and measures using large samples. The problem is that collecting data of this size is too expensive and time-consuming, making replication with different data highly unlikely. An even more straightforward solution is to limit causal-like inferences, but it is not likely that psychologists would broadly adopt such a limitation.

The other issue with multiple regressions is that by allowing researchers to hold certain variables "constant" and acknowledging a role for "error," it permits the blurring of deterministic and probabilistic relationships (Blalock, 1961). By continually introducing additional variables in order to reduce unexplained variation, the assumption of deterministic relationships is protected. As one turns from experimental to non-experimental methods in the quest to identify causal relationships, one requires more and more variables in the analysis, as there are few controls. With so many variables, theories must be simple enough to explain why they all fit together (ibid., p. 21). In other words, multiple regression techniques come with a price. They work best as a method of predicting outcomes without understanding mechanisms. They offer a fairly general and limited level of analysis. Multiple regression techniques are not especially useful in psychology when one's goal is to explain outcomes or select the best predictors of outcomes because of the typically high correlations between independent/predictor variables in the field.

Finally, as we saw earlier, there is a tendency to interpret regression coefficients as signifying the importance of specific variables, but this is only true under certain conditions. The key is that these weights are partial. As one adds more variables, r might increase, but each variable's contribution can be quite low. One important condition is the standardization of measurement units. Without this, regression coefficients are just measures of the variance in variables. Even with standardization this is still an issue. Contributions to explained variance are not indicators of causal importance (Berk, 2004). In general, regression coefficients are only "optimal" for the samples from which they were derived. They will almost always change when applied to a new sample. Generalizability, not surprisingly, tends to be inversely related to the amount of variables one includes in the regression—and positively related to increases in sample size and the representativeness of samples. Part of why people are generally not very good at these types of predictions is that they don't intuitively standardize measurements (Goldberg, 1991). It brings us back to the same issues we have returned to again and again: sampling and replication, ironically the two issues that get the least attention in psychological research.

PROBLEMS IN ACADEMIC SOURCES (II)

The Piotrowski et al. (2013) study cited in Dewar's parenting blog as evidence of the problems with permissive parenting is actually quite typical of the correlational research we have been discussing. The study, published in the *Journal of Child Family Studies* in 2013 with the more appropriate academic title "Investigating correlates of self-regulation in early childhood with a representative sample of English-speaking American families," is described well by Dewar. It is fairly typical in the sense that findings are a result of regression analysis with lots and lots of variables that are "controlled" for. The variable stew allows for lots of "findings"—correlations between self-regulation and age as well as gender but not parental education, household income, or ethnicity. The specific finding Dewar refers to is this: According to the authors, permissive parents are more likely to have children with "considerable" regulatory problems. Given their methods of data collection, however, this is dubious. The data were acquired from a telephone survey where parents were asked to assess themselves in relation to statements like "I ignore my child's bad behavior." But does this really mean the same thing to different caregivers? Can "permissiveness" really be assessed, as these authors do, by using responses to a total of seven items? To assess the outcome, self-regulation, they combine two preexisting scales while dropping a few items to make the process quicker. We are fairly certain few psychometricians would accept this as an appropriate technique for scale development and doubt that anyone has any idea what is actually being measured.

The actual correlation for permissiveness by self-regulation was a seemingly strong 0.44—yet inexplicably, at least if one accepts the logic of the general thesis, only -0.15 for authoritative and 0.23 for authoritarian. There is no attempt to explain this finding, though the only explanation that would really make sense would refer to chance. The step-wise regression included about 17 variables with 4 steps with much multicollinearity and found that when about 12 demographic variables were "controlled" for, permissiveness yielded the strongest relationship—beta = 0.34 as opposed to -0.11 and 0.09 for the other styles, though not surprisingly, all are statistically significant and treated as if they were measures of the strengths of the relationships. Perhaps the most important finding, though not reported as such by the authors: Psychologists should not be allowed to use regression analysis if they cannot lay out *in advance* a very specific theory about why the findings should be as they are. Why is the association with permissiveness stronger than authoritativeness? Why do poverty or age have stronger associations than minority status? Perhaps it's simply that poverty was entered into the step-wise regression before minority status. Why is parents' mental well-being, which one suspects would be highly associated with children's capacity for emotional regulation, not included at all?

Another study cited by Dewar found mothers of infants who increased levels of responsiveness as a result of training (measured by 10+ measures) facilitated greater growth in infant's social, emotional, and cognitive competence (measured by 10+ measures and sub-measures) than a control group

(Landry et al., 2006). The lesson here is: When in doubt, add another measure. After all, how can another positive correlation hurt? Still another study cited found a similar finding: Parents' responsiveness to distress predicted children's affect regulation, empathy, and prosocial behavior (Davidov and Grusec, 2006). Yet, according to the findings, maternal warmth did not. But maternal warmth was linked to better regulation of positive affect and greater peer acceptance, but in boys only. Also, negative affect regulation mediated between maternal responsiveness to distress and children's empathic responding while positive affect regulation mediated between maternal warmth and peer acceptance in boys. The authors conclude that the findings merit a "differentiated" approach to parenting. A better conclusion, though not one identified by the authors, is that the study offers an elegant case of the dangerous combination of small samples, too many variables, and multicollinearity.

Maccoby is correct about changes in recent methods and the weakness of the early studies, but her enthusiasm about the "complex" and differential relations identified by recent studies needs to be tempered as well. Baumrind's original studies were naturalistic and correlational, while more recent studies model complex cause-effect relationships using multivariate regression techniques. Yet, as we have suggested, this does not necessarily mean that they can confirm the role of parenting style on specific outcomes. Many of the problems we identified in multiple regression techniques are quite evident in these studies. While she views the introduction of many mediating variables as a strength, as it gets at the indirect effects of parenting, she does not seem to recognize that finding significant correlations among so many possibilities is just as easily attributable to chance, especially given that most of the theory developed is post-hoc.

What happens often, as Maccoby herself turns out to be guilty of (see Maccoby, 2000, p. 6), is that beta coefficients are treated as effect sizes. As we noted, comparing influences in this way is a problem as the values of the beta weights are partially determined by the variance in the different variables and are therefore sample-specific. If these studies were interested in prediction exclusively, this might not matter quite so much. But Maccoby is using them as evidence for the causal role parenting effects play when it comes to the outcomes. She wants to prove parents matter. Yet, such an inference is well beyond what can be determined from these studies. The more sub-samples are created as more variables are added, the smaller the samples become and the more correlations that result are simply reflections of the variance in the data.

Maccoby is correct that small correlations need not be indicative of small effects. The same is true of large ones. In fact, one might not be dealing with effects at all. But Maccoby is certainly not correct when she implies that the small correlations should be taken seriously because of the way they impact lives. Maccoby is confusing statistical prediction with explanation. If one were designing a universe and had to decide whether to give a child an authoritarian parent or an authoritative one, as these were the only options and everything else was the same, the findings suggest going with the latter, though barely. This is analogous to the example of choosing the better treatment even if its correlation with survival appears low. But this is not what is being argued. Maccoby is citing this research to demonstrate the effects of certain types of parenting. Thus she needs to establish that parenting is part of what causes the ideal outcomes. The regression analyses she cites are simply incapable of doing this.

If a researcher is interested in finding effects for certain variables in these types of studies, they will. With small samples, small effects, little replication, and the generally low power of correlations, it is really hard to know what can be gleaned from this research. Most telling of all, few of these studies ever consider any genuinely alternative models and compare them. Because many of the variables included in the analyses are conventionalized, there is little attention to the extent to which they are independent of each other. In the studies we reviewed, there was little explanation as to why certain variables were included or how the authors deal with the problem of multicollinearity. The variables are entered into computerized regressions and significant findings result. The specifics of the population sampled are simply ignored and generalizations are made about the importance of parents. These studies are not unique in these problems.

Correlations about parenting style and outcomes, even if they were high, though they rarely are, do not necessarily tell us anything about the directionality of the relationship. Are behaviors a product of parenting or is parenting a response to child behaviors? Are there whole other sets of variables not even considered? As we shall see in the next section, this is the criticism of behavioral geneticists. Are these outcomes and the styles even independent of each other given that the "styles" and the outcomes are part of the same semantic networks? Even if they are independent, does establishing a correlation between style and outcome really have any meaning? In the end, it appears the value of a particular parenting style might just be a product of faith and hope more than anything else.

CRITICISMS OF THE CRITICISMS OF ACADEMIC SOURCES

Though the parenting-style tradition continues to thrive in bookstores and blogs, in a certain sense, the idea of parental effects on children has long been out of date in psychology as a function of the confluence of several trends, including the neo-Piagetian view of infants as budding rationalists, the rise of behavioral genetics, the growing tendency to regard many infant attributes and capacities as innate, and the general influence of neuroscience. As we shall see later, however, the influence of neuroscience also allows for a return to notions of parental influence, now as providers of an environment that helps to shape brain growth. Yet, these correctives to the parenting-effects program have methodological problems of their own.

Both Baumrind and Maccoby's early positions are in line with a long-held view about the plasticity of early childhood and the residual "Lockeianism" in the field of child psychology. Yet, in the past few decades or so, the discipline has changed. Maccoby has acknowledged, Baumrind less so, the importance of including genetics, temperament, and biology in accounting for positive outcomes. The work of Judith Harris is often seen as the trigger for this change in the study of child-rearing, though in certain quarters of psychology the turn began much earlier. For example, Sandra Scarr had made similar points in the 1980s. Harris opened her 1995 article in *Psychology Review* with this provocative claim: "Do parents have any important long-term effects on the development of their child's personality? This article examines the evidence and concludes that the answer is no."

Harris's main point in the piece, as well as her 1998 follow-up, *The Nurture Assumption*, was to highlight some of the presuppositions of the field about the influence of parents and introduce the work of behavioral genetics. She acknowledged that parents who did a good job managing their lives tended to have children who do a good job of managing their lives (1998, p. 20), but asked whether one caused the other or both are the result of constitutional factors. Following the language of behavioral genetics, she argued that 50 percent of the variance in these outcomes is explained by genetics—both direct as well as indirect effects—and 50 percent environment. She then made the case that much of that non-genetic 50 percent was a result of the influence of peers rather than parents. One behavioral geneticist cited by Harris is David Rowe, another frequent critic of traditional parenting research (1994; 2001). In his work, Rowe describes various adoption and twin studies going back to the 1930s and argues that the place to find links between parents and outcomes is in gene distributions as opposed to the effects of parenting behavior.

Critics of behavioral genetics usually accept a role for genes, but argue that biology and environment are so mutually constitutive of each other their effects cannot be separated. They reject the notion that genetic and environmental effects are additive and see behavioral genetics findings as offering more of a correction than a fundamental rejection of their work (Maccoby, 2000). While this point about the mutually constitutive nature of gene-environment relationships is technically correct, it misses that behavioral geneticists are looking to explanations at a distinct level of analysis. They are interested in the "heritability" of a trait, a measure of the proportion of the variance in that trait explained by genetic differences in a population. They are not looking for the cause of that trait in an individual.

This is a distinction that often generates confusion. The notion of heritability seeks to capture the strength of genetic influence on phenotypic variation (Sesardic, 2005). It does not require that one accept that genes and environment act in isolation from each other or those genes do not require environments to express themselves in. To be fair, both sides in the debate trade in blurring this distinction as they repeatedly claim to clarify it. As Neven Sesardic (2005) points out in his defense of behavioral genetics, everyone who understands anything about biology agrees that genes and environmental influences are both necessary for development and the continued existence of any organism. The question behavioral geneticists ask is whether in particular cases the relative importance of these two factors in a population can be distinguished. The answer can offer suggestions about causal relationships, he argues, but they do not in themselves answer these questions. For instance, a trait can seem to have an obvious relationship to genetics, as say "walking" does, but have zero heritability because it cannot explain existing phenotypic *differences* in a population (Sesardic, 2005, p. 28). The same is true with eye color. Similarly, a trait can have high heritability, yet be clearly related to environmental conditions, like height.

It is not just critics of behavioral genetics that blur the distinction between "inherited" and "heritability," as well as that between the study of traits in a population or in an individual. Behavioral geneticists do so as well especially when they generalize their claims. Just a quick glance at much of their work suggests most of them already believe that many key psychological traits are caused by genes, just as parenting psychologists have long believed many key psychological traits are caused by parenting practice. Neither of these presuppositions is really falsifiable. Thus, in the case of the findings of heritability studies, there is a tendency for the "over-interpretation" of findings. There is also the confusion between a statistical interaction and a real-world one, a confusion that defenders of both positions tend to reinforce. In the case of real-world interactions, neither element can produce an effect without the other. This is obviously true of genes and environment. However, in the case of a statistical interaction, the effects of one variable changes with the variation in value of another. Thus statistical interactions do not generate problems for the idea of heritability measures, even though, in the end, real-world interactions might.

Ironically, parenting psychologists are quite comfortable using similar multiple regression techniques to ferret out causes even though they surely recognize that the actual processes involved are much more contingent and complex. They accept it as a gross measure, as it neglects any understanding of specific mechanisms, but a useful one. In fact, as we have argued, they often rely on it in cases where it is inappropriate to do so and this leads to severe misinterpretation of findings. It seems parenting psychologists hold one standard when it comes to parenting effects studies and another for gene-effects studies. Ultimately, parenting psychologists are correct in adopting a higher bar to make causal inferences as implied in their critique of behavioral genetics and one can only wish they would accept the same bar in their own work.

In the end, the debate is about an appropriate level of analysis. What behavioral genetic studies do is divide participants into hierarchically related genetic categories: monozygotic twins, dizygotic twins, step-siblings, and adoptive siblings, with each type sharing less and less genetic variation, from the most variation in the case of adoptive siblings to none in the case of identical twins. One classic model is that of comparing identical twins raised apart to fraternal ones where findings of more similarity in monozygotic twins than dizygotic twins are attributed to shared genes. There is clearly an assumption here that relevant environments cannot be correlated. This is why critics argue that identical twins are often treated the same even in different environments and that they are rarely separated from each other the moment of birth. Recent research even looks at the effects of shared versus non-shared placental environments. No matter what behavioral geneticists believe, these confounds cannot simply be accounted for through statistical solutions. Given shared environments, this methodological model breaks down as long as those environments can plausibly be regarded as phenotype influencing and trait relevant. But here is where critics of behavioral genetics are weak, as well: It is certainly plausible that the womb environment is a source of variance, yet there is still little sense of any specific mechanisms involved.

Other behavioral genetics research models look at variability in outcomes between adopted and biological siblings or between twins and siblings as a way of explaining the effects of genes versus the environment (e.g., same environment/different genes versus same environment/more similar genes) but these types of studies are not viewed as having the same power as the twins-separated-at-birth studies are, though they clearly allow for much larger samples. The point is, everyone understands that genes and environment interact in practice, but behavioral genetic studies offer a method of parceling out variance without any understanding of the mechanisms involved, for better or worse. In this sense, it mirrors the use of regression analysis in general in the social sciences (Glymour, 1997). If one rejects this type of analysis here, shouldn't one reject them everywhere? Our answer is that we should, but this is certainly not the choice of most psychologists.

The real problem with the approach of behavioral genetics is that there are other fields, like evo-devo and developmental biology, exploring some of the same phenomena, the relationship between gene and environment, at a different level of analysis that ends up spotlighting the limitations of the correlational approach. Yet, behavioral geneticists do not seem to be able to adapt. Heritability offers a way to predict the distribution of a trait in offspring by knowing its distribution in parents, a useful tool in the study of the evolution of populations, but it says nothing about the process (Lerner, 2002). When one begins to look at actual mechanisms at the molecular and cellular levels during ontogenesis, a very different picture emerges. For one, it becomes difficult to sustain the division of the variance into genetic and environmental influences. Another striking aspect is the role of chance. This is especially clear in the development of the brain where an initial proliferation of neurons and neural connections early in life accompanied by neural migration is followed by a period of selective pruning that results in the loss of neurons and neuronal connections. In fact, in recent pop psychology, this finding has led to the notion that good parenting must include helping to "build" these neural connections.

The particular pattern that results is neither the result of genetic instructions, nor a passive and deterministic response to the environment—as notions of "plasticity" are sometimes interpreted—but is probabilistic as it involves an adaptive response to resonant facets of the environment as it relates to the organism. Given a wide range of acceptable environments that provide sensory input, brain development adapts to it within certain constraints set by genes. These limits are sometimes predictable on a group level but not an individual one (Rutter, 2013). Moreover, the "environment" plays a central role in genetic expression—including the cellular environment—both in terms of which genes are active in a particular interaction, as well as more broadly, in experience-dependent brain effects like early exposure to infection or severe forms of deprivation. And still, genes play a role in terms of individual differences in environmental risk exposure.

Thus, even at a correlational level, we have at least five sources of variance: genes, environments, genetic expression as related to specific environmental conditions, environmental influences as they translate into particular genetic expression, and chance. Even the category of "environment" can be broken down into separate sources of variance. One of the more interesting findings of behavioral genetics is that environmental effects are often unshared in the same family, that is, they play a more important role in making children within the same family different as opposed to similar as had long been supposed (Plomin and Daniels, 1987). Thus one can also distinguish variance attributed to unshared and shared environmental effects. Some even distinguish between objective environmental influences and effective environmental influences, the latter inferred from similarities among children sharing that environment (Jenkins and Bisceglia, 2013).

In general, single factors don't have much effect, and by effect we mean both substantive and statistical effects. This is true of both genes and environment. It is the synergistic effect of the combination of genetic risk factors and environmental risk exposure, for example, that best explains negative psychological outcomes (Rutter, 2013). At this point, heritability figures have little value because the original point about neglecting the influence of genes has been well demonstrated. Given how these figures are constructed, they generally tend to overestimate the influence of genes. The best method available to behavioral geneticists, twin-studies, is unable to keep from violating its own assumptions about equal environments. It is conceivable that studying these factors at such a gross level of analysis has simply lost its value given what we already know about mechanisms. Finally, heritability measures are about variation, and it might just be that the focus on individual variation distracts from the focus on intra-individual mechanisms.

POPULAR VARIANTS REDUX

One way to talk about constitutional factors without getting too caught up in the specific sources of those factors is to focus on temperament. The importance of temperament is often portrayed as a corrective to the exclusive focus given to maternal behavior by attachment theorists (Karen, 1994). Two early explorers of the role of temperament were psychiatrists Stella Chess and Alexander Thomas. They identified a wide variety of variation in infant behavior, like activity level and persistence, leading them to focus on "goodness of fit" between mothers and infants. Another leading figure, Jerome Kagan (1994), distinguished between infants with higher and lower levels of reactivity. Another research program in academic psychology focused on constitutional factors seeks to identify what appear to be innate cognitive capacities in infants, like recognizing faces and understanding how the objects of physics work.

While there are serious methodological issues with the latter work, as we have discussed elsewhere (see Ausch, 2015)—a tendency to focus on small yet statistically significant effects, questionable operationalization of infant "knowledge," lack of proper variability in stimulus sampling as well as subject and context sampling, and a tendency to generalize well beyond specific findings—this new way of conceiving infancy has become wildly popular in the field. Both of these programs are useful correctives to the hyper-empiricism of prior developmental psychology, and in the case of the infancy research, the tendency to vastly underestimate infants. Yet taken too far, they can make parenting and even education seem futile.

Not surprisingly, a new genre of popular psychology books on childhood has followed the field in its focus on constitutional factors and is exemplified by the work of authors like Alison Gopnik and Paul Bloom. Gopnik introduced pop psychology readers to the new super-competent infant in her widely acclaimed *The Scientist in the Crib: What Early Learning Tells Us*

About the Mind (Gopnik et al., 1999) and her follow-up, *The Philosophical Baby: What Children's Minds Tell Us About Truth, Love, and the Meaning of Life* (2009). In these works, Gopnik describes the recent shift in the way infants are conceived by developmental and cognitive psychologists while trying to avoid stale arguments about the effects of genes and environments. Her work captures the extent of the human infant's dependence and immaturity along with its unique cognitive capacities—rapid capacity for learning, powerful imagination, plastic brain, charged levels of awareness, and less inhibitions so as not to shut all this novelty down. They allow it to thrive in all sorts of situations. Unlike many psychologists writing about children, Gopnik has a clinician's eye for details as she characterizes these early years as a unique and vital world onto itself, not simply a prequel to adulthood.

The weakness of the work is that, after all this sensitivity to difference, infants become little adults. Gopnik describes infants as reasoning about probabilities, doing experiments, and "understanding statistical ideas" (83) as reflected in their capacity to detect patterns. The studies Gopnik bases her work on tend to translate increases in the length of time an infant stares at an object into all sorts of more complex cognitive activity, though in truth, we simply do not know why an infant is staring nor do we know that found statistically significant differences are meaningful enough to make generalizations about infant's capacities. The unfortunate part of this analysis is the loss of the unique qualitative world of the infant. Yes, babies explore their world and learn from the consequences of their actions, but this does not make them little scientists. To describe them thus is to lose both an understanding of the historical and cultural variability of the term "science" as well as the fact that infants are not simply rational-adults-in-the-making. In this research, the basic form of the study is repeated over and over again, giving the feel of extensive replication, but this basic form is never altered enough to determine how sustainable the phenomenon is as the context changes nor does it tell us about the contexts where infants failed to stare.

The most surprising facet of all this nativism is that parents have made a comeback of sorts, as helping to establish to right environments to create better brains. In her history of expert advice to parents, Hubert (2003) describes a Clinton-sponsored 1997 conference designed to describe to parents, physicians, and educators the new "plastic" brain discovered by 1980s and 1990s neuroscience, creating what critic John Bruer (1999) termed in his book on the subject, *The Myth of the First Three Years.* One extremely popular version of this thesis for parents is *The Whole Brain Child: 12 Revolutionary Strategies to Nurture Your Child's Developing Mind* (2011) and its follow-up, *No-Drama Discipline: The Whole-Brain Way to Calm the Chaos and Nurture Your Child's Developing Mind* (2014) by physician Daniel Siegel and psychotherapist Tina Payne Bryson, though there are dozens of such books on the market today. In these books, the authors promise to bring the latest brain science to bear on child-rearing. What does this actually involve? Help your kids learn to integrate both the left and right hemispheres of their brain (i.e., "by redirecting emotional waves" [2011, p. 22]), as well as integrating the "upstairs" and "downstairs" brains (e.g., by not negotiating with a toddler throwing a tantrum [45]). In the latter case, Kahneman's division between S1 and S2 is turned into a source of parenting advice.

Quite frankly, most of the actual parenting advice offered could have been written by any of the defenders of the authoritative-parenting consensus we have already discussed extensively. Similar advice is offered in John Medina's (2011) hugely popular *Brain Rules for Baby: How to Raise a Smart and Happy Child from Zero to Five*, though parental influence is limited because, according to Medina, even a baby's level of happiness is constrained by genetics. Psychotherapist Sue Gerhardt's *Why Love Matters: How Affection Shapes a Baby's Brain* (2004) goes as far as trying to integrate the parenting research, attachment research, and the new brain psychology. As she puts it,

> The period from conception through the first two years—roughly speaking the first 1000 days—is uniquely significant, because this is when the nervous system is being established and shaped by experience. During this period, how parents behave has as much influence on their child's emotional make-up as his or her genetic inheritance. Their responses to their baby teach him what his own emotions are and how to manage them. . . . It is as babies that we first feel and learn what to do with our feelings, when we start to organize our experience in a way that will affect our later behavior and thinking capacities. (11)

Yet, most of the work is devoted to correlational findings about external stimuli and recorded brain activity in specific regions read through attachment theory—itself made up of correlations between measures of attachment and measures of psychological well-being. This is then turned into a defense of the nurturing-style of parenting most educated, middle class parents likely already approve of.

To be fair, variants of this thesis abound and elements of it are well established. Yes, the nervous system is developing in the first two years and yes, it is reasonable to assume parents play a role in the processes by which infants learn to regulate their emotions, but the causal arc Gerhardt is laying out well exceeds what can be established via research. Furthermore, Gerhardt is really telling a story about what makes people different, as psychotherapists do, but mostly using evidence from fairly universal neurological processes, or at best, relying on cases of extreme deprivation. The leads to claims like: "Without the appropriate one-to-one social experience with a caring adult, the baby's orbitofrontal cortex is unlikely to develop well" (56), or "A lack of positive rewarding interaction with the mother . . . can undermine the oxytocin system which is being built in the first year of life, leading to long lasting effects (140). True but trite statements like "in practice, our behavior is the result of learning: our biochemistry responds to the specific environments in which we find ourselves" (196) turn the book—who can disagree with this?—into a defense of contemporary US middle-class parenting values. Or the "mystery tonic that enables babies to flourish as soon as they get it is responsiveness" (224). Great, but what does this mean exactly?

The good news is that most middle-class children, even most working-class children, will get enough "affection," "responsiveness," and whatever else they need from parents to grow a proper brain. In fact, they will get so much that their parents probably do not matter that much in terms of the development of their brain. There is an issue with children who grow up in extreme poverty or with massive deprivation, no doubt, but the audience for this type of work is highly educated middle-class parents already anxious about giving their child a leg up in a highly competitive society. Who can deny the lure, to many parents, of helping their children build better brains? Neuroscience is quite far from understanding the workings and development of the brain to that extent. The unfortunate point is, we do not know why children turn out the way they do.

There has certainly been a long-held belief about the importance of "environmental" effects in the field despite this, suggesting that it confirms beliefs we already have. Yet defenders of various approaches to parenting, both inside and outside the academy, seem to be sure that they do know why children turn out the way they do. Correlations are a useful tool to describe data. Isn't it interesting that X varies with Y? What could this mean? Within certain constraints, regression can be useful for certain types of sorting that benefit from prediction—as we shall see in the next chapter when we consider psychological testing. But these are not tools that yield explanations. There is nothing wrong with erring on the safe side and being a loving, responsive parent with a bit of discipline in the mix as well. But such choices are probably about meeting the needs of parents just as much as children.

Chapter Six

Psychological Measurement

IQ, Personality, and Emotional Intelligence

Popular psychology of all stripes employs psychological measures, some of which are borrowed directly from the work of academic psychologists and some of which are created by the authors themselves. In terms of the work we have already reviewed: In the heuristics and biases tradition, a popular measure is the frequency of correct responses. In some of the new cognitive unconscious research, it is average speed of responses on the IAT. In happiness psychology, it is the score on a happiness assessment, as well as the F and p values resulting from comparing multiple means. And finally, in the effects of parenting research, we identified a range of measures including combinations of observed frequencies, scores on a range of assessments, measures of association and variance (regression, r, $r2$), and one in particular, the heritability coefficient. Yet, do all these numbers imply measurement has taken place?

A cursory glance across any field within the natural sciences reveals the centrality of measurement. And not surprisingly, since the origins of the discipline of psychology in the latter part of the nineteenth century to the present day, psychologists eager to position the field as a science have mostly accepted that psychology must involve some form of measurement. For much of the field, the most popular form of measurement involves counting or frequencies. It allows psychologists access to meaningful numbers with clear-cut intervals, which can then be compared to each other. A popular measure in early psychology involved time or speed. This was reflected in the allure of the measurement of reaction time. It's easy to see why these would be accepted, as they are obvious examples of quantitative phenomena. Not quite as common but also self-explanatory is distance.

In the case of psychological measures of phenomena like intelligence, anxiety, or extraversion, notions of distance on a scale are implied, however abstract and metaphorical. Numbers are assigned to individuals on the basis of tests or assessments where a position on a non-observed variable is inferred from observed scores. But how is this to be interpreted? Is this non-observed variable taken to be real or just a sum-score? If the methods by which these non-observed variables are "measured" is designed to capture differences between individuals, hence are population-derived, do these variables exist at the individual level (Dooremalen and Borsboom, 2010)? If not, is this still measurement? What could it mean to measure something that does not exist? These basic questions almost never get asked when psychologists seek to measure.

There are still other measurements in the field. In experimental psychology, some of the measurement work is performed by statistics where scores are compared across groups and inferences are made about samples and populations. In non-experimental psychology, statistics support the apportioning of the sources of variance among variables. In these cases, both the "score" implies measurement and is expressed quantitatively as does the statistic resulting from the analysis. Both are represented as numbers.

One key technology of measurement in psychology is the psychological assessment, or "test." In psychology, tests help to "explain" phenomena—that is, describe them and situate them in a network of cause-effect relations—and they are also used for prediction and sorting. Both functions have their origins in the work of Francis Galton, Alfred Binet, and early-twentieth-century intelligence testing. In the case of Galton, he treated his measures of talent as elements of reality that were inherited and unequally distributed among both individuals and groups, all still widely accepted by proponents of intelligence tests. Binet's position, on the other hand, was more ambiguous. Intelligence was the first important psychological "trait," meaning it was assumed to be enduring, stable, and resistant to change (Meier, 1994). It was also capable of being measured. The Galtonians assumption as to its normal distribution supported the notion that intelligence was biological, as this was the assumed distribution of many fixed, biological characteristics (Danziger, 1990).

In this form of psychology, traits are considered causes. Thus, intelligence is the *cause* of certain behaviors, specifically responses on an IQ test. Sometimes, however, traits are viewed as simply organizational schemes for making sense of behavior or even just descriptive summaries of behavioral frequencies. In these cases, traits are operational categories rather than real ones. One of the tendencies in psychological measurement, as we shall see, is to move back and forth between these differing conceptions of psychological traits without explicitly acknowledging it. So intelligence becomes, for example, both the cause of the failure to solve problems correctly and simply what intelligence tests measure. Having it both ways is one of the by-products of the tendency not to think too much about philosophical/theoretical issues. But this requires one to ask: What exactly is being measured if intelligence is just a statistical summary? Can you measure something that doesn't exist? Binet's tests, for example, did not require a realist take on intelligence as their strength was on differentiation for the purpose of decision-making. These were designed to be used by schools and the tasks involved were school-like tasks. American test developers were less clear about the issue because they tended to blur the distinction between the functions of sorting and explaining.

Also inherited from Galton was the use of aggregation to deal with measurement "error," meaning anything other than the trait that influences a response, a technique that influenced both Binet and Spearman. Both recognized that in large enough samples, random errors in measurement (e.g., fatigue, misinterpretation of items) tend to swamp out. However, if errors are systematic, this becomes a problem. For example, if the way data are gathered affects results, as is often clear in the cases of self-report items as opposed to behavioral frequencies, error is systematic if one cannot account for measurement-instrument-related variance (Campbell and Fiske, 1959). However, unlike experimentalists who treated individual differences as error, psychological testers looked for tasks that maximized those differences, often at the expense of context. This is why critics of standardized testing in education argue that these tests are not useful in assessing the progress of individual students (Popham, 2001). They are designed to ignore items that most students perform well on, even though this might have been the point of the curriculum in the first place, in order to find those items that better differentiate between students. In general, psychological testing is designed to distinguish between people, and so measures are relative to a population and have little meaning in any absolute sense. As we will review, this has led to problems in the interpretation of traits like intelligence and personality.

A REVIEW OF THE METHODOLOGICAL ISSUES AT STAKE (I): MEASUREMENT

What exactly does it mean to "measure" a psychological phenomenon? We will follow Joel Michell's (2010; 1999) views closely, a persistent critic of the received view of measurement in psychology. One way to express relationships between various entities is through the notion of an "attribute." Attributes can be properties of objects like length and volume, or they can be relations like nationality or gender. The first two attributes differ from the latter two in that they involve extension in space. Another way they differ is that the first two are quantitative and the latter two are classificatory. As

Michell notes, in psychology attributes are qualitative—classificatory or ordinal—or they are quantitative (2010, p. 46). Common quantitative attributes in psychology are frequencies and continuous quantities. Because frequency involves natural numbers and are observed in some form, they create a self-evident opportunity for quantification. Comparing the number of correct experimental and control group responses is a common use of frequency. It is important to note, however, that these frequencies are not direct measures of phenomena but of behavior. The experience of the phenomenon remains qualitative.

Even an intelligence test score is a frequency, a modification of the number of correct responses. Yet it is interpreted via a mathematical function as a measure of the attribute intelligence under the assumption that intelligence is a continuous quantity. Technically, this assumption is a hypothesis, as it is certainly not observed. But, as Michell explains, it is a hypothesis that is never actually subject to testing. It is simply taken for granted as the whole system of intelligence testing depends on it. The same is true of most quantitative measures in psychology. The attribute of continuous quantity and its measurement was the foundation of the scientific revolution. It allowed ratios between differences to be expressed as positive numbers. When Fechner identified continuous quantity in psychophysical phenomena, the modern science of psychology was born, even though some of the most important figures in early psychology continued to use qualitative methods of observation, including Wundt, Freud, James, Wertheimer, and Piaget, to name a few. What Fechner did, in essence, was allow ordering in a linear series to be enough to assume continuous quantity (Danziger, 1990). S. S. Stevens later termed this an "ordinal" scale.

By the late century, the quest to find measure was made easier through a shift from a focus on finding the quantitative structure of consciousness to finding the quantitative structure of human behavior. You can't count sensations the way you can count correct responses. Thus, action was structured as distinct but equivalent units of performance (Danziger, 1990, p. 142). This is what Hermann Ebbinghaus did so successfully in his study of nonsense syllables as compared to Wundt, who was still focused on measuring subjective experience. This, as Kurt Danziger explains, allowed for the juxtaposition of two distinct series of measurement: a "stimulus" series that defined the task—one that Wundt was already employing—and a "response" series that becomes known as "trials." The latter was the great contribution of Ebbinghaus to psychology, a contribution that was successfully employed by Thorndike in his learning "curves," his method for expressing cumulative responses. Thus psychology became the science of relating quantitative stimuli to quantitative responses.

In the United States, this change accelerated by the second and third decades of the twentieth century with the rise of behaviorism, basically a psychology of responses, the increasing involvement of philanthropy in the social sciences, and a generally high valuation of all things scientific. Quantitative measurement brought simplicity and scientificity, but the questions as to whether psychological objects actually contain quantitative attributes or not, or whether the cost of quantification, the loss of the directly experienced character of the object of study, were worth it was never asked or answered. Only a small few recognized that quantitative changes in psychological phenomena as expressed through instruments—sensations, personality measures, self-esteem, or anxiety—might not admit an easy comparison to each other. They tended to remain marginalized in the field. The work of psychology went on, without anyone asking about the nature of measurement itself.

Yet, the meaning of "measurement" is not so obvious. In the West, until the seventeenth century, two conceptions of measurement competed with each other. The first one viewed nature as being primarily mathematical in structure and was represented in the writings of the Pythagoreans and Plato, while the second viewed nature and having an underlying qualitative structure and was represented in the work of Aristotle. This was the case until the triumph of the quantitative view with Galileo and Newton in the seventeenth century. By the nineteenth century, measurement and science were synonymous and this view influenced the first few generations of psychologists including Fechner, Helmholtz, Galton, Thorndike, Titchner, and Binet. All of them adhered to what can be described as the classic theory of measurement. As Michell notes (2010), when the classic view of measurement in psychology was called into question by a committee established by the British Association for the Advancement for Science in the 1930s as they inquired into whether psychophysical measurement was possible, a new, more permissive "operational" version was developed that redefined measurement in such a way that it lost most of its meaning.

One can find the roots of the classical theory of measurement already laid out by Aristotle. Aristotle accepted that quantity was one of the fundamental categories of reality. He divided quantity into two categories: discrete and continuous, the former included natural numbers and the latter magnitudes like length, time, weight, and volume. What made quantities such was that they were additively composed of parts, either ones in the case of numbers or smaller magnitudes in the case of continuous quantity: so that any length is composed of smaller lengths and is infinitely divisible. Magnitudes of the same kind stand in relation of "ratio" to one another so that the magnitude of a yard relative to a foot is 3 (Michell, 1990, p. 10). Thus, the ratio of non-numerical qualities could equal the ratio between two natural numbers. This was the case with all extensive quantities whose structure is additive.

What modern science did was extend this capacity to intensive quantities, that is, quantities without an obvious additive structure. For example, while length has a simple additive structure, temperature does not. It is intensive in the sense that there are no simple operations that reflect its additive structure. You cannot summarize different temperatures by adding them together in the way you can with length. Temperature does have an additive structure but this structure is recognized through various types of evidence as opposed to the self-evident behavior of objects manifesting it. Essentially, intensive quantities were treated as length was, the exemplar for all measures of quantity. These included "physical" variables, like velocity and density, but also "psychological" variables, like sensation, pleasure, and pain. Thus, by the nineteenth century, there was no real question as to whether psychological variables could be considered quantitative. This generally involved counting responses, but as we have seen, was continually expanding in scope. But quantitative structure and measurement remained conceived from within the classical theory. Baldwin made this clear in his entry under measurement in his 1902 *Dictionary of Philosophy and Psychology*,

> In order that a concept may be measured as a mathematical quantity without ambiguity, it is essential that the special attribute by which we measure it should be conceivable as made up of discrete parts, admitting of unambiguous comparison inter se, with respect to their quality or difference of magnitude. (Baldwin, 1901, p. 58)

As Michell sees it, the collapse of the classical view of measurement in the early twentieth century was related to two things: First, the questioning of the empirical nature of number by late-nineteenth-century logicians and second, the rise of verificationism, which tended to confuse the meaning of a proposition with the observational conditions that verified it. As we noted, in psychology, this was expressed in the doctrine of operationalism. What operationalism did, in essence, was loosen the link between reality and measurement. All quantity was regarded as extensive quantity and reducible to a specific set of direct observations. While some measurements were viewed as requiring some form of derivation, as long as those measures had a direct relationship to more obvious extensive quantities like length, quantification was achieved. This initially posed a problem for psychology, as its quantitative variables had no obvious additive structure. It turns out this was exactly the finding of the Final Report of the British Association for the Advancement of Science on this question. Without some additive capacity, measurement in psychology was impossible.

The potential crisis in psychology that could have followed was quickly resolved by S. S. Stevens at Harvard. As we noted previously, Stevens (1935) defended the operationalist view in psychology. Operationalism allowed Stevens to argue that as long as a particular set of procedures yielded a number, the result was measurement. One no longer had to be concerned whether psychological variables had an additive structure as the focus was now on using numbers to represent attributes of phenomena. This can be accomplished by assigning numbers to represent the difference between attributes—what he called the "nominal" scale, or to represent order in the relationship between attributes—the "ordinal" scale, or to represent equality and order of differences between attributes—the "interval" scale, or traditional empirical and additive relationships—this was the "ratio" scale. Each scale had its own acceptable transformations and permissible statistics, though psychologists were not always willing to accept the limits implied by the latter.

As Michell puts it, these representations allowed "inferences to be made by numerical means" (1990, p. 17). Measurement became, according to S.S. Stevens, the assignment of numbers to objects or events according to a set of rules. Yet in the classical view, numbers did not involve a relationship of assignment but of predication. They are the product of the discovery of real numerical relations like ratios between things. Simple assignment does not always involve measurement. For psychology, on the other hand, the classical concept of measurement was emptied of its content. Quantitativeness was to be determined by the researcher, not the character of the entity itself. Measurement was now broad enough to include all psychological procedures. It became, as described by Michell, a "useful cosmetic" (19).

Yet there were limits. In Stevens (1939) view, for example, ordinal scales allowed only for monotonic transformations—those that preserve the order—while interval scales allowed for positive linear transformations (e.g., as you do when you convert Fahrenheit into Celsius). This does introduce an interesting question: How can psychologists use statistics like mean or standard deviation when only information about rank-order is provided as with an ordinal scale? In a representational theory of numbers, as is the case with psychology, numbers represent empirical relations and representation allows one to deduce empirical conclusions (Michell, 1990, p. 45). But in the case of an ordinal scale, computing a mean score uses the numbers to introduce information not present in the scale itself. This is the reason S. S. Stevens sought to proscribe it.

This reformulation of measurement was obviously attractive to psychologists who continued to believe that measurement was a requirement for any field to attain the status of a science. It quickly became part of conventional wisdom in psychology. This was simply what had always been regarded as measurement and the fact that before the 1930s, such measures would have been regarded as "crude" was forgotten. But in truth, measurement requires a commitment to the ontological status of a phenomenon: that it has an additive structure whose magnitudes can be expressed in ratio relationships to each other. After all, what can it mean to measure something by using numbers to "represent" it if such an entity might not have any existence outside of that representation? Certainly no scientist believes gravity has no existence outside of the operations taken to measure it. The same is probably true today of psychologists. They tend to be realists in general, operationalists only when backed into a corner.

The question is: Do proposed psychological entities like intelligence, personality, or happiness have such a structure? Can any evidence be provided to make this case? Much of the work in the natural sciences involves creating more and more sophisticated forms of measurement through the mutual development of experiment, technology, and theory, yet there has been little of such development in psychology. For one, measurement involves a causal theory: How do changes in a phenomena effect changes in a measuring instrument? For that, one needs to be able to modify stimuli of various sorts in very subtle ways. Is this possible when measuring self-esteem or social desirability or depression? This is an open question. The trick is to focus on behavior. But just because psychologists have created devices for mental measurement that yield numerical data, meaning that the attributes of the effects of behavior have a ratio character (e.g., frequency), does not mean that the mental phenomena that cause the behavior have a ratio character. The first step in figuring this out is seeking to establish whether an entity contains quantitative structure while the second involves developing procedures to estimate the ratios involved, typically by using a relationship between the attribute being quantified and another quantified attribute, for instance, the relationship between temperature, volume, and length in the case of a thermometer (Michell, 1999, p. 75).

Developers of measures of intelligence have certainly thought the most about these issues as compared to most psychologists who study traits and developers of happiness measures perhaps the least, but neither has come close to demonstrating quantitative structure. This is because there is little theory about the psychological entities themselves except in terms of the behavioral changes they cause. In the early 1900s, it was simply assumed that test scores were a form of measurement. While some in psychology turned to operationalism, test makers held on as long as they could to the notion that tests were measuring something real. Stevens's ordinal scale helped support this as did Cronbach's construct validity; the latter helped bridge the inferential leap between what a test assesses and what it's supposed to assess (Michell, 2009, p. 115).

One long-term consequence of this inferential leap was the downgrading of non-quantitative measurements and their avoidance by psychologists, even if the structures of their attributes were obviously qualitative. In the end, there is no way to know this without asking these basic questions, ones that are rarely ever asked in the field. Typically these assumptions remain hidden as theories are tailored to fit instruments rather than the other way around. The legacy of this includes tests with predictive validity but no sense of the processes or mechanisms involved (Borsboom, 2009a). Perhaps this is useful as a starting point, but to confuse this with an explanation is a mistake.

A REVIEW OF THE METHODOLOGICAL ISSUES AT STAKE (II): ASSESSMENT AND TESTING

There are instruments available to measure almost any psychological variable imaginable. Here is just a short list from Paul Kline's 2000 version of his seminal *Handbook of Psychological Testing*: verbal ability, numerical ability, memory span, form perception, warmth, dominance, boldness, differential aptitude, shrewdness, conformity, self-discipline, depression, anxiety, openness, empathy, masculinity, ego-defensive permissiveness, exhibitionism, and autonomy. Some of these involve distinct tests, but most of these are one of several variables measured by a single test. Some of these variables reflect components of cognitive ability, sometimes described as "intelligence," and are measured by combining the results of problem-solving items. Others are attributes of individuals, mostly "personality" and/or "attitude," and reflect responses to items that participants must align their own position along a continuum of strongly agree to strongly disagree. The difference between these tests is an important one. Intelligence tests actually sample problems that require "intelligence" to solve while personality tests require subjects to be truthful and insightful (Kline, 1998, p. 35). They do not elicit behaviors, for example, associated with different personality types.

The most important thing about an instrument used to measure is its accuracy. In the natural sciences, this is typically determined by comparing resulting measures with other accepted measures. Yet, without clear units of measurement, accuracy becomes difficult to ascertain (Kline, 1998). In classic psychometrics, the study and development of certain forms of psychological instruments, typically tests composed of a collection of items, this difficulty is built into the theory itself, in the division of all scores into a true score and an error score. The true score is defined as the score attained if a subject was measured along all possible items in the universe related the measure. From the perspective of classic test theory, true scores do not exist in the real world, as there is always error in measurement.

The formula for the true score is error subtracted from the expected observed score over multiple replications. Error also includes randomness from sampling from a population of subjects (Lord and Novick, 1968). The goal for psychologists is to decrease error by accounting for random errors and fixing systematic ones. The division between true score and error is at the heart of classical test theory. It creates complications though, as typically, tests are given on a single occasion and not repeated again and again, as say is the case with measurement in the natural sciences. There, the repetition generates a normal distribution, and error is regarded as random. Furthermore, again unlike in the natural sciences, true scores likely change over repetition (Borsboom, 2005).

True scores are often described incorrectly as "construct" scores, but this misses that true scores cannot be conceptualized independently of tests while psychological constructs can—in fact, classical test theory does not assume that measurement has any underlying constructs, yet another clear distinction from measurement in the natural sciences. The other problem with viewing true scores as constructs is that true scores are about reliability and constructs validity, though as Borsboom (2005) notes, the distinction is often blurred when cases are made for specific tests (see pp. 31–35). Technically people do not have a "true" or correct IQ score as much as a disposition to receive an expected value resulting from the distribution yielded from testing that person an infinite number of times (43), clearly an application of a "frequentist" approach to probability.

The more recent alternatives to classical test theory in psychometrics are the latent variable models, which uses factor analysis to identify the common causes of observed behavior and the representational measurement model, which involves developing scales or formal structures used to identify the relationship between measurements. Both of these alternatives are much more explicitly dependent on theory and remain mostly unexplored outside of psychometric circles in the field (Borsboom, 2005, p. 11). While the latent model is a realist one—latent variables are said to exist and exert a causal force on scores, the classical model, influenced by operationalism, is much more ambiguous about whether the object of measurement exists independent of the test. We will review the latent variable model in more detail when we consider intelligence testing later in this chapter.

Returning to measurement in general, the other important question about a score is its reliability: When something is measured several times, how likely is it that one will get the same results? The more reliable a test is, the more it reflects a true score and the lower its standard error. Reliability attempts to deal with the problems with the classical test theory we are discussing by always considering it in relation to a population, meaning tests are more or less reliable dependent on the population—it is meaningless to refer to "the reliability of a test," although test developers do so all the time (Borsboom, 2005, p. 23). The keys methods for determining reliability—the test-retest method, the parallel method, the split-halves method, and the internal consistency method—gloss over these problems by simply treating these divisions as if they were parallel tests—but they are not, they are the same test—and thus according to Borsboom can at best reflect the lower bounds of reliability (30).

The notion of error is meant to reflect the accuracy of a test, but it doesn't deal with the more difficult problem of validity: Does a test measure what it purports to measure? Reliability is "measured" while validity is "demonstrated." Certain forms of test development, like item response theory (IRT), allow test writers to create tests with validity "built" in, but this only ends up obscuring the problem. As a result, test developers tend to rely far more on reliability than validity when defending their tests.

All tests involve theory. Take the construct "intelligence." Tests of intelligence take people's capacity to solve problems of varying degrees of difficulty at different speeds as a measure of this construct (Kline, 1998). Clearly there are many possible paths of disagreement. What exactly do these tests measure: Verbal reasoning? Spatial reasoning? Mathematical reasoning? Fluency with language? Familiarity with types of problems on the test? Educational achievement? Economic privilege? Race? As Paul Kline notes, measuring intelligence, at best an intensive quantity if it is even that, is not the same as measuring length (28). Such ambiguity has been used by critics of such tests to argue that they are invalid. Perhaps or perhaps not—depending on whether the test is treated as a sorter, explainer, predictor, or diagnostic, this matters more or less—but it does introduce the problem of measurement invariance: Are the same test items measuring the identical attributes in different persons? If not, how can scores be compared across people? We will explore this question in full detail a bit later in this chapter.

As far as intelligence tests go, correlations with the two most successful ones, the Wechsler and the Stanford-Binet, are used to assess the validity of other tests. According to Kline, among the best intelligence tests, scores for the same individuals tend to differ on average by about five points. This is impressive, as almost all other psychological tests are far less reliable. Of course, such reliability tells us nothing about what these tests are measuring.

Kline (2000) lists the basic qualities of a "good" test: high reliability, high validity, good discriminatory power, and representative norms. High reliability includes high test-retest reliability but also internal consistency and parallel forms of reliability (e.g., correlations between different versions of same test). Internal consistency should be high, but not too high, otherwise items become highly correlated among each other and problems with regression and multicollinearity result. With respect to validity, again the much thornier problem, typically psychometricians distinguish between "face" validity—does a test look like it measures what it claims to, and again this should be high but not too high as otherwise one must deal with a subject's desire to appear a certain way, "concurrent" validity—correlation with other tests taken at same time—often high as new tests often borrow and tweak items from old ones, "predictive" validity—the capacity of a test to predict future criterions, much easier to do for intelligence tests than personality ones, "content" validity—in the case of ability or achievement testing, does it cover all relevant areas and "construct" validity—does the result of a test fit the construct being measured?

For example, Kline (1998, pp. 37–38) offers a partial list of what might be required to establish construct validity in the case of an intelligence test: 0.8 correlation with other intelligence tests, 0.5 correlation with other tests of ability, low correlation with personality tests, positive correlations with academic success, greater correlations with some subjects (e.g., physics) than others (e.g., dance), higher correlations between occupants of the same job, an 0.3 correlation with measures of authoritarianism, and a heritability of 0.7. Thus the fact that intelligence tests are good predictors of later academic achievement should not come as a surprise; they would not be considered reputable tests if they were not. Discriminatory power is a reflection of how much a test distinguishes between individual subjects. Longer tests with many dichotomous items increase discriminatory power as opposed to shorter ones with rating scales as they have too many categories. Finally, norm referencing and standardization of scores allows comparisons to be made across individuals and groups as well as between tests—most famously, intelligence tests are standardized so that means are at 100 with a standard deviation of 15.

Questions of validity are related to the purpose of a test. In the early twentieth century there were two such purposes, which corresponded with two basic types of validity. As more tests developed, this simple division grew more complex, leading to various reformulations of the term. The birth of the concept of validity was associated with growing dissatisfaction with traditional school achievement exams in the early part of the twentieth century (Newton and Shaw, 2014). The problem with exams, especially written ones, was that they introduced an element of subjectivity into evaluation and hence were seen as unfair. This made new forms of tests, those dependent on multiple-choice items, recall, sentence completion, or true/false, attractive alternatives and the construction of new tests exploded during this period. This led to a commitment on the part of test developers to promote these new objective types tests or, as they were known, "standard" tests. Standard tests were used by professional communities for assessing educational achievement as well as for diagnosis but they were also used by psychologists interested in exploring the general structure of intellectual ability and other attributes with respect to how individuals differ. From the start, there were fundamental tensions between the functions of sorting/prediction and explaining.

In 1921, concerned about the lack of consistent application of procedures in educational testing, the National Association of Directors of Educational Research published a standardized list of terms and procedures where they identified reliability and validity as the two key problems involved in educational measurement. Validity was described as "the determination of what a test measures," and reliability, "how consistently it measures" (Buckingham et al., cited in Newton and Shaw, 2014, p. 31). By 1924, this had evolved into

Giles Ruch's now classic definition of validity as "the degree to which a test or examination measures what it purports to measure" (Ruch, 1924, p. 13). Reflecting on the period years later, Thorndike described it as a time when new tests multiplied exponentially and many "sins were committed in the name of measurement by uncritical test users" (Thorndike and Hagan, 1969, p. 6).

For many, the correlation coefficient was widely used as a measure of the quality of tests. Essentially the test score was compared with another measure that reflected what the test was supposed to measure. This second measure was called a "criterion," and the correlation between the two was described as the "coefficient of validity." This later becomes known as "criterion-related validity" as new forms of validity proliferated (Newton and Shaw, 2014). This was a pragmatic understanding of validity as the selection of a criterion (e.g., another test, independent ratings) depended on what the test was to be used for. The consensus was, the higher the correlation, the more valid the test. Thus, the same test could have multiple validities, depending on its use and selected criterion.

This involved a move away from a conceptual understanding of what a test was supposed to measure to a utilitarian and atheoretical one. The correlational conception of validity, also known as the "empirical" conception of validity appealed to the developers of aptitude tests like intelligence tests who could not exactly articulate what intelligence actually was. By the third decade of the century, the Stanford-Binet test emerged as a popular criterion (because it was viewed as of "higher" quality). Today this is still the case but the same is true of the Wechsler tests as well. By the 1940s, a new generation of test developers, like Raymond Cattell and J. P. Guilford, began to criticize the empirical approach as unscientific, and instead turned to factor analysis. The power of factor analysis, first recognized by Spearman, was that psychologists could study "unobservable" or latent variables, despite the criticism of this practice by behaviorists.

An alternative conception of validity was explored during the first few decades of the twentieth century by the developers of subject-specific achievement tests used in education. They were more concerned that the tests represent the subjects they were intended to than correlate with a criterion. They viewed test construction as a process of random sampling from different areas within a field and using scaling to construct tests of different levels of difficulty. This eventually became known as logical or "content-related validity." Scaling encouraged test developers to seek out test questions or "items" with useful statistical properties that differentiated between students and hence increased variability. Items that did not "contribute" to the test, that is, differentiate between students, were removed. Each of these items could also be tested against a criterion allowing the development of more heterogeneous tests. This strategy was also attractive to developers of intelligence tests who viewed intelligence as a compilation of different capacities—thus each test contained multiple homogeneous tests. As was observed at the time with respect to education, test makers began to influence the development of curriculum itself (Newton and Shaw, 2014, p. 43).

Finally, in the growing field of personality testing, yet another interpretation of validity was being developed. Critical of self-rating personality tests, Paul Meehl and Lee Cronbach began to argue that self-ratings were not a direct sampling of behavior, as in educational tests, but an indirect sign of something deeper (Newton and Shaw, 2014). By the 1950s, this "deeper" something became a "construct" and was viewed as both a way to explain consistent responses—effects of the same "construct"—and unite criterion and content-related validity. In 1954, in a new standards document published by the American Psychological Association Committee on Test Standards chaired by Lee Cronbach, "validity" was described as the "degree to which the test is capable of achieving certain aims" (APA, 1954, cited in Newton and Shaw, 2014, p. 64). The report distinguished between four types of validity, each appropriate for different purposes: content validity—when a sample of given situations/topics is directly measured (e.g., achievement tests), predictive validity—when one is interested in predicting how an individual might perform on a future criterion (e.g., aptitude tests), concurrent validity—when one is interested in discriminating individuals on a current criterion (e.g., distinguishing between the clinically and non-clinically depressed), and construct validity—when none of the others apply and one is interested in an indicator of "psychological" constructs (e.g., personality tests).

Construct validity could incorporate the three other types, and establishing it required predictions about responses to a test based on a theory. The process, therefore, involved testing the test, but also testing the construct and the broader conceptual/empirical system or "nomological" network it was a part of. Thus it combined testing with research. Over the next few decades, more and more of the work of validation was seen as falling within the purview of construct validity, and by the 1970s, the leading figure in the theory of test development at ETS, Samuel Messick (1975), declared that all tests employ psychological constructs and hence all validity was construct validity. He was especially skeptical of predictive validity, still the favorite of educational test developers, as one could not separate prediction from measurement, thus prediction also required theoretical justification in order to make sure test scores were not inflated by construct-irrelevant variance.

Test writers also needed to focus on, argued Messick, the ethical consequences of the test and alternative explanations of what the tests were measuring. As is the current way of putting it, one doesn't validate a test but specific interpretations of outcomes from a test and validity is a matter of degree (Newton and Shaw, 2014, p. 113). The 1985 *Standards* described construct, criterion, and content as alternative forms of "evidence" of validity, not as different "kinds," and the 1999 *Standards* went even further, defining validity as dependent on the interpretations of a test. Tests are not valid or invalid the current maxim goes interpretations are.

Lost in all this was the original sense of validity: Does a test measure what it purports to measure? As Denny Borsboom (2005) notes, this notion is fairly basic and involves two assumptions: First, the attribute being measured exists and second, variations in attribute cause ordered variations in the outcome measure. Critics of Borsboom have described this as too "vague" (Sireci, 2009), as validity changes as what one is "supposed" to measure changes, as well as charge that such a definition ignores the established consensus of the past seventy years, but they miss the point. One should know what is being measured before an instrument is created. Clearly then, correlations between test scores and other established measures can provide only circumstantial evidence for validity as it requires a theory of response behavior not a theory of the relationship between measures.

As a result of the shift, many in the field have come to see construct validity as a type of criterion validity and look for correlations between test scores and other measures of the construct. The attractiveness of this to generations of psychologists is plain to see where methodological solutions are preferred to theoretical ones and strong correlations can be used as a measure of high validity. But measurement is not a two-way relationship (Borsboom, 2005, p. 162). This relationship is actually obscured by the search for predictive properties via correlation as the typical multivariate approach only ends up with multicollinearity as opposed to identifying the unique variation in the criterion.

As Borsboom forcefully puts it, validity requires the development of substantive theory and "is the one problem in testing that psychology cannot contract out to methodology" (151). Typically, measurement in psychology is an epistemological issue—it is used to gain more knowledge about something. But underneath the measurement and distinct from it is an ontological claim: Said attribute exists and has a structure appropriate for measurement. As we already noted, construct validity sidesteps all this by focusing on "constructs" in vast nomological networks that don't often exist in psychology in order to determine meaning. More generally, the operationalist bias in psychology also sidesteps this question. Psychologists confuse validation—an epistemological issue focused on determining the quality of a test, which can involve prediction or construct analysis, with validity, a state or quality not a judgment.

What classical test theory does, argues Borsboom (2006a), is shift the focus from how tests work to what a test correlates with. Thus tests are designed with correlations in mind rather than a theory of the attribute and its causal effects on a particular measure. Borsboom points to the previously discussed IAT as an example of this: No one presents any theory, psychometric or otherwise, about the relationship between observed scores and the various latent variables being studied. Instead the focus is simply on correlations with other tests. Clearly this problem extends into much of psychology, sometimes even in the name of construct validity. The idea of a simple calculation to deal with validity is just too attractive to psychologists trained in a methodological framework that eschews theory.

The issue with measurement is not one of meaning (e.g., does theory match empirical findings?) but one of reference. Does the referent exist? If attributes do not exist, that is, if we do not take a realist approach to them, how could they possibly cause the varying outcomes detected by tests and measures? And if they don't cause variable outcomes, what are the tests and outcomes measures actually detecting? Psychologists have relied on a pragmatic approach to all this for generations: If we have quantified measures, they are meaningful and the process works. But just a cursory look at what is being assumed here illustrates the incoherence of some of the most prominent underlying assumptions. The lack of a realist approach, as in the natural sciences, and the corresponding case of multiple referents for the same attributes and process, is the central problem in much of psychology in general, but it becomes especially pronounced when considering measurement. A good rule of thumb: First have a sense of what you are measuring and then try to measure it, recognizing that this understanding can change. As opposed to first designing a measure that works, meaning it has a relationship to other measures, and then determining the "construct" that is being measured, as is the case in much contemporary test construction.

Most psychological tests and measures still depend on classical test theory: trying to determine a true score by estimating error. Yet, in psychometrics, many test developers instead utilize a latent variable approach. A latent variable model typically conceives an unobserved hypothetical structure and the effects it has on a set of indicator variables. Sometimes latent variables are characterized as "unmeasurable" and a distinction is made between "traits," which are said to be real, and "constructs," which are said to exist only in the minds of researchers. Sometimes constructs are treated as a data reduction device, though they are said to measure real phenomena (Bollen, 2002). These differing descriptions imply different ways to treat latent variables and so it is important to understand what they mean. Both latent and observed variables can be either continuous or categorical. In the two most common cases, both are continuous and this is described as a "factor" model or the observed is categorical and the latent continuous and this is described as an IRT (Item Response Test) model. For example, personality tests using Likert scales tend to rely on a factor model while achievement tests, where the participant's response is either correct or incorrect, on an IRT one. Sometimes latent variables are theorized before looking at data and data are used to "test" a theory and sometimes they are derived from data—the former involves confirmatory factor analysis (CFA) and the latter exploratory factor analysis (EFA).

Unfortunately, it is very easy to misinterpret a latent variable approach and the appropriate methodological implications. Mathematically, latent models are positing the expectation that one set of variables is a function of another set of variables and the relationship is usually identified through some regression function (Borsboom, 2008). What makes the relationship different from other similar statistical relationships is not so much that the latent variable is "theoretical" or "unobservable" as is usually assumed (e.g., IQ score is an observed variable while intelligence is a latent one), as most variables are not "observed"—one cannot see "age" or "SES"—but reflect the level of certainty one has as to the location of a person within that variable structure: latent = less certain (Borsboom, 2008, p. 30). As Borsboom notes, it is an epistemological distinction more than an ontological one, that is, the distinction is partly a function of the observer. One way to explain this is that variables considered latent today might be considered observable with improved measurement capacity (Bollen, 2002).

Some of this is decided by convention and some decided by whether the causal structure that produces the changes in the indicators is viewed deterministically, as the only causally relevant one and as having equivalent variable positions as indicators have data patterns—this "matching up" is what is often meant by an "observable" variable (Borsboom, 2008, p. 33). In contrast, "latent" variables tend to have a probabilistic relationship to indicators, though they are usually taken to have the only systematic relationship to indicators—this is known as "unidimensionality" and is important because without it, an item might be measuring several latent variables and scores become impossible to interpret. Also, latent variables have "local independence" meaning indicators are statistically independent of each other when the latent variable is held constant (Bollen, 2002).

The key point is, the distinction is not meant to be read through the logic of operationalism—as it frequently is—that latent variables are any less real than observed ones. As if they are not "real," how can they have a causal relationship with observed variables, which, as we have seen, makes measurement possible? In other words, all this involves laying out theoretically the structure of the latent variable itself and its relationship to data patterns via parameter estimation and modeling, and then using multiple approaches to test these models. "Real" does not mean they are localized in space and time, although it does mean they occupy certain places in a variable structure and that by following a certain measurement procedure, the resulting indicator values are fixed and the relationship is a lawful one (Borsboom, 2008, p. 44).

This is a slightly different definition of causality than that of the push-pull type of Newtonian physics but better explains the kinds of causes one finds in psychology where causes are the consequences of multiple variables connected by parameters within which individuals are located (Pearl, 2000). Psychology must deal with causes if it is to measure. The confusion lies when such causes are described as being "in" individuals as opposed to "pertaining to" individuals, so that intelligence need not be "inside" individuals to have a causal relationship to IQ. Different forms of variation—over time, over people and over situations, yet with different variable structures and thus different causal explanations and inferences across these contexts, should be made with an explicit theoretical rationale (Borsboom, 2008, p. 47). Thus, measures of variance within groups likely mean little when it comes to individuals or a finding of lack of variance over time tells us little about variance across situations. We will discover that these confusions tend to extend into popular psychology involving testing and measurement as well and we start with the most established psychological measure of all, intelligence.

CASE STUDY ONE: INTELLIGENCE (I) POPULAR VARIANTS

The measurement of intelligence is, by far, the most successful measure ever developed by psychology if we grade success by influence, familiarity outside the field, and predictive validity. Yet, it is also invokes the most controversy outside of psychometric quarters, especially with respect to its distribution among certain groups, and yet it is also a widely accepted metaphor in popular psychology. Add the noun "intelligence" and one has identified a new measurable construct: emotional intelligence, social intelligence, musical intelligence, spatial intelligence, and so on. Defining intelligence has been a notorious problem for the field. Paul Kline offers this simple one: the general reasoning ability that is useful in the solution of problems (1998, p. 100). The four key elements in this definition are that it is an "ability" that involves reasoning, is general, and is used to solve problems.

Psychometricians usually see Charles Spearman's 1904 paper using factor analysis to catalog human abilities as the start of this tradition and following Spearman they prefer to use factor analysis to specify intelligence further, though his technique of computing tetrad differences was quite arduous. Spearman was seeking to explain the "positive manifold," or the fact of high positive correlations among test scores on cognitive tasks. They must be due to the same cause, he reasoned. He essentially devised a method of computing multiple correlations across tests and people so as to reveal a common cause. Spearman identified two such factors: *g* or a general factor and *s*, specific factors or the residual variance unexplained by *g*. He believed that his discovery of *g*—including its heritability and its biological basis in mental "energy"—as the key to making psychology a science as well as protecting the status of a classical education in Britain (as it supported the strengthening of *g*).

Since the days of Spearman there have been debates as to how many kinds of intelligence there are. Two recent examples in this debate are those of Howard Gardner and Robert Sternberg. Sternberg distinguishes between analytic, creative, and practical intelligence and developed a test to measure them. Gardner (1983) claims he explicitly chose the word "intelligence" because he felt the concept had to be broadened. Gardner introduced the idea of multiple intelligence in his 1983 bestseller *Frames of Mind.* The additional forms of intelligence he identifies did not come from the factor analysis of test data, as was the case with traditional forms, but his survey of cultural and colloquial ways of thinking about valuable abilities. Thus psychometricians tend to reject them. In fact, one of the criticisms of Gardner, other than the lack of measures and either exploratory or confirmatory factor analyses, is precisely his conflation of ability and intelligence—though some studies have found correlations between many of these and *g* (e.g., Visser et al., 2006). He lists nine: musical-rhythmic, visual-spatial, verbal-linguistic, logical-mathematical, bodily-kinesthetic, interpersonal, intrapersonal, naturalistic, and existentialist. Gardner argues that they are independent of each other while Carroll (1993) and others argue that they are not.

As Perry Klein (1998) has noted, there is a tautological quality to this: Having high musical intelligence means one is good at music, yet if one is good in music it is explained as caused by high musical intelligence. Other critics view the list as fairly arbitrary. Linda Gottfredson (2009) has argued that despite public controversy, most psychologists still view IQ tests as valid and useful ways to assess student potential and accept that *g* remains the best predictor of academic achievement. Even the APA in 1995 accepted that at least 40 percent of the variance in IQ is genetic and that the genetic differences become a greater source of variance as children age. Gottfredson views Gardner's influence as a reassuring salve against the consistent finding in the 1960s and 1970s that attempts to raise the IQ scores of poor and minority children were fruitless.

In general, part of this "broadening" is also related to the quest to improve it. In schools, theories of multiple intelligence translate into the notion of multiple learning styles and are more palatable than using IQ scores to explain the lack of success in school among certain children. For Gottfredson, the danger is that schools downplay the analytic and verbal abilities that are required for success in school and beyond at the expense of focusing on what student's already excel at, a kind of feel-good education. Despite Gottfredson's insistence that genes cause these individual differences, which the study of population genetics cannot actually reveal, Gottfredson is correct about the difference between how schools and teachers view intelligence and how it is presented to first-year psychology students. The latter accepts the notion of multiple intelligences, but certainly take the idea of a stable IQ divided into one or two major factors as well as its predictive validity as a given. The theory of MI survives, argues Gottfredson, because it is untestable and its implied argument, that IQ tests are too "narrow," is attractive to many. Certainly the prevalent view that IQ testing is associated with racism and eugenics doesn't help.

This brings us to a very important point: Intelligence testing is designed to differentiate between people. The conception is biased toward capacities that some people do much better than others as opposed to those most people are good at. They were designed for sorting not the evaluation of individuals. And they remain good at sorting. Industrial societies seem to require sorting with respect to education, as different jobs require very different types of education. Most other Western societies are more comfortable with educational sorting than is the case is the United States. But the widespread use of tracking, AP classes, community colleges, and special education, as well as categories like "learning disabled," "differentiated learning," and "remedial education," is just sorting in more palatable terms. Perhaps there is a sense that a disability or "differentiation" can be treated and therefore is less hopeless?

The APA's recently published *Correcting Fallacies about Educational and Psychological Testing* (Phelps, 2009) treads similar ground. Phelps, the editor and well-known defender of standardized testing in education, chooses not to include even one entry critical of testing. An entry by Linda Gottfredson summarizes recent survey's involving experts who view IQ scores as reliable, valid, unbiased, stable, not very modifiable, highly heritable, and correlated with neurological activity, and the best single predictor of key life outcomes (Gottfredson, 2009). And these surveys are probably correct as they tend to define expertise fairly narrowly: Since Spearman, the fallback position on intelligence for intelligence theorists has linked the reliability of scores and its predictive validity to a one- or two-factor model that is mostly genetic and different across racial groups. Spearman seemed to think that it were these assumptions that made the psychology of intelligence a real science.

The psychology of intelligence, at least in the past decade, is not a major theme in popular psychology. This is not surprising given the view among psychometricians that copious quantities of it are not widely distributed in the population at large. There are a host of writers trying to cull out more democratic variants. For example, Anne Cianciolo and Robert Sterberg's (2004) *Intelligence: A Brief History* seeks to provide a broad introduction to the field. To convey pluralism, they offer a set of metaphors for capturing intelligence—geographic, computational, biological, epistemological, sociological, anthropological, and systems—and present them as equally valuable. Most of the book is taken up with the "geographic" though, as this serves as a placeholder for traditional theories of intelligence. They describe a hierarchical view of intelligence—with *g* at the top followed by more specific abilities like verbal, fluid, or crystallized intelligence at the next level of the hierarchy. They describe a "radix" model with *g* at the center and other forms radiating out.

In a section on the problems with intelligence testing, they note a disagreement between the public and intelligence theorists about whether the "geographic" metaphor's focus on abstract, general reasoning alone is an appropriate way to conceive intelligence as the public believe—coincidentally just like Sternberg—intelligent behavior involves everyday thinking as well. They argue that because the public has "such implicit theories . . . [it] can lead to the view that intelligence is not being completely captured by the dominant testing practices. That intelligence tests are not better predictor of performance in school and on the job suggests that there is likely some truth to this view (54). As to whether intelligence can be improved, they turn to the view of Alfred Binet that it can, as opposed to that of Galton and Spearman who viewed it as fixed by heredity, and defend Sternberg's "system" view, which suggests improvements are possible.

As far as the more traditional view about hereditarianism and racial differences, they acknowledge that some variability is due to genes but question the validity of twin studies, the immutability of genetic effects, and the overly simplistic division of the source of the variance into two categories, genes and environment. In terms of racial differences they reference the 15-point average difference in score between whites and blacks and highlight that those differences tend to be larger on those items that are *g* loaded. They describe these differences as the result of a "complex web" of biological and societal factors that are not easily disentangled but not a function of test bias (133). This view seems to represent the consensus of those academics that write for a broader audience.

Another very different but recent entry in this genre, *IQ Testing 101* (2009) written by Alan Kaufman, a student of David Wechsler and developer of the popular K-ABC test for children, has a much more explicitly clinical focus. The book is filled with jokes about how people think IQ tests are evil and dangerous and Kaufman clearly views part of his role and trying to make them more palatable. The book is a defense of Wechsler's WISC and WAIS and their distinction between verbal and performance IQ as well as providing a host of subscores that make them far more practical than the Stanford-Binet. He argues that quality IQ tests are individual tests and not group tests and so he will stay out of the group comparison controversy. He defends IQ testing for diagnostic and selection related activity, though argues that many interpretations of tests over the years have been, in his words, "stupid." He advocates for "intelligent" testing, which basically means bringing a clinicians perspective to testing rather than a statistical one and one he attributes to Wechsler who accepted *g* but considered IQ as part of a broader assessment of individuals.

An intelligent approach avoids common misinterpretations of tests including the tendency to ignore normal variations in subtest score and to confuse the identification of *g* with what is actually useful in assessing the bulk of children who are referred for psychological evaluation. What they need, argues Kaufman, is an "ipsative" approach that identifies relative strengths and weaknesses instead of comparing them to external norms as psychometricians do. He criticizes test developers for holding on to items that do not connect with the views of cognitive and neuropsychology. Kaufman himself is anti-*g*, which he views as coming out of the "ivory tower" rather than the real world of intelligence testing in schools and clinics. Intelligent testing also involves linking testing to current research in cognitive processes as opposed to simply creating tests with high *g* loads—Kaufman estimates that the right number of abilities to test is more than two but less than seven (100).

While his clinical approach is refreshing, Kaufmann accepts many basic findings of the traditional view including the link between scores and occupation—but recognizes we can't identify cause and effect—as well as racial differences—which interestingly are cut by half on his K-ABC tests (173) and which he argues, against the Jensen consensus, are actually a function of class not race. In terms of heritability, his estimate is that 50 percent of intelligence is inherited, but wisely cautions that estimates are culturally and historically specific. He also reviews recent research about variance in IQ related to whether twins share a placenta or not, making the case that the question of what is inherited is more complex that typically recognized by behavioral geneticists. Kaufman also reviews the so-called "Flynn effect," the finding by James Flynn (2007) that on average, IQ scores in the United States are increasing by about 3 points a decade from the 1930s to the 2000s. One aspect of this is that IQ norms become outdated fairly quickly and another, perhaps the more attractive, is that these changes are clearly not a result of changes in gene frequencies and so explanations of this tend to view it as an effect of industrialization and scientific progress as well as changes in nutrition and the availability of education.

Then there are a few recent books that attempt to broaden the notion of intelligence further, making it much more widely distributed, like writer David Shenk's (2010) popular psychology tract, *The Genius in All of Us*. Shenk describes intelligence as a process, not a "thing" that, in his view, undermines any kind of hereditarian argument. Like Scott Kaufman's (2013) *Ungifted: Intelligence Redefined*, he challenges the notion of "giftedness" as a static endowment and instead views it as the result of complex dynamic between interior and exterior forces. Nature versus nurture needs to be replaced, argues Shenk, by "dynamic" development (27). After a promising start however, Shenk's solutions to modifying intelligence and creating a "culture of excellence" seem more like solutions he borrowed from positive psychology: set high expectations while showing compassion, creativity, and patience, he advises (123). Kaufman, a student of Robert Sternberg, focuses on the limitations of traditional one or two-factor models and argues that they not only misrepresent the phenomena, but also influence the way teachers and parents treat children, becoming a kind of self-fulfilling prophecy. The problem, as proponents of traditional IQ tests love to point out, no "multiple" intelligence model offers any measurement-based alternative to the current model, which is often what schools and parents want (though probably not teachers). The history of intelligence testing suggests that their success is related to their utility not necessarily their capacity to assess something important.

Viewing IQ tests as a clinical tool seems reasonable, especially in schools, as IQ tasks were designed to measure the cognitive skills needed to excel in school in the first place. Defenders of this view need only turn to Binet's original research, much more a product of the clinical approach of French psychiatry than German experimentalism or Anglo-American Galtonianism. Like Piaget, Binet was really interested in the qualitative elements of thinking and the processes those tested were engaged with were much more important than the responses. And in fact, Piaget borrowed many of Binet's specific problems. Binet and Simon's 1905 scale, the one borrowed and transformed by the Americans, was a product of fifteen years of research involving endless variations of similar problems given to children. Binet himself criticized US researchers for their sterile testing conditions and obsession with simple and precise quantifiable results, which ironically he helped extend even further by allowing intelligence to be conceived as a single entity (Wolf, 1973). Still, Binet never forgot the link between the data and the actual cognitive processes they required while at the same time, always attending to individual differences.

The debate about *g* seems beside the point with respect to these concerns as more factors create a better clinical picture. What about the question of modifiability? Can capacity with respect to these factors be improved? This question does seem to get to the heart of the value of education itself. Because IQ tests are linked to capacities for mathematical, verbal, and conceptual abstraction, and development in these areas is built into the curriculum, it would be hard to imagine schooling does not raise scores. And they do. Norm referencing downplays these increases and focuses more on individual increases as related to cohort increases. But then one enters the mess of explaining how inter-individual differences translate into intra-individual differences, which seems to be ignored by most defenders of norm-referenced testing in general. Even clinical applications require caution, but in terms of comparison, selection, and prediction, it does seem fair to require some understanding of how psychological variables cause variance on measuring instruments, and even that those variables are capable of being quantified in the first place, before using it to limit people's opportunities in life, as is the case when IQ-like tests are used for school and job selection. If this has not yet been achieved with respect to intelligence testing, and as we shall see, it surely has not, one can only imagine how far this is from being the case in other forms of psychological testing.

CASE STUDY ONE: INTELLIGENCE (II) AND RACE

Probably the most widely known issue around IQ testing in the past half a century is the question of racial differences in the distribution of intelligence scores. Spearman (1927) was actually the first to suggest that there were racial differences in intelligence, though he foolishly suggested that Asians have less of it than Europeans, already pointing to the historical and cultural specificities of these claims. In his now infamous, "How much can we boost IQ and scholastic achievement?" Jensen (1969) "discovered" a 15- to 18-point difference in IQ scores between whites and blacks that he claimed increased with tasks "saturated" with *g*. When SES was controlled for, claimed Jensen, the differences were reduced slightly. A similar case was made by Charles Herrnstein and Richard Murray (1994) nearly twenty-five years later in *The Bell Curve,* though as we will review, the latter also had problems with some of the regression techniques employed.

Jensen was undoubtedly the more careful of the three and his actual claims were much more qualified than some of his critics recognized. For example, he never denied the impact of environmental factors, nor the interaction between environmental and genetic factors, but argued the genetic ones were predominant in terms of influence. Even this, he recognized, could not be established, at least as far as intergroup differences, so much as inferred from the high intragroup heritability scores. His main argument was not about denying certain groups an education, as it is sometimes presented, but tailoring education to different levels of ability, a fairly acceptable idea today, as long as those abilities don't seem to match up too much with attributes like race or class. He also refers to *g* as a "hypothetical construct" (1969, p. 10), though he has not always been consistent about this.

The response of the scientific community to Jensen's work was overwhelmingly negative. Jensen claimed that he was simply presenting findings that he stumbled on without any concern for the politics but this was not convincing given that Jensen's paper was published a few years after the battles to desegregate schools in the South and just as the backlash against the Civil Rights Movement was starting to grow as well as a frustration among certain whites that tax dollars were being spent on social programs. One expression of this backlash was the questioning of the value of programs like Head Start, and Jensen knew that his findings would be used to make exactly that point (Alland, 2002). To call this "nonpolitical" is disingenuous at best.

Stephen J. Gould's (1981) critique of Jensenism, *The Mismeasure of Man*, is probably better known at this point than Jensen's 1969 *Harvard Educational Review* paper. Gould argues that, over history, the method of factor analysis has led intelligence testers to confuse a statistical abstraction—the primary factor to emerge from the factor analysis—with a real world entity. He terms this "reification." He seems to suggest that by definition statistical abstractions cannot be real world entities. But this is a strange assertion. Even psychometricians would view factor analysis as a necessary but not sufficient condition for determining the reality of something. They would require, at the very least, the establishment of concurrent and predictive validity. Ironically, many psychometricians are themselves ambivalent as to the reality of their constructs and, given the influence of operationalism in the field, would happily argue that the reality of intelligence is not relevant, only its predictive validity, as it is a mechanism for making distinctions between individuals and nothing more.

In his *Straight Talk About Mental Tests* (1981), Jensen attempted a less technical defense of his ideas. Like Spearman before him, he views the high positive correlations between the capacity to perform mentally complex tasks, as the basis for the argument of a single-factor approach to intelligence. He describes the existence of this trait—as either one or two factors—as one of the most generally acknowledged findings in the field of psychology and he is probably right. He also acknowledges that IQ is most related to children's performance in school because these types of tasks are emphasized in school, but this does not mean they are limited to schooling. He also describes the claim that observed differences among persons on intelligence are largely "attributable to genetic inheritance" as one of the least controversial facts in the IQ controversy (1981, p. xii), but this depends on how you interpret what this statement means. The term "attributable" is not directly a causal claim so much as a statement about explaining variance in a statistical sense. There is also the difference between the claims that the "observed" differences in scores are attributable to genes or the claim that differences in intelligence are largely attributed to genes let alone caused by genes. The latter claims are inferred from the first but they are treated as identical by critics of Jensen.

Defenders of intelligence tend to trade on slippery distinctions between intelligence as a test score, intelligence as a statistical abstraction, intelligence as a concept, and intelligence as a bio-psychological entity. Jensen is no exception. The method of factor analysis easily supports this confusion (Glymour, 2010). Intelligence tests are not biased against minorities argued Jensen (1981). Part of Jensen's goal was to make clear the difference between a statistical bias and the public's conception of bias. Bias does not mean that the average score of one group is lower than the average of another. This, says Jensen, is simply a finding. It does mean, again in a statistical sense that score values consistently over or under estimate true score value. It is a systematic error in measurement. He goes as far as accepting that there probably are no scientifically satisfactory explanations for group differences in scores because definitive experimental evidence is impossible to obtain, but because of the strong feelings aroused by this issue, it is difficult to even search openly for these causes (Jensen, 1981, p. 213). For him, the genetic hypothesis is more likely because of the difficulty of detailing how experience can produce those differences, but clearly his critics would make the same point about genetics. In fact, this is precisely Jensen's claim: defenders of the environmentalist thesis do not offer detailed mechanisms as to how a particular environmental variable causes changes in IQ scores yet accuse him of not doing so with respect to genetics. He is right in the sense that all of these debates are taking place at the wrong level of analysis.

Yet, many in behavioral genetics seem to do this again and again. In a 2003 collection of essays in tribute to Jensen with entries from well-known figures in the fields of genetics and intelligence like Robert Plomin, John Carroll, and Robert J. Sternberg, there are some entries that could have easily been written by Jensen himself, especially those about race and IQ (Rushton, 2003) and criminality and IQ (Ellis and Walsh, 2003). It seems that many of Jensen's positions are still within the range of acceptable positions in the field. Quite frankly, the general findings reviewed in this work have not changed much since 1969. What is going on with behavioral genetics? Are they defenders of an unpopular truth as some of them see it or a field of racists and bad scientists? In his *Misbehaving Science* (2014), Aaron Panofsky tries to explain this in relation to the conflict-riddled history of the discipline.

As the field was founded after the Second World War, it faced several challenges. It sought to bridge together researchers from diverse fields—much as cognitive science tried to do later—continue to support both animal and human research, build up new academic departments, and move away from its past associations with eugenics and hereditarianism. Part of this success was due to an attempt to avoid politics and issues of race entirely. The one battle they were willing to fight was against extreme environmentalism, as this challenged the very basis of the field. The Jensen article disrupted this consensus. Critics attacked not only Jensen's conclusions, but the basic methods of the field itself, particularly the notion of heritability.

While many in the field rejected Jensen's analysis, they refused to attack his work publicly as they began to believe the very survival of the field was in play. They were willing, however, to challenge what they viewed as the radical environmentalism of critics and this often made them come across as glib and out of touch with the politics involved. Ironically, as Panofsky notes, during the 1950s, some in the field had already argued that the concept of heritability had long outlived its usefulness, but the battles of the 1970s ended up creating a "bunker" mentality in the field, where nothing was open to challenge anymore (64). By the 1980s, the field had rallied around Jensen and accepted three of his points: the importance of heritability estimates, a causal interpretation of heritability, and that the black/white IQ gap could be explained partially by genetics (86). They also accepted Jensen's argument that findings from the study of individual differences could be extended to groups as well as could explain intra-individual processes. As those who disagreed with these theses were no longer taken seriously in the field, they were no longer able to integrate the more complex models of cognition coming out of cognitive or developmental science, nor were they able to introduce any methodological reformulations into their research.

In the case of Herrnstein and Murray, there is the behavioral genetics argument—borrowed from J. Philippe Rushton's (2003) work on the genetic hierarchy of races—but there is also the dependence on regression techniques to infer causal relationships, specifically between IQ and all that is good and bad, an approach taken, to be fair, by the vast majority of social scientists who use regression. Regressions do not yield causal relationships or even somewhat causal-ish relationships. A high correlation or beta value is not evidence for cause nor is a low value evidence for its absence. There are a few who try to develop statistical techniques to infer causal relationships—like Judea Pearl or Clark Glymour, but their work is not well known outside of statistics. Predictors are not causes. It is perfectly conceivable to imagine a predictor without any association between the variables—e.g., if one controls for an intervening variable it is possible that a nonzero regression coefficient can result between two non-associated variables (Glymour, 2010). If that value is high enough you can be sure a case for causality will be made. This is the problem with the lack of substantive theory, and this is exactly what Herrnstein and Murray go on to do.

Their argument revolves around Herrnstein's thesis, first made in a 1971 *Atlantic* article, that success in a meritocratic society is a result of intelligence, and intelligence is inherited, thus success is inherited. He never actually mentions race and it takes until the 1990s for him to make the connection explicit when he gets involved in debates over affirmative action (Alland, 2002). He needed only add that there were racial differences in intelligence to his basic argument and affirmative action, for him, became a danger to the meritocracy. Even more than Jensen, Herrnstein, and Murray play with the public's confusion about heritability. At one point in *The Bell Curve* they explain clearly that heritability is about population variances, not genetic causes. Later, they treat heritability estimates as a constant when dealing with racially different populations despite the fact that the data they used was gathered from an all-white sample (cited in Alland, 2002, p. 150).

In other words, after saying that heritability was population specific, they go on to ignore it. Perhaps there are grounds for this, as Jensen had argued as well, but they never go on to defend this. Still, they clearly say—whether to take them at their word is another matter—that they are "agnostic" about whether the cause of IQ differences is genetic or environmental and that it only appears that as of now, the hereditarian hypothesis is the most likely one. Yet, in the book, they seem much more critical of studies that show the influence of environmental factors on the variance in IQ as opposed to those focused on genes, and they make certain assumptions that inflate heritability-like including both additive and non-additive genetic variation and ignoring shared-placental related variation (Daniels et. al., 1997).

At base *The Bell Curve* is based on several causal claims. Not only that racial differences in IQ are genetic or that they are not malleable—which doesn't necessarily follow, nor does the idea that "environmental" causes are malleable for that matter, they are just repeating the claims of Jensen here—but that IQ is the cause of a range of positive outcomes including job success, lack of criminality, stable marriage, competency of parenting, wealth, etc. Their concern is that if these high IQ scorers breed only with each other, more inequality will result, a concern shared by Francis Galton. This is where the regression comes in. Regression does not eliminate human judgment, but it can disguise it (Glymour, 1997). A key judgment in this case obviously involves the choice of variables to include in the regression. This is often a function of the causal assumptions made, but can never be tested by the data.

For example, in the case of correlated error, the error term in the regression is correlated with one or more of the regressors (270). This could mean that the association between regressors and outcome may be a function of an omitted variable. Other possible errors in human judgment that generate serious issues include using the outcome variable to determine which units to include in the sample (i.e., selecting subjects who only differ in a specific way), ignoring how the data were generated in determining whether causal inferences are possible, or even just getting the direction between predictors and outcomes wrong. *The Bell Curve* makes almost all of these errors: on a basic level, the list of possible omitted variables is extensive and the assumption that IQ is cause and not effect certainly cannot be derived from the data.

Most readers of Jensen, Herrnstein, and Murray in the media do not typically take note of their caveats and take inter-individual differences and treat them like intra-individual differences, as say one does when making a latent trait the cause of behavior or arguing that traits are biological in origin. But this leap is something that requires theoretical elaboration and cannot simply be assumed. Part of the problem is that these traits are assumed to be stable and individual variation is treated as error (Borsboom et al., 2009b, p. 15). But why make this assumption given the evidence from developmental psychology that cognitive processes change qualitatively over the course of development? One obvious reason is that intelligence is not a cognitive structure but a statistical measure of differences between people. Jensen himself went back and forth between the argument that intelligence was a statistical concept used only to measure differences between people/groups and that it was a cognitive one that caused these differences (see Jensen, 1998). Again, this is a fairly extensive problem in psychology that involves measurement based on tests focused on between-group differences. This includes intelligence and personality testing where psychologists just assume homogeneity.

The problems with Jensen, Herrnstein, and Murray's work with respect to the controversy over racial differences lies not in their "racism" or "reification"—though they are all clearly political conservatives—but in their neglect of the notion of measurement invariance. Interpreting group differences on test scores is not a simple as they make it seem: simply compare observed scores. The idea of measurement invariance is an attempt to solve a fairly obvious problem with respect to testing different types of people. It attempts to answer the question: Are observed differences in scores attributable to differences in the properties of what is being measured? (Borsboom, 2006b). In order for this to be the case, the same attribute must relate to the same set of observations across different groups. The only way to know this is to test whether items function differentially across groups by using various statistical and modeling strategies. Bias is not always a problem, especially in trying to understand a particular phenomenon with respect to within-group differences. Sometimes multiple biases can even swamp themselves out.

The real problem, as Borsboom notes, is the lack of measurement invariance in tests used for selection/sorting purposes where the test ends up measuring attributes that groups possess in different degrees (e.g., like education or language proficiency). The test score then measures both the latent variable being studied and the one possessed by the groups in different degrees. In this case, the test violates the basic principle of unidimensionality—test items should only measure one variable—in each of the groups as well as the comparison between groups (2006b, p. 179). This will translate into bias in the ordering of people within-group as they can be identical with respect to the latent variable but different with respect to the unanalyzed one. When such tests are used for making decisions about individuals, fairness requires that psychometric standards be much higher than they typically are in the study of populations as they involve real-world consequences.

Measurement invariance is an ideal. It is almost always violated. The question is to what degree is this tolerable. The approach of Jensen and others is simply to confuse measurement invariance with predictive invariance, that is, check whether predictions between scores and criterion are comparable across groups, or in the case of Herrnstein and Murray, whether regressing a criterion on observed scores yields similar regression parameters. But as Millsap (1997) explains, prediction invariance and measurement invariance should actually conflict with each other. For instance, if two groups differ on intelligence, there should not be predictive invariance between the groups at all and regression parameters should actually be different. If this is not the case, the test must have bias with respect to a particular group (Borsboom, 2006b), meaning measurement invariance cannot be established. Despite this, the APA and AERA continue to view investigating predictive invariance as the appropriate path to determining test bias. The lack of serious consideration of these issues is a reflection of the narrow focus in the field of intelligence psychology itself and its closed nature.

CASE STUDY ONE: INTELLIGENCE (III) ACADEMIC VARIANTS

It was Spearman's correlational-based technique much more than *g* that vastly transformed psychology's capacity for measurement and hence its status as a science (Hearnshaw, 1979). The *g* factor came under attack decades later as Leon Thurnstone (1947) identified an alternative technique for factoring: One could posit a single factor and identify the amount of correlations accounted for and continue to add factors until there were no more correlations to explain. This is the basis for exploratory factor analysis (EFA). In this method, a large matrix of correlations is factored in order to account mathematically for those correlations in terms of a smaller number of factors or linear sums of variables. The strength of a factor is measured by its "loading" or correlation with a variable. Thus one goal is to minimize the number of factors required to account for the correlations in the correlation matrix (Kline, 1998). So that *g,* for example, is described by its defenders as common to all the variables in the matrix.

In EFA, factors are statistical abstractions. These factors can also be "rotated," meaning along an axis of a graphic representation of factors, where factors loadings can change, although they remain mathematically equivalent, thus generating multiple models that need to match up to what Thurnstone termed "simple structure"—only a few factors with high loadings. Multiple factors can be correlated with each other—termed oblique, or uncorrelated—termed orthogonal. In EFA, common factor variance is distinguished from error variance, while in PCA (principal component analysis) the factors account for all the variance, including error. One can obtain correlations between primary factors to identify second-order factors (or third-order ones as is the case with *g*). Thurstone demonstrated that *g* can be made to disappear under a multi-trait model and model selection was as much about aesthetics as it was about science. The justification for a model had to come from elsewhere. Furthermore, decisions about sampling—size, types of subjects, variables included—as well as selecting the number of factors and types of rotations can yield widely divergent results.

In recent years, a general consensus from factor analysis of cognitive abilities has emerged focused on the following abilities and their highest loading factors: *g* (third-order)—induction, visualization, quantitative reasoning, and verbal ability—not quite as large but also emerging: flexibility of closure, numerical facility, associative memory, word fluency, speed of closure, sequential reasoning, and spatial relations—followed by a first order level of more specific abilities (Caroll, 1993). Carroll calls the second-order factors the different flavors of *g*. It is also possible to interpret the findings of factor analysis, following Cattell, as identifying two second-order abilities, fluid intelligence or *Gf*—which includes induction, visualization, and quantitative reasoning—and crystallized intelligence or *Gc*—which includes verbal ability, language development, reading comprehension, sequential reasoning, and general information, the latter said to be more directly related to schooling. Whether one follows Spearman's single-factor model or Cattell's two-factor model is probably a matter of taste more than anything else, though debates in the psychometric world about *g* continue to go on.

Paul Kline (1998) summarizes some of the other generally accepted findings among psychometricians: an approximately 0.6 correlation between intelligence and academic performance—and this is not caused by a third variable like home environment or SES, intelligence test results are the best predictor of job success, the heritability of intelligence test scores range from 0.5 to 0.8—monozygotic twins raised apart show a correlation of 0.78 on IQ versus 0.22 for dizygotic twins, probably the most impressive finding—yet Robert Plomin's (2003) more influential view puts it at 0.86 for MZs and 0.60 for DZs and puts heritability at 0.50, making the finding slightly less impressive. The numbers might be confounded a bit by shared placenta effects and similar treatment of identicals, which Plomin claims puts heritability at about 48 percent. Also accepted is that shared environment contributes little to the variance in intelligence (as opposed to non-shared environment like accidents, disease, mental health, etc., though this is a better predictor of dissimilarity) and crystallized intelligence scores are the most "improvable" (111–114). Kline acknowledges that if psychometricians had a better idea of the specific cognitive processes involved—including if they should be conceptualized as linear the way factor analysis does—as well as if intelligence tests had clear units of measurement and additive structure they would be superior (115).

Findings on specific biological pathways of *g* have not been especially impressive. Britt Anderson (2003), looking at various studies of brain size, suggests a 0.35 correlation between brain size and IQ, Richard Haier (2003) claims people with high IQ utilize brain glucose more efficiently, and Arthur Jensen (1998) had already identified a relationship between IQ and reaction time, though none of these findings have been well accepted outside of psychometric circles. Certainly the view of general intelligence asserted by Jensen and others seems out of line with the recent emphasis on modularity in cognitive science and neuropsychology as well as system-emergent models in developmental biology. In the end, correlational data will not explain the complex relationship between cognitive differences, cognitive mechanisms, and neurological ones, and this divergence is one example of the "two cultures" of psychology that Lee Cronbach identified in the 1950s.

The success of *g*, its defenders argue, is related to the fact that it offers the best explanation for the positive manifold. Van der Mass et al. (2006) have developed a "mutualism" theory as an alternative to *g* that views the emergence of the manifold as a result of a dynamic set of beneficial interactions between independent cognitive processes over development. In other words, establishing *g* psychometrically, as the result of factor analysis, is not enough if it doesn't line up with developmental and psychological models. The mutualism model, they argue, does a better job of explaining the finding of the generally poor predictability with respect to adult intelligence from early child performance as well as the finding that the heritability of IQ seems to increase with age. These effects should be regarded as population specific. In other words, like any other phenomena in the organic world, intelligence develops and that development involves both plasticity and constraint. In the end, both approaches are impossible to falsify and the continued acceptance of *g*-based model in psychometrics demonstrates the power of Spearman's original vision of the field

Either way, the problems we are interested in are methodological. As Borsboom et al. (2009b) describes it, the process of the measurement of intelligence begins with a construct and a set of indicators like a set of items on an IQ test. Once a factor analysis is performed, the single largest factor to emerge is deemed to represent that original construct. This is how *g* emerged. Afterward, the test scores are correlated with a number of relevant variables—grades, job performance, SATs—and if the correlations are in the right direction—they don't have to be especially high—the test is regarded as a measure of intelligence. The picture is completed, explains Borsboom et al., by computing heritability values. In this standardized practice the investigation ends because within the construct validity framework, there is nowhere left to go other than fitting new psychometric models or correlating scores with more measures (Borsboom et al., 2009b, p. 156).

But looking at correlations is a poor way to determine what a test measures. After all, it is entirely possible that two distinct but highly correlated variables are associated with similar outcome variables. The only way to resolve this is through an actual investigation of the mechanisms involved, specifically the relationship between variance in the constructs and the variance in the indictors. Is it possible to explain the former as a cause of the latter? The problem with intelligence testing is that it offers only one level of analysis and refuses to go any further where that further development is clearly warranted. Certainly this would help determine if a construct or model designed to capture between subject differences says anything about within subject differences, necessary if it is to tell us anything about how intelligence works. Again, to cite Borsboom et al. (2009),

> For instance, it could well be that John's performance on IQ measures is determined by both speed of information processing and neural efficiency (i.e., John represents a two-factor model) and Paula's performance is determined by information processing, neural efficiency and working memory (i.e., Paula represents a three-factor model), while the analysis of individual differences between the Johns and the Paulas of the world would fit a single factor model nearly perfectly. (158)

Simply because a one-factor model fits between-subjects data, it is premature to conclude that such a factor sits inside the heads of individuals. In personality testing this line of reasoning goes even further. Somehow a specific trait (or lack of it) is regarded as the single or primary cause of a behavior; a trait discovered via analysis of between subject differences but is taken to have a counterpart in explaining within subject differences, a counterpart that somehow causes the ticking of a response category on a personality questionnaire. This all represents a gigantic leap, yet it goes on mostly unchallenged in the field of personality measurement. The unasked question is this: What causes the variation in the responses? And are those causes always identical? It might be that those processes are so heterogeneous and complex it is not really appropriate to describe this process as "measurement" (ibid, p. 162). IQ scores likely represent complex composites made up of elements whose measures represent a multiplicity of processes and no single traits, all the more so in the case of personality.

CASE STUDY TWO: PERSONALITY (I) POPULAR VARIANTS

Explaining individual differences via theories of personality has a long history in the West. From Galen's humourology to astrological star charts and

Gall's phrenology, even Freudianism, proto-personality theories have helped to make relationships more ordered and predictable. In the West until recently, personality theories were often typological: People belonged to a single, static type. Jung's typology is a modern example of this, as is psychiatric diagnosis. Typology tends to be more holistic in its approach. Yet in much of twentieth-century personality psychology, a correlational "trait" approach dominates, which tends to downplay the importance of context and change. With respect to the trait approach to personality, two assumptions are key: First, traits are additive, and second, verbal descriptions are consonant with psychological reality. This requires that sources of variance be considered additive of each other as well because alternate sources of variance—like that between different raters for example—can be very explicit (Danziger, 1990). One solution to this issue was the notion of inter-rater reliability, a much simpler solution than considering the ambiguities of language itself.

Recent popular psychology on personality tends to borrow the "Big Five" model that as we shall see later, dominates the field. Susan Cain's (2012) *Quiet: The Power of Introverts in a World That Can't Stop Talking* is one example of the application of the Big Five to new domains in popular psychology. One of her key points, psychology tends to value extraversion over introversion, is a fair one. She claims to be inspired by Betty Freidan's *The Feminine Mystique* and sees introverts as second-class citizens who are often pathologized by the helping professions and popular psychology. If one considers Dale Carnegie's advice in *How to Win Friends and Influence People*, you see her point. By the end of 2012, *Quiet* turned up on many of the year's bestseller lists. She has also become a TED Talk All-Star.

Cain's book has a mournful quality. She estimates that two out of every three Americans are extraverts and the rest are just faking it so that they can live up to what she calls the "extravert ideal." Her version of extraversion, however, is less Costa and McCrae and more Jung, though she tries to bridge them by referring to Kagan's (1994) thesis that infants are born with either low-reactive or high-reactive temperaments. Presumably the introverts are highly reactive and need to withdraw from others or risk feeling overwhelmed. Eyensenck, too, accepted a version of this thesis. She warns that too much extraversion leads to groupthink, less creativity, and is the possible source of so much financial loss among Wall Street bankers during the economic collapse of 2008 while introvert Warren Buffett profited. Why? It turns out extraverts become more dependent on "dopamine" responses than introverts (Cain, 2012, p. 160).

Sam Gosling, psychology professor, developer of very brief measures of the Big Five (Gosling et al., 2003) and consultant on the MTV show *Room Raiders*—where contestants are allowed to look through the rooms of potential dates—has taken personality testing to a new place with his (2008) *Snoop: What Your Stuff Says About You.* He calls himself a snoopologist and offers to train readers on the art of snooping. The reader, he promises, will learn to distinguish between fake and real messages, what a messy desk means, what discrepancies between people's front and backyards really mean, as well as what car radio presets tell us. He will do all this, he says, by linking with the discoveries psychologists have unearthed and cutting-edge contemporary research on behavior (8), which is actually research into the Big Five and its behavioral correlates. He offers the Big Five a more contemporary take: Openness becomes the "Leonardo" factor, Conscientiousness becomes the "Robocop" factor, Extraversion becomes the "Beverly Hills Cop" factor, Agreeableness becomes the "Mr. Rogers" factor, and Neuroticism, of course, becomes the "Woody Allen" factor. Clearly these will turn out to be culturally invariant and likely have a genetic basis.

Sometimes a "type" can be generated by combining factors—i.e., high agreeableness and neuroticism becomes a "sensitive/sentimental" type while low on both becomes an "unemotional" type. Gosling is never explicit about whether the types emerged from exploratory factor analysis, but one suspects not. Each trait has several lower-order "facets," though again no specific methodology is offered in terms of how they were discovered. The exciting part is the snoopologist's personality test. For example, people who score high on different traits will be found in different places: Openness high scorers in the philosophy section of a bookstore, Conscientiousness at Office Depot in the filing supplies section, and high Agreeableness scorers saving baby seals. What about snooping? If you're looking for an extravert, a swinging arm is a good place to start. Focus on whether they lift their leg when they walk as opposed to the more obvious question of the showiness of their dress. With Conscientiousness, look for formal dress but do not be distracted by a controlled sitting posture or fluent speech. With Agreeableness, focus on friendly expression but not on a pleasant voice. And for Neuroticism, dark garments should be your focus (93–94).

Gosling borrows some of this from a 1992 study by Peter Borkenau and Anette Liebler on trait inferences among strangers where participants rated the personalities of strangers seen on videotape. In terms of the Big Five, participants tended to agree the most over which strangers should be rated high in extraversion followed by conscientiousness and least over emotional stability, openness, and agreeableness but when these ratings were compared to actual NEO-FFI scores taken by the "strangers," ratings of extraversion were most in line with actual scores followed by agreeableness, while much less so for the others (though neuroticism was the only non-significant correlation at 0.10, a very low bar indeed). They then looked at correctness of judgment in terms of specific physical attributes by specific personality traits. Some of the highest correlations included extraversion and facial expression, attractiveness, and showy dress. In general, facial expressions and sympatheticness tended to produce better estimates than specific physical features, dress, or movement, and extraversion tended to correlate the strongest with specific physical features. While this might suggest interesting questions about what extraversion actually means, Borkenau and Liebler are not interested in this and simply conclude that in general physical traits can mislead subjects with respect to some traits as opposed to others. Gosling's interpretation of the findings as a snooping guide is a bit of a stretch, to say the least.

Annie Murphy Paul (2005) offers one of the few critical takes on personality tests in the popular psychology tradition. The title says it all: *The Cult of Personality: How Personality Tests Are Leading Us to Miseducate Our Children, Mismanage Our Companies, and Misunderstand Ourselves*. She describes personality testing as a form of modern phrenology, but she is being too generous to personality testing. Whether correct or not, phrenology painted complex clinical portraits of individuals and certainly did not reduce them to five factors. It also was the first quasi-scientific tradition to make a convincing case that the brain is the source of most psychological processes. Paul directs most of her attack against the Myers-Briggs, which she describes as therapeutic rather than diagnostic, and this is not a positive thing. Given its low reliability and virtually no validity, at least in traditional terms, its widespread use is hard to understand. Costa and McCrae's Big Five do not fare much better in her view. She points to the bizarre attempt to find similar traits in animals, the new NEO-4 that drops neuroticism entirely to make it more attractive to career counselors, and Costa and McCrae's total lack of interest in the origins of personality, all of which we will review in the next section.

She also points out that Costa and McCrae's hyperboles about the definitiveness of their model are partially a result of the fact that NEO PI-R is a big money-maker for them. Patenting tests and assessments while conducting research on their value does seem like a conflict of interest, at the very least. She also calls into to question the process of generating personality characteristics from a study of lexical terms, which as we shall see, is where the Big Five derive from. Is there really such a clear-cut relationship between language, psychology, and biology? Finally, she cites critics who describe the popularity of the Big Five and its measures as a "social phenomenon" and not of especially well designed tests. This is certainly the case. As compared with the most successful intelligence tests, they have fairly low predictive or concurrent validity. There is little sense of what these traits actually are, if they exist, and certainly no sense of how variations in the traits cause variations in scores. IQ items require intelligence for a response, so there is a vague causal theory there. Self-report items on personality tests certainly do not require traits for a response in the same way. Defenders of the Big Five claim these five factors have emerged from years of factor analysis and that may be correct but this doesn't make them any more than summaries of data. They might very well be reflections of how we in modern, Western societies talk about personality, but as of yet, there is no evidence that they refer to anything more than this.

CASE STUDY TWO: PERSONALITY (II) ACADEMIC VARIANTS

Unlike intelligence testing where performances are viewed as an inherent property of the subject, in personality testing performances are taken to reflect inherent properties of the task so that the task changes for those with differing traits (ibid., p. 161). Because the study of particular traits tends to reflect the interests of psychologists in a specific time or place, especially given the lack of theoretical basis for their identification, until recently, there has been much fluctuation of the traits under investigation. As Danziger notes, during the 1920s and 1930s one finds traits like extraversion, ascendance, and submission being measured while in the 1940s and 1950s, attention shifts to traits like emotionality and psychoticism, not surprising given the increased influence of psychoanalysis as well as a shift from personnel selection to psychiatric diagnosis in terms of their use (163). The contrast with German psychology is striking. A key figure in this shift was Gordon Allport. He brought together the Galtonian tradition and the old moral discourse of character into a new science of personality. He influenced the major figures in twentieth-century personality psychology including Raymond Cattell, Hans Eysenck, Paul Costa, and Robert McCrae, though most of them have decisively rejected Allport's attempt to fuse a mathematical approach to personality with a qualitative individual-focused one. Allport's views, in turn, had been shaped by those of his teacher, William Stern, the first major post-Wundtian psychologist to make personality his focus.

William Stern founded the Institute for Applied Psychology in Berlin in 1906. He published detailed diaries of his observations of his own children in 1907 and tried to develop a coherent method for such investigations. His focus moved away from the study of the universal subject of experimental psychology and to the study of individuality (Lamiell, 2003, pp. 6–10). After 1910, he led the Society for School Reform with Ernst Meumann and sought to reform education using the principles of Fichte, Humboldt, and Pestalozzi. Their mission was to "humanize" education, developing whole persons. After World War One, Stern sought to apply the lessons of his study of individuality to determining the suitability of persons for specific jobs, especially in the army. It was during the 1920s that Gordon Allport came to Germany to study with Stern.

Stern's most important work, *Persons and Things*, was published in three volumes from 1906 to 1924. The essence of his position was the importance of making the distinction between persons and things. This meant that people could not be studied via the methods of physics as things were. He called his system "personalism." Part of the problem with experimental psychology, argued Stern, was that it saw individual differences as a source of error that needed to be eliminated (Lamiell, 2003, p. 36). Instead, psychology needed to focus on various typologies of personhood that express variations in human functioning. For this, the techniques of the experiment and quantification might be appropriate as this study was seeking to uncover law like regularities. And yet, individuality was a singularity and could not be grasped this way. Thus, personalist psychology must also study individuals in their totality and not simply see them as a composition of various types. This position was in line with a general move in Weimar Culture to value anti-mechanical and holistic sciences rather than experimental ones. Stern's personalism had two goals: to understand basic variation in human nature and to use that understanding to help people realize practical ends.

Thus, unlike the laboratory psychology of Wundt and his followers, this psychology was intended to be applied from the start. By the mid-1920s, Stern began to see that personality psychology was being dominated by testing and quantitative approaches that lost sight of the whole person. He viewed these tests as helpful to a point as they only provided a momentary snapshot of persons and focused more on reactive rather than spontaneous behaviors (Lamiell, 2003, p. 71). Psychologists were exaggerating what they could achieve, complained Stern, so that they can promote more testing. This was an issue that Gordon Allport would also find in US personality psychology, though unlike Stern, he gradually capitulated to this trend. For Stern, comparing individuals to each other was beside the point. The point of these measures was to study the attributes of personality, not to rank persons against each other. He also bemoaned the fact that the techniques used to do this were taken up by researchers who had little understanding of their limitations.

When Gordon Allport returned to the United States and published *Personality: A Psychological Interpretation* in 1937, he made sure to distinguish his "trait" approach from Stern's "personalistic" one, though in a way that made it clear that he was influenced by the German distinction between the sciences of nature and culture. He did this by distinguishing between two approaches to the study of personality, an idiographic and nomothetic one, a distinction he borrowed from neo-Kantian Wilhelm Windelband. Both were equally valid, but the first focused on studying individuals intensively and the second on comparing individuals to each other using tests and measurement. The idiographic approach was Allport's version of personalism, and it employed a "clinical method" that focused on the expression of traits in various individuals using intuition and looked to psychotherapy for methodological inspiration.

The nomothetic approach in contrast, examined "common" traits, that is, dimensions of psychological functioning that could be compared across people (Allport, 1937). These traits had a biophysical reference and were to be established statistically (Lamiell, 2003, p. 86). In this 1937 version, Allport devoted a bit of space to Stern's personalism, though was quite critical of it, but by the 1960s version, he barely mentions Stern at all (ibid., p. 92). Allport developed various tests to measure common traits like introversion/extraversion—borrowed from Jung—and ascension/submission. He was careful, however, not to characterize traits as distinct entities. Even though traits were "real" and involved "volition," they were best conceived as higher order habits (Nicholson, 2003, p. 154).

Personality was certainly the right topic for the times. Although only appearing in university catalogs in the 1920s, by the end of the 1930s, 31 percent of leading colleges offered a course in personality and ten out of eleven leading psychology textbooks devoted a chapter to it (Nicholson, 2003, p. 4). In fact, Allport's 1924 dissertation was the first completed in the US to make personality its principal topic. The key thing about the term "personality" as opposed to the older term "character" was that it was intentionally divested of its moral undertones. It was supposed to be descriptive rather than normative. In retrospect we can easily see this is not correct and that many common traits (e.g., neuroticism, agreeableness) have fairly obvious moral resonances. As Nicholson (2003) notes, the concept of "character" tends to call more on community-based notions of duty and service while "personality" became a way to talk about the self as distinct from others (e.g., as in "I have an 'attractive' personality"). It was a more salient way to talk about selfhood in an urbanized and industrialized age that focused on distinguishing people from each other and helping people become more "adaptable" (Nicholson, 2003, p. 6). Unlike character, personality was flexible, morally light, and modern, a perfect category for psychology (ibid., p. 38).

By the mid-1940s, Allport's idiographic approach was under attack. It was deemed unscientific and an impediment to psychology's advance as a science. Holt called it "a vestige of Romantic science" (Lamiell, 2003, p. 100) and others argued that although all events in nature are singular, the nature of science is to focus on general laws. One of Allport's most virulent critics was German-born but London-based clinical psychologist Hans Eysenck. Eysenck's teachers, Charles Spearman and Cyril Burt, were both pivotal in the extension of the Galtonian approach to new domains. As we have discussed, Spearman's factor analysis was a way of dealing with much larger volumes of data but also expressing intercorrelates of various attributes within the same person. Eysenck developed his own factor theory of personality, describing two key dimensions with which all persons could be measured. The first was a "body organized personality" or neuroticism, and the second, introversion/extraversion, was distilled from Jung (Gibson, 1981, p. 122). He later added a third dimension: psychoticism. Eysenck believed that he would eventually discover the foundations of these factors in neurological mechanisms. He also claimed that his factors had a heritability of 80 percent, a claim that has not been widely accepted. Recent personality theorists tend to reject Eysenck's specific dimensions, but are impressed with his discovery of a large number of behavioral correlates.

The currently popular five-factor personality model emerged from the study of the natural language of personality description in the 1930s (Baumgarten, 1933; Allport and Odbert, 1936). Beginning with about 18,000 dictionary terms involving personality, Allport and Odbert identified four basic categories: states, traits, judgments, and marginally relevant terms. In the 1940s, Raymond Cattell used the list of trait terms as a starting point and eventually identified thirty-five variables, which became the basis for his Sixteen Personality Factor Questionnaire (John, 2011). Seeking further synthesis, by the 1950s, several personality researchers converged on five or six factors and by the 1960s they were identified as extraversion, agreeableness, conscientiousness, emotional stability, and culture (Norman, 1963). The "culture" factor, which becomes "openness to experience" in Costa and McCrae, described traits like intellectual, polished, and open-minded. By 1980s, they were known as the Big Five. The principal technique for these reductions was exploratory factor analysis.

Independent of these lexical analyses, Costa and McCrae were developing a personality test, the NEO Personality Inventory (Neuroticism, Extraversion, Openness) based in Cattell's work. By the late 1980s, they added tests for agreeableness and conscientiousness and in 1992 published their popular NEO Personality Inventory-Revised (NEO-PI-R). They also developed the shorter NEO-FFI that contains a 12-item scale (60 items altogether). While there were still some debates in the field as to what these factors actually were, by the late 1990s personality test writers had consolidated around Costa and McCrae's version of the Big Five and several other personality tests were developed that correlated fairly well with the NEO-PI-R (John, 2011). Costa and McCrae (2011) have gone further than just viewing the Big Five as convenient summaries of data, as many in the field still do, and have developed the Five Factor Model (FFM) into a total trait theory of personality, which views these traits as real and the cause of the data patterns. They view these traits as stable, biologically and evolutionarily based, and presenting fairly early in life. Defenders of this view point to twin studies suggesting the high heritability of the Big Five—around 50 percent (Bouchard and McGue, 2003) as well as brain research linking the Big Five to specific neurological structures (DeYoung, 2010).

The factors most commonly accepted by personality test writers are those of extraversion-introversion followed by "neuroticism," also known as "anxiety" or "emotional instability." The three most common trait theories of personality upon which personality tests are based—Eysenck's three factors, Cattell's sixteen factors, and Costa and McCrae's OCEAN—all accept them.

Again, Eysenck conceived them as biologically based, extraversion related to arousal levels of the central nervous system, and neuroticism to the instability of the autonomic nervous system (Kline, 1998). This is why they could plausibly be described as inherited. Costa and McCrae's have not been able to link their additional factors—conscientiousness, openness to experience, and agreeableness—to any biological ground, though still view them as highly heritable. Recent work has attempted to "find" these traits in children, but it involves conflating FFM with theories of temperament that have a radically different theoretical and methodological foundation and seems to go against the spirit in recent developmental psychology of developing more sophisticated analyses of the relationship between disposition and environment (Block, 2010).

The most common reservation about Costa and McCrae's additional measured traits is that they are, not surprisingly, highly correlated with each other, especially agreeableness and consciousness as well as openness and both extraversion and intelligence (Kline, 1998, p. 167). Kline offers this work as an example where the simple yielding of factors without psychological theory is presented as a finding. Why these factors and not others? It violates what Kline describes as the requirement for simple structure. Eysenck (1991) has long claimed that E and N along with psychoticism (P) account for much of the variance in test scores, thus a five-factor model adds unnecessary complexity (he views C and A as part of P).

On one hand, these correlations generate problems with measurement, but on the other, they make perfect sense given that in actual persons, these traits are not functionally independent of each other. But the use of factor analysis obscures this by examining them independently of each other (Block, 2010). While Costa and McCrae have a trait "theory," the actual five dimensions are quite a-theoretical. They are products of factor analyses already oriented toward finding them. Moreover, the scaling high-low approach cannot make distinctions between low neuroticism (a good thing) and insufficient neuroticism (not necessarily a good thing) or high agreeableness (a good thing) or excessive agreeableness (maybe not so good) (Block, 2010). In fact, it is the reliance on everyday personality language that creates much of this obscurity.

Do these terms mean the same things to different populations? Does the fact that these categories emerged from samples of college students limit their reach? Some critics of Costa and McCrae's Big Five personality traits, for example, have found that within-subject variability can better be explained by an approach that is tailored to specific individuals over time: Some people are "one-factor" people while others are two- or three-factor people (Moleenar et al., 1997). If so, how can such traits then be considered universal and/or biological? To make this inference one must at least have homogeneity across both the individual and group levels. This means that measurement structures are invariant across individuals. Otherwise one is not measuring the same thing.

Even defenders of the Big Five admit that the criterion validity of personality tests tends to range between 0.20 and 0.30, leaving the great bulk of variance unexplained. In fact, in their book on adult personality, McCrae and Costa (2003) barely mention validity and only do so when discussing the problem of social desirability in their defense of self-reports. The correlations between scores over time, sometimes described as the stability coefficient, tends to be fairly high, even among people who describe themselves as having changed "a good deal"—between 0.56 and 0.90 for the NEO-PI (McCrae and Costa, 2003, p. 127). The problem, the same test is being given over again generating a fairly large confound. The findings would be more impressive if they came from different tests. This has led to periodic criticisms that behavior is mostly situation-dependent. But writing in 2003, McCrae and Costa describe the empirical status of the Big Five as equivalent to the fact that there are seven continents (201) and offers studies of the identification of the Big Five across cultures as "proof" of its predictive validity. Their major defense of any limitations is that the theory is "young" and much more is to come. While there are obvious problems with limiting talk of validity to criterion-related validity, defenders of the FFM can barely provide this convincingly. There is simply no attempt to explain how variance in traits causes variance in test scores.

Another source of confusion in personality trait psychology is methodological, often a function of a limited understanding of psychometric techniques among psychologists. For example, how does one identify the latent variables that make up personality? As we have been suggesting, the first step is the development of theory. Yet, a popular method employed, principal components analysis (PCA), starts with the data. PCA is essentially a data reduction technique. It provides a set of principal components expressed as weighted sub-scores. However, trait psychologists often interpret these components as latent variables (Borsboom, 2006a). For example, Costa and McCrae's analyses yielded five components, which they identify as OCEAN and describe as biologically based tendencies (McCrae et al., 2000). The problem with PCA is that it is a "formative" model, meaning it conceptualizes constructs as caused by observations. It is not a reflective one that views observations as constructed by constructs (Borsboom, 2006a, p. 426).

This subtle distinction is important as when one is talking about latent variables and one is implying a causal relationship between the variation in the variable and the variation in the score. Latent variables are not simple summaries of observed scores. This is obvious in the case of intelligence where defenders of the concept are clearly positing a causal relationship between *g* and IQ scores. The more appropriate technique to identify develop a latent variable theory structure is factor analysis. Turns out, when Confirmatory Factor Analysis (CFA) was used by McCrae, the results did not support the notion of the "big five," but McCrae et al.'s reaction was to question whether CFA was appropriate to the study of personality (McCrae et al., 1996, p. 563). One reason for this, though not explicitly acknowledged, is that the identification of latent variables requires much larger samples than psychologists typically work with, whereas the adding up of sum-scores does not (Borsboom, 2006a, p. 433). When multiple measures are used, a latent variable approach requires that with respect to a particular position on a latent variable, there are no correlations between indicators: This is termed "local independence" (Pearl, 2000). Thus, whether factors are or are not correlated with each other is an important question. Clearly in the case of the Big Five, they are.

Borsboom offers the example of conscientiousness. One might have an intuitive sense of the behaviors involved and thus some sense of what needs to be measured (2006a, p. 434). But there is still much to consider in terms of the relationship between latent variable and measure. Are the test items to be a sampling of behavior where the trait is viewed as a proportion of "conscientiousness" related behaviors? Is conscientiousness a product of certain behaviors, or is it the cause of certain behaviors? This would determine whether one uses a formative or reflective model. Is it an attribute with only between-person variance or within-person variance as well (e.g., say, over time)? Is it a continuous variable or a categorical one? Does it have ordinal structure? Interval structure? Additivity? Is it a monotonic function? A logistic function (S-shaped)? Borsboom describes this as an "embarrassment of psychometric riches" (435). The problem is not that personality test developers do not settle these issues. They do so implicitly by the models and statistics they select. The real problem is that personality traits are treated like reflective latent variables with a continuous structure without any sense about why this must be so other than convenience.

Personality psychology is one area particularly affected by the divide between the experimental branch of psychology and the testing branch manifested as the difference between viewing personality as revealed by average dispositions to act or specific actions taken by individuals in a context where the identical behaviors have different causes and functions (Borsboom, 2006a). Those who lean toward the former approach rely more on correlations and factor analysis, the latter on experiment and case study. Though both these groups use the term "personality" to identify what they study, the actual referents are quite distinct. These two approaches are incommensurable as are the explanatory frameworks they employ. Their findings are largely irrelevant to each other. Knowing where people are ordered on a line tells us nothing about how they got to that place in the line or concern itself with how they produced responses to specific test items as long as they don't affect the order. The same extraversion score, for example, can involve completely distinct social and emotional processes across individuals. Perhaps the practical value of tests that discriminate between people makes these types of questions moot.

CASE STUDY THREE: EMOTIONAL INTELLIGENCE (I) POPULAR VARIANTS

In contrast with intelligence, emotional intelligence is a frequent topic in popular psychology. The idea of emotional intelligence developed through several sources. In a sense, personality tests, originally designed to measure what intelligence tests missed, might be said to be the first attempt to measure this attribute. The recent surge of theories of emotional intelligence (EI) began in academic psychology and well as popular psychology in the 1990s. In fact, in the past few decades, papers and books published on EI or one of its measures, EQ, far outnumber those published on intelligence or IQ. It clearly speaks to psychologists, educators, parents, and others right now in a way traditional IQ doesn't. But is EI a type of intelligence? Is this meant literally? What might that mean?

The term was first introduced in the 1960s (Beldoch, 1964). For the public and even most academics, it all began with the publication of Goleman's *Emotional Intelligence: Why it can matter more than IQ*, in 1995. Goleman famously claimed that IQ was responsible for 20 percent of success in life, EI the other 80 percent! The success of his book helped to establish a mini–Emotional Intelligence industry. EI became a staple in popular psychology of all types. Landy (2005) prefers to distinguish between the "academic" wing of EI and the "commercial" wing, but as we saw in other cases, the distinction is not especially clear-cut. Part of what makes the construct attractive is that it is a type of intelligence that anyone can possess. It has a more democratic feel, unlike the "elitist" IQ. It is notable that while gender differences have been found across EI measures, there is no widespread movement to repudiate EI for its gender bias. The other characteristic of measured EI that makes it attractive, in contrast to IQ, is that it is regarded as highly malleable. In popular psychology, the term EQ is often used, making the link with IQ even more explicit, yet emotional intelligence measures have nothing close to the history of research that IQ measures have, despite their problems. The more popular variants tend to stress the importance of EI for life success, and given its resonance with certain psychotherapeutic themes, this seems plausible, yet there has been little independent evidence of this.

One interesting element of popular EI is its quick diffusion into the business world. This is partly due to the influence of Daniel Goleman. In the 1990s, Goleman had been a staff writer at *Psychology Today* and a science writer at the *New York Times*. In 1995, he published *Emotional Intelligence*, in which he made bold claims about the importance of EI but also argued that it was independent of IQ. Since then his work has made its connection with business and management philosophy very explicit. He followed it up with titles like *Social Intelligence* (2007), *Leadership: The Power of Emotional Intelligence* (2011), and *Primal Leadership* (2013). His latest book, *Focus: The Hidden Driver of Excellence*, encourages leaders to develop "open awareness" an Eastern-ish version of attentiveness. In a *Harvard Business Review* piece in 2013, he makes the connection between emotional intelligence and focus explicit:

> Emotional Intelligence begins with self-awareness—getting in touch with your inner voice. Leaders who heed their inner voices can draw on more resources to make better choices and connect with their authentic selves. . . . Hearing your inner voice means paying careful attention to internal physiological signals. The subtle cues are monitored by the insula, which is tucked behind the frontal lobes of the brain. . . . How well people can sense their own heartbeats has, in fact, become a standard way to measure their self-awareness. (2013b)

The paper, like the new book, is filled with the strange combination of Westernized Buddhism, EI language, neuroscience, therapeutic talk, corporate-talk, and language borrowed from the heuristics and biases tradition about the importance of listening to your gut. No doubt, Goleman will earn a lot of money training corporate executives to focus. Something that one sees a lot of in popular psychology, but is especially evident here, is taking words from all different variants of psychology that have little relationship to each other but appear to be semantically linked and pulling them together into a singular theory. In this case we have: *openness*, *authenticity*, *cognitive control*, *attention*, *empathy*, *intuition*, and *social*—throw in talk of *brain centers*, *networks*, *circuits*, and *connections*, along with *mindfulness* and *positivity*, and you have a bestseller.

Other recent popular psychology books on the topic include *Emotional Intelligence 2.0* (Bradberry and Graeves, 2009), *Raising an Emotionally Intelligent Child* (Gottman and Declaire, 1998), and a range of books in the last few years titled *Emotional Intelligence* with subtitles like: *Increasing your EQ by Mastering Emotions*, *A Practical Guide to Making Friends with Your Emotions*, *Quick Guide to Develop Your EI and Apply It Today*, and of course, *Emotional Intelligence for Dummies*. There is even a 2014 book titled *The Emotional Intelligence of Jesus*.

A not-so-friendly 1999 review of Goleman's work in *Slate* magazine by Ann Murphy Paul accuses him of excelling at "Promotional Intelligence" more than anything else and twisting the academic version beyond recognition. Goleman borrowed an idea developed by psychologist John Mayer for a book he was writing about emotion in the early 1990s. Goleman readily admits that he borrowed the term but claims that he did not borrow the specific construct. Paul sees the popularity of EI in late 1990s popular psychology as a kind of reaction against the pessimism of Herrnstein and Murray's *The Bell Curve*. In addition, there was the attractiveness of bringing together emotion and intellect, traditionally viewed as opposites and the message that you don't have to be smart to succeed. Being a nice person is enough.

CASE STUDY THREE: EMOTIONAL INTELLIGENCE (II) ACADEMIC VARIANTS

Currently there are three basic models of emotional intelligence with a tension between an "ability" approach and a "trait" one: the EI ability model by John Mayer and Peter Salovey (1997), the Emotional-Social Intelligence model (ESI) by Reuven Bar-On (1997), and the emotional competencies model based in Daniel Goleman (1998). Alongside these there are others with a more popular focus like Cooper and Sawaf's (1997) Executive EQ, Emotionally Intelligent Parenting (Elias et al., 1999), and Shapiro's (1997) Child EQ. Of the academic variants, the EI ability model seems to have generated the most research and appears to have been the first to be developed (Salovey and Mayer, 1990). This model views EI as a mental ability involving the capacity to perceive, appraise, and express emotion as well as the ability to understand and regulate emotion. The model comprises four hierarchically organized abilities with respect to emotion: perception, assimilation, understanding, and regulation (Mayer and Salovey, 1997; Mayer et al., 2008). Because EI is a type of intelligence, its assessment involves the kinds of performance-based tasks associated with intelligence testing in general. To this end, Mayer et al. (2001) developed the Mayer-Salovey-Caruso Emotional Intelligence Test (MSCEIT). In terms of responses, correctness is determined either by comparison with a normative sample of the population or with an expert panel.

Reuven Bar-On's ESI model, another fairly researched one, is broader than the EI ability one and tends to incorporate a broader set of social and emotional skills and moves away from a purely cognitive approach. In this case, ESI comprises five high-level factors—interpersonal skills, intrapersonal skills, adaptability, stress management, and general mood. Each of these is divided in turn into fifteen sub-factors. Bar-On's (2000) focus is on how these interact together to generate individual well-being. His most popular measure is the Emotional Quotient Inventory (EQI), a self-report measure consisting of 133 items that evaluate the five components and has more in common with typical personality tests than intelligence ones.

Finally, Goleman's competency model tends to focus on EI in the workplace. The model was laid out in his second book on the topic, *Working with Emotional Intelligence*, which developed a list of competencies based on research in organizations that lead to individual success. The four major ones are self-awareness, social awareness, self-management, and relationship management. Each of these has sub-competencies as well and they are learned based in emotional intelligence. Assessing them involves the Emotional Competence Inventory 2.0, which uses measures based on external raters (Boyatzis et al., 2000). It also consists of a self-report section that allows for a comparison between the perspective of employees and their superiors. Out of the three, this model seems to have inspired the least empirical research.

John Mayer and his colleagues (Mayer et al., 2008) defend their approach viewing EI as a specific ability as opposed to a trait and criticizes those approaches that try to broaden it to the point where it becomes difficult to determine what is and what is not EI, a criticism made frequently (Locke, 2005; Landy, 2005). In their early work, they made a point to explicitly identify EI as a form of intelligence and contrast it with a trait like extraversion, which they described as a preference, though they suspect the two might be correlated along with a trait like openness (Salovey and Mayer, 1990). By viewing EI this way, they link its study to the much more psychometrically respected work in intelligence testing. Some of this respect is due to its reliance on "objective" performance measures as opposed to "subjective" self-report ones.

They blame the popularity of Goleman's work for some of this confusion, as he did borrow from Mayer's work, though added various trait-like qualities to EI as well. Golemen, along with Bar-On, offer what Mayer et al. term "mixed" models (Mayer et al., 2008, p. 504). Mixed-model indicators, insists Mayer et al., voicing a criticism of self-report assessments in general, especially in personality testing, are not able to distinguish between the traits they are interested in, construct-irrelevant variance, subject's capacity for self-reflection, language skills, and the meaning assigned to items. Critics of Mayer argue that many of the items the MSCEIT characterized as performances are actually disguised self-reports (Brody, 2004) and that it confuses the distinctions between attributes, traits, states, and skills that intelligence researchers have developed over the course of the twentieth century (Locke, 2005). Thus for intelligence testers, even Mayer's work doesn't measure up.

The field's reputation was not helped by Goleman's grand claims for the predictive value of EI. Defenders of mixed models, argues Mayer et al., rarely offer any theoretical justification for why certain characteristics are included in EI, thus these variants have little construct validity and even the Bar-On version, the best of the lot, defends his model based exclusively on predictive validity as opposed to theoretical grounds (Mayer et al., 2008, p.

505). They defend their analogy with intelligence as even defenders of *g* view it as inclusive of multiple first- and second-order factors and EI, they insist, should be viewed as one of such factors.

In point of fact, the MSCEIT shows higher correlations with measures of intelligence (0.35 between MSCEIT and verbal intelligence) than personality measures (509)—though the highest correlations with the Big Five personality model are found between EI and Agreeableness as well as Openness (0.29 between the MSCEIT and Openness on the NEO-PI-R as opposed to O.16 for Bar-On's EQI). The EQI correlates even less with intelligence leading Bar-On (2000) to offer this as evidence of a trait view. Interestingly, in earlier formulations of the Big Five, Openness was viewed partially as a measure of intelligence, so the correlation between openness and the MSCEIT can also be used to argue for a trait view (John et al., 2011). Clearly, both high and low correlations with other constructs can be turned into evidence for any position, helping point to the weakness of the notion of concurrent validity.

Either way, this view fits nicely with a notion like Gardner's multiple intelligence and even contains elements of two of his types: interpersonal intelligence and intrapersonal intelligence. In fact, variants of EI have been implied in the past like Edward Thorndike's suggestion of a "social" intelligence distinct from "abstract" and "mechanical" intelligence in *Harpers* magazine in 1920, an idea that was rejected by much of the field at the time. In his conception of social intelligence, Thorndike included a cognitive and a behavioral component. He was concerned about the narrowness of intelligence testing and the fact that it was tested in a way that overemphasized the verbal elements (Landy, 2005). Intelligence testing, wrote Thorndike, required more genuine situations. Why didn't Thorndike's call have more influence? As Landy explains, Thorndike was not really suggesting a different form of intelligence so much as different approaches to test intelligence. For him, intelligence was a singular phenomenon. Spearman acknowledged social intelligence as well, but viewed it as a part of *g*.

Several tests of social intelligence were developed in the following years, including an "ability to sell" test, but by the 1930s, most were viewed as either tests of personality or poor measures of intelligence. Attempts to resurrect it under names like "social insight" or "psychological ability" never took off, as critics either dismissed it as either general intelligence applied to social situations or as a vague and unmeasurable construct. In his multiple factor approach, Guiliford described it as "cognition of behavioral relationships" and provided some evidence for its independence from other factors, though again the idea never took off among psychometricians. As with EI today, critics also mentioned the confusion in the concept between "knowing" and "doing" (Landy, 2005). Also, in defense of the concept, then and now, there is a tendency to focus more on divergent validity as opposed to convergent validity; in other words, demonstrating it is not correlated with other tests as opposed to whether it measures anything relevant.

Not surprisingly, therefore, those that lean toward a single or dual factor model of intelligence almost never accept EI as a distinct factor of intelligence. While defenders of the ability approach don't seem to recognize it, the "correctness" of a response to a logical reasoning problem is not the same as the "correctness" of a response to interpreting the emotions in a picture of a face. The MSCEIT determines the "correctness" of some of the responses using a pool of twenty-one emotional researchers (Mayer et al., 2008), hardly a broad sampling of views on emotion. Also, the MSCEIT never reveals the variance in expert opinion. It also tends to discriminate better between low scorers than high scorers—though it's not clear how people who score low on EI are supposed to reflect on their own capacities, a bigger issue with the self-report EQ-1. Nor is it clear that too much emotional intelligence is always a good thing as with IQ. The correlations between MSCEIT and EQ-I when personality factors are controlled for is negligible, which begs the question: Is there any single construct being studied—though Mayer views this as evidence for the distinction between an ability and trait approach. In general, there is too little substantive theoretical work to figure any of this out.

Predictive validity for the MSCEIT is not especially high—between 0.22 and 0.38 with the SCL-90-R, a self-report psychopathology assessment published by Pearson (Mayer et al., 2008, p. 511) as opposed to between 0.50 to 0.80 for IQ and its criterion—though in the world of testing a 0.30 correlation between a test and a criterion is considered outstanding and a correlation of .015—2 percent of variance explained—is considered acceptable in terms of validity (Meyer et al., 2008). Yet, when controlling for other measures (e.g., personality and intelligence), the added levels of variance explained (termed incremental validity) drops to between 1 percent and 6 percent. Clearly, such scores will not yield many successful predictions when applied to individuals, nor do they reveal why one should bother with the MSCEIT. The highest correlations are with "deviant" behaviors like drug use and getting into physical fights (between 10–16 percent of variance).

Mayer and his colleagues insist that EI is a component of intelligence, thus presumably a latent variable as well, yet they are not clear on how variance in EI relates to variance in the instrument. For one, IQ items are not always recognized as tests of complex intelligence. Many of the items involve responses to simple information processing for example. They also accept that measures of the same latent variables need change over time (Brody, 2004). Moreover, intelligence is viewed as a cause not a summary. Part of this is evidenced by high correlations with divergent tests but also the recognition that the relationship between intelligence and IQ is a complex one. None of this complexity appears to be acknowledged by defenders of

EI. In fact, even in academic variants, psychometric and statistical techniques are misapplied.

For example, in an analysis of the construction of the Ability Emotional Intelligence Measure (AEIM), Antonakis and Dietz (2010) found a host of errors including: lack of control when testing incremental validity, confusion of stepwise and hierarchical regression, complete neglect of heteroscedasticity and measurement error, and neglect of the relationship between theoretical and empirical claims. This led the authors to widely overstate their case for the measure. There is also little sense of measurement invariance across gender, race, SES, or age, but it is likely that responses across these groups are not measuring the same thing, thus any findings on group differences are biased. While the methodological problems with validating the AEIM are extreme, other measures have similar problems, specifically a lack of broad theoretical considerations when using regressions to determine validity and little thought to measurement invariance.

There are still other methodological issues. The self-report measures seem to elicit socially desirable responses. There is a tendency to rely on unrepresentative samples. There is also the tendency to define EI by its separate subscales, but then use a total score when reporting relationships with other measures (Day, 2004). There is arbitrariness to the number of factors different models focus on, and little theoretical defense of these choices. And there is an assumption that the relationships between EI and its criterion are linear without any justification. Again, who is to say excessive EI is a good thing? In general, the predictive validity of EI measures are mixed and get worse when other factors are controlled for, yet they are regularly touted as great tests of leadership and character (Rode et al., 2007).

Just one or two of these issues would make for a poor test in psychometric circles; put them all together and we have tests that don't measure anything, or if they do, we can't say what it is. As is the case with intelligence and research into cognitive processes, emotional intelligence relates awkwardly to the experimentally based research on affect regulation in infancy and early childhood. Clearly, EI acquires added value through this relationship, though the actual referents are quite distinct, even in the ability model. There is no focus on any of the processes involved and the correlational approach reveals nothing about causes and mechanisms. What we have is a measure that offers a score, but for what exactly it is impossible to say.

Conclusion

How to Read Pop Psychology (and all psychology perhaps?)

This monograph explored the confluence of popular psychology, academic psychology, and methodology. To start with, we summarize the findings of our review of the problems with the academic sources of pop psychology in the various genres we explored. Given certain conditions, people can make "errors" in judgment that are often related to the application of probability and sampling. At times, these "errors" can be highly adaptive, at other times less so. Changing the conditions by which the problems are presented can mitigate most of these "errors," as can changing the norms by which they are evaluated. Given that much of the field is focused on demonstrating their pervasiveness, there is little attention given to the possible cognitive processes or mechanisms involved in these judgments, and therefore, the findings provide for exciting demonstrations and salacious warnings about "bad" thinking but little else. In general, little attention is paid in this tradition to where the data actually come from and the effects of context.

Terms like "unconscious" or "intuitive" are fairly vague and bring with them assumptions that have long been associated with conceptions of a hidden as well as reflex-driven mind in the West. The actual referents with respect to these terms tend to differ across particular sub-disciplines in the field and even among researchers within those sub-disciplines. There is a tendency to characterize processes with one-word terms like "associative" or "fast" but there is little theoretical development in terms of the mechanisms involved. This tradition repeats the homunculus fallacy and simply assigns to the unconscious and conscious systems attributes that rightly belong to organisms operating in an environment. Despite these issues, popular psychology writers encourage readers to develop their intuition or avoid their intuition but offer little sense of what that actually means.

Happiness is yet another vague concept that is radically under-theorized in the field. Measures of happiness tend to be crude and evidence from interventions into happiness tend to reveal small effects, often exaggerated by measures employed, that achieve statistical significance, but do not necessarily have any convincing real-world effects. Moreover, interpretations of findings of statistical significance tend to reveal profound confusion about what they actually mean, particularly the confusion between the correct interpretations, given the null how likely are the findings and the more attractive one, and given the findings how likely is the null? This is exacerbated by a convention to focus on the binary logic of accepting or rejecting the null rather than degrees of belief in a hypothesis as well as by low-powered studies where actual effects are unlikely to be found. Yet, pop psychology writers typically ignore this and offer people vague and supposedly science-based findings that translate into advice about achieving happiness. Critics often ridicule the silliness of some of the findings, yet miss that the more serious methodological issues are quite pervasive in much of psychology.

Giving advice to parents is easy, but demonstrating that those practices have real-world effects is not. Given the historical bias for environmentalist explanations in Anglo-American psychology, the importance of parenting is often accepted as a given despite weak evidence. Critics of these explanations who turn to genetic ones often end up repeating similar mistakes. In both cases, given the absence of experiment, psychologists rely on correlational relationships that are treated as causal ones where one variable is designated the "predictor" and the other the "outcome" based in presuppositions that are themselves never called into question. The most popular technique for such analysis, regression, is approached as if the statistics themselves reveal cause-like factors, when in fact findings are often related to the unrecognized assumptions imposed on the data by researchers. This is especially true when psychologists employ too many variables and there is not enough data to distinguish an effect for each from zero. Overfitting, that is, selecting too many parameters with respect to observations, distorts the effects of variables on outcomes by forcing researchers to predict the data they do not have, as opposed to the data they do have, making the particularities of the sample even more influential. In the end, there is little acknowledgment that we simply do not know why children turn out the way they do, especially in popular psychology, where taken-for-granted assumptions mined from American middle class child-rearing values are presented as the findings of research.

Finally, psychologists treat measurement as if it involves the simple imposition of number on a phenomenon rather than an understanding of the structure of the entity one seeks to measure. Not all psychological phenomena lend themselves to meaningful quantitative measurement. With the exception of intelligence tests, most psychological tests and assessments have little predictive validity, and the focus on predictive validity is itself a distraction from the more basic question of whether psychological tests measure what they are supposed to measure. Effective measurement involves a belief that the variable to be measured exists and a sense of how variation in that variable causes variation in instrument scores. This has not yet been achieved with measures of intelligence, let alone measures of emotional intelligence or personality. Despite this, works of popular psychology treat these instruments as if they are clear about what is actually being measured and that the resulting "measurements" are meaningful.

Extrapolating a bit, when reading pop psychology, one can consider the following questions:

1. Where do the data come from and how were they gathered?
2. Are findings the result of differential conditions with respect to sample, design, and stimuli? What kinds of inferences are permissible given the choice of sample, design, and stimuli?
3. What is the relationship between symbol and referent? Is this referent so specific that it has little generalizability across contexts?
4. What are the ontological claims made in the work? Do proposed psychological entities exist? Are they assigned attributes appropriate to that level of analysis? Do they exert causal effects on other entities?
5. Do findings of statistical significance translate into meaningful differences?
6. Are probable relations characterized as deterministic ones? Are the findings of one study treated as if they were subjected to extensive replication?
7. Can the statistics employed carry the inferential weight they are asked to bear? Are alternative explanations seriously considered? Are the assumptions of various statistical tests met? Are the variables employed independent of each other?
8. Do measured items have an internal structure that warrants measurement? Are they treated as statistical entities yet assumed to have causal power with respect to instruments?
9. Is the notion of measurement invariance taken seriously? Has the research considered whether observed differences in measures are attributable to properties unrelated to the phenomenon being measured?
10. Is the phenomenon appropriately studied using experimental techniques and quantitative measures? Is it better captured by methods that acknowledge its qualitative nature, the indissolubility of context, and the meanings assigned to it by the individuals involved?

These questions apply well to psychological research in general. Underlying these questions are several basic problems. Not all psychological phenomena can be best understood lifted from the context within which they are studied. The human world is not the same as the nonhuman one. One cannot simply pretend that mind, language, and interpretation—all central to the human experience—do not call into question the assumption that psychological phenomena operate in the same way that the traditional objects of the natural sciences do, or can be studied in the same way for that matter. In the case of psychological phenomena, decontextualization and generalization require an argument based in theory and evidence, not hope or wish. The same is true of measurement. It is simply not clear that most objects studied by psychologists lend themselves to ratio or additive structure, at least if one expects that those ratios are meaningful. Moreover, the objects of psychology are treated as the cause of variation in measures, yet some psychologists are not even willing to acknowledge in an unambiguous way that they are real.

Then there is the problem of uncertainty in general, a far more difficult one. How does one integrate notions of chance into a discipline that seeks to convince others outside the discipline of their findings? Unlike the natural sciences, applications of psychology and popularizations of psychology have been integral to its success as a discipline. How does one convey stochastic processes to people comfortable with deterministic ones? How does one educate psychologists so that they better understand the conceptual foundations of the techniques that they use? Moreover, how does one integrate notions of uncertainty into an institutional structure—publications, funding, promotion—that encourages determinism and clear cut findings?

The struggle to integrate notions of chance is not a new one. Judeo-Christian thought had long been skeptical of the thoroughgoing determinisms of the ancient world—where causes were usually a function of the actions of gods or fate and a way to assign responsibility—and sought to retain notions of freedom and will in its stead. The transfer of causal power from gods and humans to physical objects began with developments in engineering and these new causal agents naturally took on some of the characteristics of the older ones including force, responsibility and even purpose (Pearl, 2000, p. 333). In other words, in addition to being sources of responsibility, causes became carriers of physical forces. The victory of the scientific worldview was a victory for determinism, one based not in God or magic but natural law. But it also laid the ground for the weakening of that determinism by turning causality from questions about purpose to questions about how things work, from explanations to descriptions, all this culminating in Hume's reduction of causality to a psychological category.

Yet, in the scientific worldview of the seventeenth and eighteenth centuries, chance was still regarded as vulgar and superstitious (Hacking, 1990). The mass acceptance of the scientific worldview by the end of the nineteenth century led to the widespread acceptance of mechanistically based determinisms. The world was composed of natural forces, some of which were related to each other as causes and effects, and they were knowable with certainty. If there was uncertainty, it was a function of error in measurement. But, also in the nineteenth century, this view was being undermined by the spread of the notion of uncertainty, both in the human world with the rise of social statistics, and in the natural one with the collapse of the Newtonian paradigm and the rise of biometry. In parts of the social sciences, including psychology, there was a gradual turn to the study of regularity, average and standard deviation rather than law, even in the case of experiments, long held up as the only route to causality. What looked like necessity and law was actually a by-product of chance (Hacking, 1990, p. 11). Randomness was not a function of error or ignorance, but built into the very nature of the world itself.

And yet, statistical regularities, in essence just descriptions, came to be treated as if they reflected underlying determined relationships. Correlates were treated as causes. Probable relations that applied to a series were treated as if they reflected something about individuals. The problem of induction was deferred. Perhaps the issue was that science was taking up the role of authority with respect to knowledge, and authority must speak with certainty, especially when speaking to the non-scientific public. Either way, popular psychology has taken advantage of this confusion or perhaps some academic psychologists are confused by it as well.

Some psychologists are moving in this direction. There are various groups of psychologists working on replicating influential studies—the findings so far do not inspire confidence—making sure data are made public as well as publishing failed studies. Others are developing Bayesian-based models of significance testing and other practices that conceive findings in terms of degrees of belief rather than accept or reject. As is clear in the case of the natural sciences, corroboration of a theory requires multiples levels of evidence of differing quality with extensive replication. The recent emphasis on meta-analysis, however, is not the solution to low-powered studies because they tend to inflate results and effect sizes not to mention cannot account for publication bias.

On the other hand, measurement does require a certain level of determinism. It involves, at base, a theory of cause and effect that must be supported by evidence. No matter, psychology probably has a lot less to say with a lot less certainty than is currently the practice. A more restrained psychology, unfortunately, goes against the ever-expanding spirit of the university: more students, more faculty, more publications, more funding, and infinitely more psychological science, no matter what the quality.

Works Cited

Abelson, R. (1997). On the surprising longevity of flogged horses. *Psychological Science*, 8(1), 12–15.

Abbott (1988). *The System of Professions*. Chicago, IL: University of Chicago Press.

Achen, C. (1977). Measuring representation. *American Journal of Political Science*, 21, 805–815.

Achen, C. (1986). *The Statistical Analysis of Quasi-Experiments*. Berkeley: University of California Press.

Alland, A. (2002). *Race in Mind*. New York: Palgrave Macmillan.

Allport, G. (1937). *Personality*. New York: H. Holt.

Allport, G. & Odbert, S. (1936). Trait names. *Psychological Monographs*, 47(1), 1–171.

Anderson, B. (2003). Brain Imaging and *g*. In H. Nyborg (ed.). *The Scientific Study of Intelligence*. Amsterdam: Pergamon.

Anisfeld, E., Casper, V., Nozyce, M., & Cunningham, N. (1990). Does infant carrying promote attachment? *Child Development*, 61(5), 1617–1627.

Ankin, L., Norton, M., & Dunn, E. (2009). From wealth to well-being? *Journal of Positive Psychology*, 4, 523–527.

Antonakis, J. & Diaz, J. (2010). Emotional intelligence. *Industrial & Organizational Psychology*, 3(2), 165–170.

Ariely, D. (2008). *Predictably Irrational*. New York: Harper Collins.

Asendorpf, J. (2013). Recommendations for increasing replicabilty in psychology. *European Journal of Personality*, 27(2), 108–119.

Ausch, R. (2015). *An Advanced Guide to Psychological Thinking: Critical and Historical Perspectives*. Lanham, MD: Lexington Books.

Ayton, P. (2000). Do the birds and bees need cognitive reform? *Behavioral and Brain Sciences*, 23(5), 666–667.

Ayton, P. (2004). The hot hand fallacy and the gambler's fallacy. *Memory and Cognition,* 32 (8), 1369–1378.

Azar, B. (2011). Positive psychology advances, with growing pains. *APA Monitor*, 44(4), 32.

Bakan, D. (1966). The test of significance in psychological research. *Psychological Bulletin*, 66, 423–437.

Bakker, M., Dijk, A., & Wicherts, J. (2012). The rules of the game called psychological science. *Perspectives on Psychological Science*, 7(6), 543–554.

Baldwin, A. (1948). Socialization and the parent-child relationship. *Child Development*, 19, 127–136.

Baldwin, J. M. (1901). *Dictionary of Philosophy and Psychology*. New York: Macmillan.

Bargh, J. (1997). The automaticity of everyday life. In R. Wyer (ed.). *Advances in Social Cognition.* Volume 10. Mahwah, NJ: Erlbaum.
Bargh, J. (2005). Bypassing the will. In R. Hassin, J. Uleman & J. Bargh (eds.). *The New Unconscious.* Oxford: Oxford University Press.
Bargh, J. & Morsella, E. (2008). The unconscious mind. *Perspectives on Psychological Science*, 3(1), 73–79.
Bar-On, R. (1997). *The Emotional Intelligence Inventory.* Toronto: Multi-health Systems.
Bar-On, R. (2000). Emotional and Social Intelligence. In R. Bar-On & J. Parker (eds.). *The Handbook of Emotional Intelligence.* San Francisco: Jossey-Bass.
Barr, R. (2013). Mother and child. In D. Keating (ed.). *Nature and Nurture in Early Child Development.* New York: Cambridge University Press.
Baumgarten, F. (1933). The character traits. In *Beitraege Zur Charakter*, 1. Bern: Francke.
Baumeister, R., Vohs, K., & Tice, D. (2011). The strength model of self-control. *Current Directions in Psychological Science,* 16(6), 351–355.
Baumrind, D. (1966). Effects of authoritative parental control on child behavior. *Child Development*, 37, 887–907.
Baumrind, D. (1967). Child care practices anteceding three patterns of preschool behavior. *Genetic Psychology Monographs*, 75, 43–88.
Baumrind, D. (1968). Authoritarian vs. authoritative parental control. *Adolescence*, 3, 255–272.
Baumrind, D. (1970). Socialization and instrumental competence in young children. *Young Children*, 26, 104–119.
Baumrind, D. (1971). Current patterns of parental authority. *Developmental Psychology Monographs*, 4, 1–103.
Baumrind, D. (1972). An exploratory study of socialization effects on black children. *Child Development*, 43, 261–267.
Baumrind, D. (1978). Reciprocal rights and responsibilities in parent-child relations. *Journal of Social Issues*, 34, 179–196.
Baumrind, D. (1996). A blanket injunction against disciplinary use of spanking is not warranted by the data. *Pediatrics*, 98, 828–831.
Baumrind, D. (2013). Authoritative parenting revisited. In R. Larzelere, A. Morris & A. Harrist (eds.). *Authoritative Parenting.* Washington, D.C.: APA Books.
Bechara, A., Tranel, D., Damasio, H., & Damasio, A. (1996). Failure to respond autonomically to anticipated future outcomes following damage to prefrontal cortex. *Cerebral Cortex*, 6, 215–225.
Beldoch, M. (1964). Sensitivity to expression of emotional meaning in three models of communication. In J. Davitz (ed.). *The Communication of Emotional Meaning.* Westport, CT: Greenwood Press.
Bennett, D. (1998). *Randomness*. Cambridge, MA: Harvard University Press.
Berk, R. (2003). *Regression Analysis.* Thousand Oaks, CA: Sage.
Birnbaum, M. (1992). Should contextual effects in human judgments be avoided? *Contemporary Psychology*, 37, 21–23.
Birnbaum, M. (1999). How to show that 9 > 221. *Psychological Methods*, 1(3), 243–249.
Birnbaum, M. & Mellers, B. (1983). Bayesian inference. *Journal of Personality and Social Psychology*, 45, 792–804.
Blalock, H. (1961). *Causal Inferences in Nonexperimental Research.* Chapel Hill: The University of North Carolina Press.
Blantan, H. & Jaccard, J. (2006). Tests of multiplicative models in psychology. *Psychological Review*, 113, 155–169.
Block, J. (2010). The five-factor framing of personality and beyond. *Psychological Inquiry*, 21, 2–25.
Bluemke, M. & Friese, M. (2005). Do features of stimuli influence IAT effects? *Journal of Experimental Social Psychology,* 42, 163–176.
Bolier, L., Haverman, M., Westerhof, G., Riper, H., Smit, F., & Bohlmeijer, E. (2013). Positive psychology interventions. *BMC Public Health*, 13(119), 1–20.
Bollen, K. (2002). Latent variables in psychology and the social sciences. *Annual Review of Psychology*, 53, 605–634.

Borkenau, P. & Liebler, A. (1992). Trait inferences: Sources of validity at zero acquaintance. *Journal of Personality and Social Psychology*, 62(4), 645–657.
Borsboom, D. (2005). *Measuring the Mind.* Cambridge: Cambridge University Press.
Borsboom, D. (2006a). The attack of the psychometricians. *Psychometrika*, 71(3), 425–440.
Borsboom, D. (2006b). When does measurement invariance matter? *Medical Care*, 44(11), 176–181.
Borsboom, D. (2008). Latent variable theory. *Measurement*, 6, 25–53.
Borsboom, D., Cramer, A., Kievit, R., Scholten, A., & Franic, S. (2009a). The end of construct validity. In R. Lissitz (ed.). *The Concept of Validity*. Charlotte, NC: IAP.
Borsboom, D., Kievit, R., Cervone, D., & Hood, S. (2009b). The two disciplines of scientific psychology. In J. Valsiner, P. Molenaar, M. Lyra, & N. Chaudary (eds.). *Developmental Process Methodology in the Social and Developmental Sciences.* New York: Springer.
Bouchard, T. & McGue, M. (2003). Genetic and environmental influences on human psychological differences. *Journal of Neurobiology*, 54(1), 4–45.
Box, G. (1976). Science and statistics. *Journal of the American Statistical Association*, 71, 791–791.
Boyatzis, R., Goleman, D., & Rhee, K. (2000). Clustering competence in emotional intelligence. In R. Bar-On & J. Parker (eds.). *The Handbook of Emotional Intelligence.* San Francisco: Jossey-Bass.
Bridgman, P. (1927). *The Logic of Modern Physics*. New York: MacMillan.
Bridgman, P. (1954). Remarks on the present state of operationalism. *Scientific Monthly*, 79, 224–226.
Bridgman, P. (1959). *The Way Things Are.* Cambridge, MA: Harvard University Press.
Brody, N. (2004). What cognitive intelligence is and what emotional intelligence is not. *Psychological Inquiry*, 15, 234–238.
Bruer, J. (1999). *The Myth of the First Three Years*. New York: The Free Press.
Bruner, J. (1957). On perceptual readiness. *Psychological Review*, 64, 123–152.
Burnham, J. (1987). *How Superstition Won and Science Lost.* New Brunswick, NJ: Rutgers University Press.
Cain, S. (2012). *Quiet.* New York: Crown.
Campbell, D. & Fiske, D. (1959). Convergent and discriminant validation by the multitrait-multimethod matrix. *Psychological Bulletin,* 56(2), 81–105.
Carroll, J. (1993). *Human Cognitive Abilities.* Cambridge: Cambridge University Press.
Carroll, J. (2003). The higher-stratum structure of cognitive abilities. In H. Nyborg (ed.). *The Scientific Study of Intelligence*. Amsterdam: Pergamon.
Carver, R. (1974). Two dimensions of tests. *American Psychologist*, 29(7), 512–518.
Carver, R. (1978). The case against statistical significance testing. *Harvard Educational Review*, 48(3), 378–399.
Chao, R. (1994). Beyond parental control and authoritarian parenting style: Understanding Chinese parenting through the cultural notion of training. *Child Development*, 65, 1111–1119.
Chua, A. (2011). *Battle Hymn of the Tiger Mother*. New York: Penguin.
Chugani, H., Behen, M., Muzik, O., Juhasz, C., Nagy, F., & Chugani, D. (2001). Local brain functional activity following early deprivation. *NeuroImage*, 14, 1290–1301.
Christopher, J. & Hickinbottom, S. (2008). Positive psychology, ethnocentrism and the disguised ideology of individualism. *Theory & Psychology*, 18(5), 563–589.
Cianciolo, A. & Sternberg, R. J. (2004). *Intelligence: A Brief Survey.* Oxford: Blackwell.
Clark, H. (1973). The language-as-fixed-effect fallacy. *Journal of Verbal Learning and Verbal Behavior*, 12, 335–359.
Cleermans, A. & Jimenez, L. (2002). Implicit learning and consciousness. In R. French and A. Cleermans (eds.). *Implicit Learning and Consciousness*. Hove, UK: Psychology Press.
Cohen, J. (1977). *Statistical Power Analysis for the Behavioral Sciences.* New York: Academic Press.
Cohen, J. (1990). Things I have learned so far. *American Psychologist*, 45(12), 1304–1312.
Cohen, J. (1994). The earth is round ($p < .05$). *American Psychologist*, 49(12), 997–1003.

Cohen, L. (1981). Can human irrationality be experimentally demonstrated? *Behavioral and Brain Sciences*, 4, 37–70.

Conger, R. & Elder, G. (1994). *Families in Troubled Times*. Hawthorne, NY: Aldine.

Conger, R. & Conger, K. (2002). Resilience in Midwestern families. *Journal of Marriage and Family*, 64(2), 361–373

Cooper, C. McCord, D., & Socha, A. (2011). Evaluating the college sophomore problem. *The Journal of Psychology*, 145(1), 23–37.

Cooper, R. and Sawaf, A. (1997). *Executive EQ*. New York: Grosset Putnam.

Cosmides, L. & Tooby, J. (1996). Are humans good statisticians after all? *Cognition*, 58(1), 1–73.

Coulson, M., Healey, M., Fidler, F., & Cumming, G. (2010). Confidence intervals permit but do not guarantee better inference than statistical significance testing. *Frontiers of Psychology*, 2, doi:10.3389.

Coyne, J. (2013). Positive psychology is mainly for rich white people. *PLOS Blogs*, posted August 21, 2013.

Cronbach, L. & Meehl, P. (1955). Construct validity in psychological tests. *Psychological Bulletin*, 52, 281–302.

Craven, H. (1978). *The Triumph of Evolution*. Philadelphia: University of Pennsylvania Press.

Criss, M. & Larzelere, R. (2013). Introduction. In R. Larzelere, A. Morris, & A. Harrist (eds.). *Authoritative Parenting.* Washington, D.C.: APA Books.

Cronbach, L. (1982). *Designing Evaluations of Educational and Social Programs*. San Francisco: Jossey-Bass.

Cronbach, L. (1986). Social inquiry by and for earthlings. In D. Fiske & R. Shweder (eds.). *Metatheory in Social Science.* Chicago: University of Chicago Press.

Cumming, G., William, J., & Fidler, F. (2004). Replication and researchers' understanding of confidence intervals and standard error bars. *Understanding Statistics*, 3, 299–311.

Csikszentmihalyi, M. & Larson, R. (1987). Reliability and validity of the experience-sampling method. *The Journal of Nervous and Mental Disease,* 175(9), 526–536.

Damasio, A. (1999). *The Feeling of What Happens*. New York: Houghton Mifflin.

Daniels, M., Devlin, B., & Roeder, K. (1997). Of genes and IQ. In B. Devlin, S. Fienberg, D. Resnick, & K. Roeder (eds.). *Intelligence, Genes and Success.* New York: Springer.

Danziger, K. (1987). Statistical Method and the Historical Development of Research Practice in American Psychology. In L. Kruger, G. Gigerenzer & M. Morgan (eds.). *The Probabilistic Revolution: Volume Two.* Cambridge, MA: MIT Press.

Danziger, K. (1990). *Constructing the Subject.* Cambridge: Cambridge University Press.

Darling, N. & Steinberg, L. (1993). Parenting style as context: An integrative model. *Psychological Bulletin*, 113, 487–496.

Davidov, M. & Grusec, J. (2006). Untangling the links of parental responsiveness to distress and warmth to child outcomes. *Child Development*, 77(1), 44–58.

Dawes, R. (1988). *Rational Choice in an Uncertain World.* New York: Harcourt Brace.

Dawes, R., Mirels, H., Gold, E., & Donahue, E. (1993). Equating inverse probabilities in implicit personality judgment. *Psychological Science*, 6, 396–400.

Dawes, R. (1998). Behavioral decision making and judgment. In D. Gilbert, S. Fiske, & G. Lindsey (eds.). *The Handbook of Social Psychology*. 4th Edition. Volume 2. Boston, MA: McGraw Hill.

Dawes, R. (1994). *House of Cards*. New York: The Free Press.

Dawes, R. (2001). *Everyday Irrationality*. Boulder, CO: Westview Press.

Day, A. (2004). The measurement of emotional intelligence: The good, the bad and the ugly. In G. Geher (ed.). *Measuring Emotional Intelligence*. New York: Nova.

Debner, J. & Jacoby, L. (1994). Unconscious perception. *Journal of Experimental Psychology*, 20(2), 304–317.

DeYoung, C. (2010). Personality neuroscience and the biology of traits. *Social and Personality Psychology Compass*, 4(12), 1165–1180.

Diancos, P. (1985). Theories of data analysis from magical thinking to classical statistics. In D. Hoaglin, F. Mosteller, & J. Tukey (eds.). *Exploring Data Tables, Trends and Shapes.* New York: Wiley.

Dijksterhuis, A. (2004). Think different. *Journal of Personality and Social Psychology*, 87, 586–598.

Donaldson, M. (1978). *Children's Minds*. New York: W. W. Norton.

Dooremalen, H. & Borsboom, D. (2010). Metaphors in psychological conceptualization and explanation. In A. Toomela & J. Valsiner (eds.). *Methodological Thinking in Psychology: 60 Years Gone Astray?* Charlotte, NC: IAP.

Druckerman, P. (2012). *Bringing Up Bebe*. New York: Penguin.

Duhigg, C. (2012). *The Power of Habit*. New York: Random House.

Dunn, B., Dalgleish, T., & Lawrence, A. (2006). The somatic marker hypothesis. *Neuroscience and Biobehavioral Reviews*, 30, 239–271.

Ebel, D. (1961). Must all tests be valid? *American Psychologist*, 16(10), 640–647.

Ehrenreich, B. (2009). *Bright-Sided*. New York: Metropolitan Books.

Elias, M., Tobias, S., & Friedlander, B. (1999). *Emotionally Intelligent Parenting*. Easton, PA: Harmony.

Ellis, L. & Walsh, A. (2003). Crime, delinquency and intelligence. In H. Nyborg (ed.). *The Scientific Study of Intelligence*. Amsterdam: Pergamon.

Erderlyi, M. (1992). Psychodynamics and the unconscious. *American Psychologist*, 47(6), 784–787.

Evans, J. & Over, D. (1996). *Rationality and Reasoning*. Hove, UK: Psychology Press.

Evans, J., Clibbens, J., Kattani, A., Harris, A., & Dennis, I. (2003). Explicit and implicit processes in multicue judgment. *Memory & Cognition*, 31(4), 608–618.

Evans, J. & Stanovich, K. (2013). Dual processing theories of higher cognition. *Perspectives on Psychological Science*, 8, 223–241.

Evans, J. (2013). *Reasoning, Rationality and Dual Processes*. New York: Taylor & Francis.

Eysenck, H. (1957). *Sense and Nonsense in Psychology*. Middlesex, UK: Penguin.

Eysenck, H. (1991). Dimensions of personality. *Personality & Individual Differences,* 12, 773–790.

Fanelli, D. (2010). "Positive" results increase down the hierarchy of science. *PLOS ONE*, 5(3), e10068.

Fidler, F. (2005). From statistical significance to effect estimation. Unpublished Dissertation.

Fiedler, K. (2011). Voodoo correlations are everywhere. *Perspectives on Psychological Science*, 6(2), 163–171.

Fodor, J. & Charles, C. (1965). Operationalism and ordinary language. *American Philosophical Quarterly*, 2, 281–295.

Francis, G. (2012). Too good to be true. *Psychonomic Bulletin and Review,* 19, 151–156.

Frankish, K. & Evans, J. (2009). The duality of mind. In K. Frankish & J. Evans (eds.). *In Two Minds*. New York: Oxford University Press.

Fredrickson, B. & Losada, M. (2005). Positive affect and the complex dynamics of human functioning. *American Psychologist*, 60(7), 678–686.

Friese, M. & Fiedler, K. (2010). Being on the lookout for validity. *Experimental Psychology*, 57, 228–232.

Fuchs, H., Jenny, M., & Fidler, S. (2012). Psychologists are open to change yet wary of rules. *Perspectives on Psychological Science*, 7, 639–642.

Gable, S. & Haidt, J. (2005). What (and why) is positive psychology? *Review of General Psychology*, 9, 103–110.

Galak, J., Leboeuf, R., Nelson, L., & Simmons, J. (2012). Correcting the past. *Journal of Personality and Social Psychology*, 103(6), 933–948.

Gardner, H. (1983). *Frames of Mind.* New York: Basic Books.

Gazzaniga, M. (1985). *The Social Brain*. New York: Basic Books.

Gelman, A. & Loken, E. (2013). The garden of forking paths. Unpublished Paper.

Gerhardt, S. (2004). *Why Love Matters.* London: Routledge.

Gibson, H. (1981). *Hans Eysenck*. London: Peter Owen.

Gigerenzer, G. (1987). Probabilistic thinking and the fight against subjectivity. In L. Kruger, G. Gigerenzer, & M. Morgan (eds.). *The Probabilistic Revolution: Volume Two.* Cambridge, MA: MIT Press.

Gigerenzer, G. (1991). How to make cognitive illusions disappear. *European Review of Social Psychology*, 2, 83–115.

Gigerenzer, G. (1996). On narrow norms and vague heuristics. *Psychological Review*, 103, 592–596.

Gigerenzer, G. (2000). *Adaptive Thinking*. New York: Oxford University Press.

Gigerenzer, G. (2007). *Gut Feelings*. New York: Viking.

Gigerenzer, G. & Hoffrage, U. (1995). How to improve Bayesian reasoning without instruction: frequency formats. *Psychological Review*, 102, 684–704.

Gigerenzer, G. & Murray (1987). *Cognition as Intuitive Statistics*. Hillsdale, NJ: Erlbaum.

Gigerenzer, G., Swijtink, Z., Porter, T., Daston, L., Beatty, J., & Kruger, L. (1989). *The Empire of Chance.* Cambridge: Cambridge University Press.

Gilovich, T., Griffin, D., & Kahneman, D. (2002). *Heuristics and Biases*: Cambridge: Cambridge University Press.

Gilbert, D. (2006). *Stumbling on Happiness*. New York: Knopf.

Gilbert, D. (2014). Interview published in *The Atlantic,* accessed at: http://www.theatlantic.com/education/archive/2014/03/psychology-an-owner-s-manual-for-your-own-mind/284329/.

Gilovich, T. (1991). *How we know what isn't so.* New York: The Free Press.

Gilovich, T., Valone, R., & Tversky, A. (1985). The hot hand in basketball. *Cognitive Psychology*, 17, 295–314.

Gladwell, M. (2000). *The Tipping Point*. New York: Little Brown.

Gladwell, M. (2005). *Blink*. New York: Back Bay.

Glymour, C. (1997). Social statistics and genuine inquiry: Reflections on *The Bell Curve*. In B. Devlin, S. Fienberg, D. Resnick, & K. Roeder (eds.). *Intelligence, Genes and Success.* New York: Springer.

Glymour, C. (2010). *Galileo in Pittsburgh.* Cambridge, MA: Harvard University Press.

Goldberg, L. (1991). Human mind versus regression equation. In D. Cicchetti & W. Grove (eds.). *Thinking Clearly About Psychology.* Minneapolis: University of Minnesota Press.

Goldie, P. (2002). *The Emotions*. Oxford: Clarendon Press.

Goleman, D. (1995). *Emotional Intelligence*. New York: Bantam Books.

Goleman, D. (1998). *Working with Emotional Intelligence*. New York: Bantam Books.

Goleman, D. (2013a). *Focus.* New York: Harper.

Goleman, D. (2013b). The focused leader. *Harvard Business Review*, December, 2013.

Goodie, A. & Williams, C. (2000). Some theoretical and practical implications of defining aptitude and reasoning in terms of each other. *Behavioral and Brain Sciences*, 23, 675–676.

Gould, S.J. (1981). *The Mismeasure of Man.* New York: W. W. Norton.

Gosling, S. (2008). *Snoop*. New York: Basic Books.

Gosling, S., Rentfrow, P., & Swann, W. (2003). A very brief measure of the big five personality domains. *Journal of Research in Personality,* 37, 504–528.

Gottredson, L. (2000). Intelligence. In E. Borgatta & R. Montgomery (eds.). *Encyclopedia of Sociology*. New York: MacMillan.

Gottfredson, L. (2009). Logical fallacies used to dismiss the evidence on intelligence testing. In R. Phelps (ed.). *Correcting Fallacies About Educational and Psychological Testing.* Washington, D.C.: APA Books.

Gopnik, A., Meltzoff, A., & Kuhl, P. (1999). *The Scientist in the Crib.* New York: William Morrow.

Gopnik, A. (2009). *The Philosophical Baby*. New York: Farrar, Strauss and Giroux.

Green, C. (1992). Of immortal mythological beasts. *Theory & Psychology*, 2, 291–320.

Greenwald, A. (1992). New Look 3. Unconscious cognition reclaimed. *American Psychologist*, 47(6), 766–779.

Greenwald, A. & Banaji, M. (1995). Implicit social cognition. *Psychological Review*, 102(1), 4–27.

Greenwald, A. & Farnham, S. (2000). Using the IAT to measure self-esteem and self-concept. *Journal of Personality and Social Psychology*, 79(6), 1022–1038.

Greenwald, A., McGhee, D., & Schwartz, J. (1998). Measuring differences in implicit cognition. *Journal of Personality & Social Psychology*, 74(6), 1464–1480.

Greenwald, A. & Nosek, B., (2001). Health of the IAT at age 3. *Zeitschrift fur Experimentelle Psychologie*, 48, 85–93.
Greenwald, A., Nosek, B. & Banaji, M. (2003). Understanding and Using the IAT. *Journal of Personality and Social Psychology*, 85, 197–216.
Griggs, R. (1989). To "see" or not to "see." That is the selection task. *Quarterly Journal of Experimental Psychology*, 41A, 517–529.
Ferguson, M., Bargh, J., & Nayak, D. (2005). After-effects. *Journal of Experimental Social Psychology*, 41, 182–191.
Flynn, J. (2007). *What is Intelligence?* New York: Cambridge University Press.
Frankish, K. (2009). Systems and levels. In K. Frankish & J. Evans (eds.). *In Two Minds*. New York: Oxford University Press.
Hacking, I. (1975). *The Emergence of Probability*. Cambridge: Cambridge University Press.
Hacking, I. (1990). *The Taming of Chance*. Cambridge: Cambridge University Press.
Haidt, J. (2001). The emotional dog and its rational tail. *Psychological Review*, 108, 814–834.
Haidt, J. (2006). *The Happiness Hypothesis*. New York: Basic.
Haidt, J. (2012). *The Righteous Mind*. New York: Pantheon.
Haier, R. (2003). Positron emission tomography studies of intelligence. In H. Nyborg (ed.). *The Scientific Study of Intelligence*. Amsterdam: Pergamon.
Hale. M. (1980). *Human Science and the Social Order*. Philadelphia, PA: Temple University Press.
Harris, A. & Hahn, U. (2011). Unrealistic optimism about future life events: A cautionary note. *Psychological Review*, 118(1), 135–154.
Harris, J. (1998). *The Nurture Assumption*. New York: The Free Press.
Hassin, R. Uleman, J., & Bargh, J. (2005). *The New Unconscious*. Oxford: Oxford University Press.
Hassin, R., Ferguson, M., Shidlovski, D., & Gross, T. (2007). Subliminal exposure to national flags affects political thought and behavior. *Proceedings of the National Academy of Sciences*, 104(50), 19757–19761.
Hearnshaw, L. (1979). *Cyril Burt*. Ithaca, NY: Cornell University Press.
Hedges, L. (1987). How hard is hard science, how soft is soft science? *American Psychologist*, 42(5), 443–455
Henle, M. (1962). On the relation between logic and thinking. *Psychological Review*, 69, 366–378.
Henrich, J., Heine, S., & Norenzayan, A. (2010). The weirdest people in the world? *Behavioral and Brain Sciences*, 33, 1–75.
Henry, C. & Hubbs-Tait, L. (2013). New Directions in authoritative parenting. In R. Larzelere, A. Morris & A. Harrist (eds.). *Authoritative Parenting*. Washington, D.C.: APA Books.
Herrnstein, R. & Murray, C. (1994). *The Bell Curve*. New York: Simon & Schuster.
Hertvig, (2000). The questionable utility of "cognitive ability" in explaining cognitive illusions. *Behavioral and Brain Sciences*, 23(5), 678–679.
Hetherington, E., Henderson, S., & Reiss, D. (1999). *Adolescent Siblings in Stepfamilies*. New York: Wiley.
Hoeve, M., Dubas, J., Eichelsheim, V., van der Laan, P., Smeenk, W., & Gerris, J. (2009). The relationship between parenting and delinquency. *Journal of Abnormal Child Psychology*, 37(6), 749–775.
Horowitz, M. (2014). *One Simple Idea*. New York: Crown.
Hornstein, G. (1988). Quantifying Psychological Phenomena. In J. Morawski (ed.). *The Rise of Experimentation in American Psychology*. New Haven, CT: Yale University Press.
Hulbert, A. (2003). *Raising America*. New York: Knopf.
Ioannidis, J. (2005). Why most published research findings are false. *PLOS Medicine*, 2(8). 696–701.
James, W. (1902). *The Varieties of Religious Experience*. New York: Lonomans.
Jastrow, J. (1900). *Fact and Fable in Psychology*. New York: Houghton and Mifflin.
Jastrow, J. (1928). *Keeping Mentally Fit*. Garden City, NY: Garden City Press.

Jenkins, J. & Bisceglia, R. (2013). Understanding within-family variability in children's responses to environmental stress. In D. Keating (ed.). *Nature and Nurture in Early Child Development.* New York: Cambridge University Press.

Jensen, A. (1969). How much can we boost IQ and scholastic achievement? *Harvard Educational Review*, 39(1), 1–123.

Jensen, A. (1981). *Straight Talk about Mental Tests.* New York: The Free Press.

Jensen, A. (1998). *The g Factor.* Westport, CT: Praeger.

John, L., Loewenstein, G., & Prelec, D. (2012). Measuring the prevalence of questionable research practices with incentives for truth-telling. *Psychological Science*, 23(5), 524–532.

John, O., Nauman, L., & Soto, C. (2011). Paradigm shift to the integrative big five trait taxonomy. In O. John, R. Robins, & L. Pervin (eds.). *Handbook of Personality.* Third Edition. New York: Guilford.

Kagan, J. (1994). *Galen's Prophecy.* New York: Basic Books.

Kagan, J. (1998). *Three Seductive Ideas*. Cambridge, MA: Harvard University Press.

Kahneman, D. & Tversky, A. (1974). Judgment under uncertainty, *Science*, 185 (1974), 1124–1131.

Kahneman, D., Slovic, P., & Tversky, A. (1981). *Judgment Under Uncertainty.* Cambridge: Cambridge University Press.

Kahneman, D. (2011). *Thinking, Fast and Slow.* New York: Farrar, Straus & Giroux.

Kahneman, D. & Fredrick, S. (2002). Representativeness revisited. In T. Gilovich, D. Griffin, & D. Kahneman (eds.). *Heuristics and Biases*: Cambridge: Cambridge University Press.

Kahneman, D. & Krueger, A. (2006). Developments in the measurement of subjective well-being. *Journal of Economic Perspectives*, 20(1), 3–24.

Kaufman, A. (2009). *IQ Testing 101.* New York: Springer.

Kaufman, S. (2013). *Ungifted.* New York: Basic Books.

Karen, R. (1994). *Becoming Attached.* New York: Oxford University Press.

Kendler (1981). The reality of operationalism. *Journal of Mind & Behavior*, 2, 331–341.

Keren, G. & Schul, Y. (2009). Two is not always better than one. *Perspectives on Psychological Science*, 4, 533–550.

Kihlstrom, J. (1987). The cognitive unconscious. *Science*, 237, 1145–1451.

Kim, K. & Rohner, R. (2002). Parental warmth, control and involvement in schooling. *Journal of Cross-Cultural Psychology*, 33(2), 127–140.

King, G. (1986). How not to lie with statistics. *American Journal of Political Science*, 30, 666–687.

Kline, P. (1998). *The New Psychometrics*. London: Routledge.

Kline, P. (2000). *Handbook of Psychological Testing*. London: Psychology Press.

Knapp, T. & Sawilowsky, S. (2001). Constructive criticisms of methodological and editorial practices. *Journal of Experimental Education*, 70, 65–79.

Kochanska, G. (1997). Mutually responsive orientation between mothers and their young children. *Child Development*, 68, 908–923.

Kochanska, G. & Thompson, R. (1997). The emergence and development of conscience in toddlerhood and early childhood. In G. Grusec & L. Kuczunski (eds.). *Parenting and Children's Internalization of Values.* New York: Wiley.

Kohn, A. (2005). *Unconditional Parenting.* New York: Atria Books.

Kohn, A. (2014). *The Myth of the Spoiled Child.* New York: De Capo.

Krause, M. & Howard, K. (2003). What random assignment does and does not do. *Journal of Clinical Psychology*, 59(7), 751–766.

Koch, S. (1999). *Psychology in Human Context.* Chicago, IL: University of Chicago Press.

Kordi, A. & Baharudin, R. (2010). Parenting attitudes and style and its effects on children's school achievements. *International Journal of Psychological Studies*, 2(2), 217–222.

Kutieleh, S. & Egege, S. (2008). Dimming down difference. In L. Dunn & M. Wallace (eds.). *Teaching in Transnational Higher Education.* New York: Routledge.

Lakatos, I. (1970). Falsification and the methodology of scientific research programmes. In I. Lakatos & A. Musgrave (eds.). *Criticism and the Growth of Knowledge.* Cambridge: Cambridge University Press.

Lakoff, G. (1996). *Moral Politics*. Chicago, IL: University of Chicago Press.

Lamiell, J. (1987). *The Psychology of Personality.* New York: Colombia University Press.

Lamiell, J. (2003). *Beyond Individual and Group Differences.* Thousand Oaks, CA: Sage.

Landry, S., Smith, K., Swank, P. (2006). Responsive parenting. *Developmental Psychology*, 42(4), 627–642.

Landy, F. (2005). Some historical and scientific issues related to research on emotional intelligence. *Journal of Organizational Behavior*, 26(4), 411–424.

Leahey, T. (1980). The myth of operationalism. *Journal of Mind & Behavior*, 1, 127–143.

Leahey, T. & Leahey, G. (1983). *Psychology's Occult Doubles.* Chicago, IL: Nelson Hall.

Ledoux, J. (1996). *The Emotional Brain.* New York: Simon and Schuster.

Lehrer, J. (2010). The truth wears off. *The New Yorker*, December 13.

Lerner, R. (2002). *Concepts and Theories of Human Development.* 3rd Edition. Mahwah, NJ: Erlbaum.

Leventhal, L. & Huynh, C. (1996). Directional decisions for two-tailed tests. *Psychological Methods*, 1(3), 278–292.

Levine, M. (2008). *The Price of Privilege.* New York: Harper Collins.

Levitan, D. (2014). *The Organized Mind.* New York: Dutton.

Levitt, S. & Dunbar, S. (2005). *Freakonomics.* New York: William Morrow.

Levitt, S. & Dunbar, S. (2014). *Think Like a Freak.* New York: William Morrow.

Lewis, C. (1981). The effects of firm-parental control. *Psychological Bulletin*, 90, 547–563.

Libet, B., Wright, E., & Gleason, C. (1982). Readiness-potentials preceding unrestricted spontaneous vs. pre-planned voluntary acts. *Electroenchephalograpy and Clinical Neurophysiology*, 54(3), 322–335.

Libet, B. (1985). Unconscious cerebral initiative and the role of conscious will in voluntary action. *Behavioral and Brain Sciences*, 8, 529–539.

Lilienfeld, S., Lynn, S., Ruscio, J., & Beyerstein, B. (2010). *50 Great Myths of Popular Psychology.* Chichester, UK: Wiley Blackwell.

Locke, E. (2005). Why emotional intelligence is an invalid concept. *Journal of Organizational Behavior*, 26(4), 425–431.

Loeber, R. & Dishion, T. (1983). Early predictors of male delinquency. *Psychological Bulletin*, 94, 68–99.

Loevinger, J. (1957). Objective tests as instruments of psychological theory. *Psychological Reports*, 3, 635–694.

Loftus, E. & Klinger, M. (1992). Is the unconscious smart or dumb? *American Psychologist*, 47(6), 761–765

Lord, F. & Novick, M. (1968). *Statistical Theories of Mental Test Scores.* Reading, MA: Addison-Wesley Publishing.

Lykken, D. (1968). Statistical significance in psychological research. *Psychological Bulletin*, 70, 151–159.

Lykken, D. (1991). What's wrong with psychology anyway? In D. Cicchetti & W. Grove (eds.). *Thinking Clearly About Psychology.* Volume 1. Minneapolis: University of Minnesota Press.

Lyubomirsky, S. (2008). *The How of Happiness.* New York: Penguin.

Lyubomirsky, S. (2013). *The Myths of Happiness.* New York: Penguin.

Lyubomirsky, S. & Ross, L. (1997). Hedonic consequences of social comparison. *Journal of Personality & Social Psychology*, 73, 1141–1157.

Machery, E. (2007). 100 years of psychological concepts. *Studies in History and Philosophy of Biological & Biomedical Sciences*, 38, 63–84.

Maccoby, E. & Martin, J. (1983). Socialization in the context of the family. In P. Mussen (ed.). *Handbook of Child Psychology.* Volume 4. New York: Wiley.

Maccoby, E. (2000). Parenting and its effect on children. *Annual Review of Psychology*, 51, 1–27.

MacLean, P. (1973). *A Triune Concept of Brain and Behavior.* Toronto: University of Toronto Press.

Manktelow, K. & Over, D. (1991). Social roles and reasoning with deontic conditionals. *Cognition*, 35, 85–105.

Margolis, H. (1987). *Patterns, Thinking, and Cognition.* Chicago, IL: University of Chicago Press.

Marszalek, J., Barber, C., & Kohlhart, J. (2011). Sample size in psychological research over the past 30 years. *Perceptual & Motor Skills*, 112(2), 331–348.

Maslow, A. (1954). *Motivation and Personality*. Ann Arbor: University of Michigan.

Maxwell, S. (2004). The persistence of underpowered studies in psychological research. *Psychological Methods*, 9(2), 147–163.

Mayer, J. & Salovey, P. (1997). What is emotional intelligence? In P. Salovey & D. Sluyter (eds.). *Emotional Development and Emotional Intelligence.* New York: Basic Books.

Mayer, J., Salovey, P., & Caruso., D. (2002). *Mayer-Salovey-Caruso Emotional Intelligence Test*. Toronto: Multi-health Systems.

Mayer, J., Salovey, P., & Caruso., D. (2008). Emotional intelligence: new ability or eclectic traits? *American Psychologist*, 63(6), 503–517.

Mayer, John D. (2014). *Personal Intelligence.* New York: Farrar, Straus, and Giroux.

Mcdonald, D. (1997). Haldane's lungs. *Multivariate Behavioral Research*, 32, 1–38.

McCrae, R., Zonderman, A., Costa, P., Bond, M., & Paunonen, S. (1996). Evaluating replicability of factors in the revised NEO Personality Inventory. *Journal of Personality and Social Psychology*, 70(3), 552–566.

McCrae, R., Costa, P., Ostendorf, F., Angleitner, L., Kusdil, N. & Avia, M. (2000). Nature over nurture. *Journal of Personality & Social Psychology*, 78, 173–186.

McCrae, R. & Costa, P. (2003). *Personality in Adulthood.* 2nd Edition. New York: Guilford Press.

McCrae, R. & Costa, P. (2011). The five factor theory of personality. In O. John, R. Robins & L. Pervin (eds.). *Handbook of Personality*. Third Edition. New York: Guilford Press.

McLeod, B., Wood, J., & Weisz, J. (2006). Examining the association between parenting and childhood anxiety. *Clinical Psychology Review*, 27, 155–172.

McNemar, Q. (1946). Opinion-attitude methodology. *Psychological Bulletin*, 43, 289–374.

Medina, J. (2011). *Brain Rules for Baby*. Seattle, WA: Pear Press.

Meehl, P. (1967). Theory-testing in psychology and physics. *Philosophy of Science*, 34, 103–115.

Meehl, P. (1978).Theoretical risks and tabular asterisks. *Journal of Consulting and Clinical Psychology*, 46(4), 806–834 (p. 817).

Meehl, P. (1990). Why summaries of research on psychological theories are often uninterpretable. *Psychological Reports*, 66, 195–244.

Meier, S. (1994). *The Chronic Crisis in Psychological Measurement and Assessment.* San Diego, CA: Academic Press.

Mellers, B., Hertvig, R., & Kahneman, D. (2001). Do frequency representations eliminate conjunction effect? *Psychological Science*, 12(4), 269–275.

Messick, S. (1975). The standard problem. *American Psychologist*, 30, 955–966.

Mlodinow, L. (2008). *The Drunkard's Walk*. New York: Pantheon.

Mlodinow, L. (2012). *Subliminal*. New York: Pantheon.

Michell, J. (1990). *An Introduction to the Logic of Psychological Measurement*. Mahwah, NJ: Erlbaum.

Michell, J. (1999). *Measurement in Psychology*. Cambridge: Cambridge University Press.

Michell, J. (2008). Is psychometrics pathological science? *Measurement: Interdisciplinary Research & Perspective*, 6 (1), 7–24.

Michell, J. (2009). Invalidity in validity. In R. Lissitz (ed.). *The Concept of Validity*. Charlotte, NC: IAP.

Michell, J. (2010). The quantity/quality interchange: A blind spot on the highway of ccience. In A. Toomela & J. Valsiner (eds.). *Methodological Thinking in Psychology: 60 Years Gone Astray?* Charlotte, NC: IAP.

Miller, A. (2008). A critique of positive psychology. *Journal of Philosophy of Education*, 42(3–4), 591–608.

Mills, J. (1991). Operationalism, scientism, and the rhetoric of power. In C. Tolman (ed.). *Positivism in Psychology*. New York: Springer

Millsap, R. (1997). Invariance in measurement and prediction revisited. *Psychometrika*, 72(4), 461–473.

Mitchell, J., Nosek, B., & Banaji, M. (2003). Contextual variations in implicit evaluation. *Journal of Experimental Psychology*, 132(3), 455–469.

Moleenar, P. (1997). A manifesto on psychology as an idiographic science. *Measurement: Interdisciplinary Research and Perspectives*, 2(4), 201–218.

Mook, D. (1983). In defense of external invalidity. *American Psychologist*, 38, 379–387.

Morris, A., Cui, L., & Steinberg, L. (2013). Parenting research and themes. In R. Larzelere, A. Morris, & A. Harrist (eds.). *Authoritative Parenting.* Washington, D.C.: APA Books.

Morrison, D. & Henkel, R. (eds.). (1970). *The Significance Test Controversy*. London: Butterworths.

Moshman, D. (2000). Diversity in reasoning and rationality. *Behavioral and Brain Sciences*, 23, 689–690.

Mosier, C. (1947). A critical examination of the concepts of face validity. *Educational and Psychological Measurement*, 7(2), 191–205

Mudge, J. Baker, L., Edge, C., & Houlahan, J. (2012). Setting an optimal alpha that minimizes errors in null hypothesis significance tests. *PLOS One*, 7(2), e32734.

Murray, J. (1963). *The Power of Your Subconscious Mind.* New York: Prentice Hall.

Neisser, U., Boodoo, G., Bouchard, T., Boykin, A., Brody, N., Ceci, S., Halpern, D., Loehlin, J., Perloff, R., Sternberg, R., & Urbina, S. (1996). Intelligence knowns and unknowns. *American Psychologist*, 51(2), 77–101.

Newell, B. & Shanks, D. (2014). Unconscious influences on decision-making. *Behavioral and Brain Sciences*, 37(1), 1–19.

Newstead, S. (2000). Are there two different kinds of thinking? *Behavioral and Brain Sciences*, 23, 690–691.

Newton, P. & Shaw, S. (2014). *Validity in Educational and Psychological Assessment*. Thousand Oaks, CA: Sage.

Nicholson, I. (2003). *Inventing Personality*. Washington, D.C.: APA Books.

Nisbett, R. & Ross, L. (1980). *Human Inference*. New York: Prentice-Hall.

Nisbett, R. (2003). *The Geography of Thought*. New York: The Free Press.

Nisbett, R., Aronson, J., Clancy, B., Dickens, W., Flynn, J., Halpern, D., & Turkheimer, E. (2012). Intelligence. *American Psychologist,* 67(2), 130–159.

Norem, J. (2001). *The Power of Negative Thinking*. Cambridge, MA: Basic Books.

Norenzayan, A., Smith, E., Kim, B., & Nisbett, R., (2002). Cultural preferences for formal versus intuitive reasoning. *Cognitive Science*, 26, 653–684

Norman, W. (1963). Toward and adequate taxonomy of personality attributes. *Journal of Abnormal & Social Psychology*, 66, 574–583.

Nosek, B., Greenwald, A., & Banaji, M. (2002). Harvesting implicit group attitudes and beliefs from a demonstration website. *Group Dynamics*, 6(1), 101–115.

Nyborg, H (2003). The sociology of psychometric and bio-behavioral sciences. In H. Nyborg (ed.). *The Scientific Study of Intelligence*. Amsterdam: Pergamon.

Oakes, M. (1986). *Statistical Inference*. Chichester, UK: John Wiley & Sons.

O'Connor, R. (2014). *Rewire*. New York: Hudson Street Press.

Osman, M. (2004). An evaluation of dual-process theories of reasoning. *Psychonomic Bulletin and Review*, 11(6), 998–1010.

Ozer, D. (1985). Correlation and the coefficient determination. *Psychological Bulletin*, 97(2), 307–315.

Panofsky, A. (2014). *Misbehaving Science*. Chicago, IL: University of Chicago Press.

Patterson, G. & Bank, L. (1989). Some amplifying mechanisms for pathologic processes in families. In M. Gunnar & E. Thelen (eds.). *Systems and Development.* Hillsdale, NJ: Erlbaum.

Patterson, G. & Forgash, M. (1995). Predicting future clinical adjustment from treatment outcome and process variable. *Psychological Assessment*, 7, 275–285.

Paul, A. (2005). *The Cult of Personality.* New York: The Free Press.

Pearl, J. (2000). *Causality*. Cambridge: Cambridge University Press.

Pedersen, J. (2013). *The Rise of the Millennial Parents.* Lanham, MD: Rowman & Littlefield Education.

Peterson, C. (2012). *Pursuing the Good Life.* New York: Oxford University Press.

Peterson, C. & Seligman, M. (1984). Causal explanations as a risk factor for depression. *Psychological Review*, 91, 347–374.

Peterson, C. & Seligman, M. (2004). *Character Strengths and Virtues*. Washington, D.C.: APA Books.

Peterson, J. (2011). *The necessity of virtue.* Online Lecture: You Tube (https://www.youtube.com/watch?v=gwUJHNPMUyU).

Petit, G., Bates, J., & Dodge, K. (1997). Supportive parenting, ecological context and children's adjustment. *Child Development*, 68, 908–923.

Perkins, A., Forehand, M., Greenwald, A., & Maison, D. (2008). The influence of implicit social cognition on social behavior. In C. Haugtvedt, P. Herr, & F. Kardes (eds.). *Handbook of Consumer Behavior.* Hillsdale, NJ: Erlbaum.

Phelps, R. (2009). (ed.). *Correcting Fallacies About Educational and Psychological Testing.* Washington, D.C.: APA Books.

Piaget, J. (1969). *The Early Growth of Logic in the Child.* New York: W. W. Norton.

Piotrowski, J., Lapierre, M., & Linebarger, D. (2013). Investigating correlates of self-regulation in early childhood with a representative sample of English speaking families. *Journal of Child and Family Studies,* 22(3), 423–436.

Plomin, R. (2003). Molecular genetics and *g*. In H. Nyborg (ed.). *The Scientific Study of Intelligence*. Amsterdam: Pergamon.

Plomin, R. & Daniels, D. (1987). Why are children from the same family so different from one another? *Behavioral & Brain Sciences*, 10(1), 1–16.

Popham, J. (2001). *The Truth about Testing*. Alexandria, VA: ASCD.

Porter, T. (1986). *The Rise of Statistical Thinking*. Princeton, NJ: Princeton University Press.

Porter, T. (2003). Statistics and Statistical Methods. In T. Porter & D. Ross (eds.). *The Cambridge History of Science: Volume Seven.* Cambridge: Cambridge University Press.

Poulton, E. (1994). *Behavioral Decision Theory*. Cambridge: Cambridge University Press.

Prescott, J. (1971). Early somatosensory deprivation as an ontogenetic process in the abnormal development of brain and behavior. In I. Goldsmith and J. Moor-Jankowski (eds.). *Medical Primotology 1970*. Basel: Karger.

Prescott, J. (1996). The origins of human love and violence. *Pre- and Perinatal Psychology Journal*, 10(3), 143–188.

Prentice, D. & Miller, D. (1992). When small effects are impressive. *Psychological Bulletin*, 112(1), 160–164.

Reber, A. (1967). Implicit learning of artificial grammars. *Journal of Verbal Learning and Verbal Behavior*, 6, 855–863.

Reber, A. (1993). *Implicit Learning and Tacit Knowledge*. New York: Oxford University Press.

Reiss, D, Hetherington, E., Plomin, R., Howe, G. & Simmons, S. (1995). Genetic questions for environmental studies. *Archives of General Psychology*, 52, 925–936.

Rode, J., Mooney, C., Arthaud-Day, M., Near, P., Ribin, R., & Baldwin, T. (2007). Emotional intelligence and individual performance. *Journal of Organizational Behavior*, 28, 399–421.

Rogers, T. (1991). Antecedents of operationism. In C. Tolman (ed.). *Positivism in Psychology*. New York: Springer.

Rogers, T. (1995). *The Psychological Testing Enterprise*. Belmont, CA: Wadsworth.

Rosenthal, R. (1966). *Experimental Effects in Behavioral Research*. New York: Appleton.

Rosenthal, R. (1979). The "file drawer problem" and tolerance for null results. *Psychological Bulletin*, 86, 638–641.

Rosenthal, R. (1993). Cumulating evidence. In G. Keren & C. Lewis (eds.). *A Handbook for Data Analysis in the Behavioral Sciences.* Hillsdale, NJ: Erlbaum.

Rosenthal, R. & Rosnow, R. (2009). *Artifacts in Behavioral Research*: New York: Oxford University Press.

Rosenthal, R. & Rubin, D. (1979). A note on percent variance explained as a measure of the importance of effects. *Journal of Applied Social Psychology*, 9(5), 395–396.

Rosnow, R., Rosenthal, R., & Rubin, D. (1982). Contrasts and correlations in effect size stimulations. *Psychological Science*, 11(6), 446–453.
Rowe, D. (1994). *The limits of Family Influence.* New York: Guilford Press.
Rowe, D. (2001). *Biology and Crime.* Los Angeles: Roxbury.
Rozeboom, W. (1960). The fallacy of the null hypothesis significance test. *Psychological Bulletin*, 57, 416–428.
Rozenwald, G. (1986). Why operationalism won't go away. *Philosophy of the Social Sciences*, 16, 303–330.
Rucci, J. & Tweney, R. (1980). Analysis of variance and the "second" discipline of psychology. *Psychological Bulletin*, 87, 166–184.
Ruch, G. (1924). *The Improvement of the Written Examination.* Chicago, IL: Scott, Foresman.
Rushton, J. P. (2003). Race differences in *g* and the "Jensen effect." In H. Nyborg (ed.). *The Scientific Study of Intelligence.* Amsterdam: Pergamon.
Rutter, M. (2013). Biological and experiential influences on psychological development. In D. Keating (ed.). *Nature and Nurture in Early Child Development.* New York: Cambridge University Press.
Ryan, B. & Adams, G. (1995). The family-school relationships model. In B. Ryan, G. Adams, T. Gullotta, R. Weissberg, & R. Hampton (eds.). *The Family-School Connection.* Thousand Oaks, CA: Sage.
Sailor, D. (2003). *Supporting Children in their Home, School and Community.* New York: Prentice Hall.
Salovey, P. & Mayer, J. (1990). Emotional intelligence. *Imagination, Cognition and Personality*, 9, 185–211.
Schacter, D. (1987). Implicit memory. *Journal of Experimental Psychology*, 13(3), 501–518.
Schacter, D. & Tulving, E. (1994). What are memory systems of 1994? In D. Schacter & E. Tulving (eds.). *Memory Systems.* Cambridge, MA: MIT Press.
Schaefer, E. (1959). A circumplex model for maternal behavior. *Journal of Abnormal & Social Psychology*, 59, 226–235.
Scheines, R., Spirites, P., Glymour, C., Meek, C., & Rochardson, T. (1998). Reply to comments. *Multivariate Behavioral Research*, 33(1), 165–180.
Schneider, W. & Shriffin, R. (1977). Controlled and automatic human information processing. *Psychological Review*, 84, 1–66.
Schultz, D. (1969). The human subject in psychological research. *Psychological Bulletin*, 72, 214–228.
Schimmack, U. (2012). The ironic effect of significant results on the credibility of multiple-study articles. *Psychological Methods*, 17(4), 551–566.
Schmidt, F. (1996). Statistical significance testing and cumulative research in psychology. *Psychological Methods*, 1(2), 115–129.
Schmidt, F. & Hunter, J. (1996). Measurement error in psychological research. *Psychological Methods*, 1, 199–223.
Schoch, R. (2007). *The Secrets of Happiness.* London: Profile Books.
Schwartz, N. (1996). *Cognition and Communication.* New York: Erlbaum.
Schwartz, N., Strack, D., Hilton, D., & Naderer, G. (1991). Base rates representativeness and the logic of conversation. *Journal of Psycholinguistic Research*, 15, 47–92.
Sears, R., Maccoby, E., & Levins, H. (1957). *Patterns of Child Rearing.* Evanston, IL: Peterson.
Sears, W. (1997). *The Complete Book of Christian Parenting and Child Care.* Nashville, TN: B&H Books.
Sears, W. & Sears, M. (1993). *The Baby Book.* New York: Little Brown.
Sedlmeier, P. & Gigerenzer, G. (1989). Do studies of statistical power have an effect on the power of studies? *Psychological Bulletin*, 105, 309–316.
Seligman, D. (1992). *A Question of Intelligence.* New York: Birch Lane Press.
Seligman, M. (1970). On the generality of the laws of learning. *Psychological Review*, 77, 406–418.
Seligman, M. (1975). *Helplessness.* San Francisco: Freemen.
Seligman, M. (1991/2006). *Learned Optimism.* New York: Knopf.

Seligman, M. (2002/2007). *Authentic Happiness*. New York: The Free Press.

Seligman, M. (2011). *Flourish*. New York: The Free Press.

Seligman, M. & Csikszentmihalyi, M. (2000). Positive psychology. *American Psychologist*, 55(1), 5–14.

Seligman, M., Steen, T., Park, N., & Peterson, C. (2005). Positive psychology progress. *American Psychologist*, 60(5), 410–421.

Senior, J. (2006). Some dark thoughts on happiness. *New York Magazine*. 17573.

Sesardic, N. (2005). *Making Sense of Heritability*. Cambridge: Cambridge University Press.

Shapiro, L. (1997). *How to Raise a Child with High EQ*. New York: HarperCollins.

Shenk, D. (2010). *The Genius in All of Us*. New York: Doubleday.

Siegel, D. & Bryson, T. (2011). *The Whole-Brain Child*. New York: Delacorte Press.

Simon, H. (1947). *Administrative Behavior*. New York: MacMillan.

Sin, N. & Lyubomirsky, S. (2009). Enhancing well-being and alleviating depressive symptoms with positive psychology interventions. *Journal of Clinical Psychology*, 65(5), 467–487.

Sireci, S. (2009). Packing and unpacking sources of validity evidence. In R. Lissitz (ed.). *The Concept of Validity*. Charlotte, NC: IAP.

Skinner, B. F. (1954). Critique of psychoanalytic theories and concepts. *Scientific Monthly*, 79, 300–305.

Skinner, B. F. (1971). *Beyond Freedom and Dignity*. New York: Knopf.

Skinner, B. F. (1974). *About Behaviorism*. New York: Random House.

Sloman, S. (1996). The empirical case for two systems of reasoning. *Psychological Review*, 119, 3–22.

Smart, R. (1966). Subject selection bias in psychological research. *Canadian Psychologist*, 7a, 115–121.

Snyderman, S. & Rothman, M. (1988). *The IQ Controversy, the Media, and Public Policy*. Edison, NJ: Transaction.

Sorkhabi, N. & Mandara, J. (2013). Are the effects of Baumrind's parenting styles culturally specific or culturally equivalent? In R. Larzelere, A. Morris, & A. Harrist (eds.). *Authoritative Parenting*. Washington, D.C.: APA Books.

Spearman, C. (1904). General intelligence, objectively determined and measured. *American Journal of Psychology*, 15, 201–293.

Spearman, C. (1927). *The Abilities of Man*. London: MacMillan.

Spencer, H. (1963/1860). *Education: Intellectual, Moral, and Physical*. Paterson, NJ: Littlefield, Adams.

Spera, C. (2005). A review of the relationship among parenting practices, parenting styles and adolescent school achievement. *Educational Psychology Review*, 17(2), 125–146.

Spirites, P., Glymour, C., & Scheines, R. (2001). *Causation, Prediction and Search*. 2nd Edition. Cambridge, MA: MIT Press.

Stanovich, K. & West, R. (1998). Individual differences in rational thought. *Journal of Experimental Psychology*, 112, 1–36.

Stanovich, K. & West, R. (2000). Individual differences in reasoning. *Behavioral and Brain Sciences*, 23, 645–726.

Stanovich, K. (2009). Distinguishing the reflective, algorithmic and autonomous minds. In K. Frankish & J. Evans (eds.). *In Two Minds*. New York: Oxford University Press.

Starr, P. (1983). *The Social Transformation of Medicine*. New York: Basic Books.

Stearns, P. (2004). *Anxious Parents*. New York: NYU Press.

Steele, C. (1997). A threat in the air. *American Psychologist*, 52(6), 613–629.

Steinberg, L., Lamborn, S., Dornbusch, S., & Darling, N. (1992). Impact of parenting practices on adolescent achievement. *Child Development*, 63, 1266–1281.

Steinberg, L. (1996). *Beyond the Classroom*. New York: Simon and Schuster.

Steinberg, L. (2001). We know some things: Parent-adolescent relationships in retrospect and prospect. *Journal of Research on Adolescence*, 11(1), 1–19.

Steinberg, L. (2004). *The 10 Basic Principles of Good Parenting*. New York: Simon and Schuster.

Sterling, T. (1959). Publication decision and the possible effects of inferences drawn from tests of significance—or vice versa. *Journal of the American Statistical Association*, 54, 30–34.

Sterling, T., Rosenbaum, W., & Weinkam, J. (1995). Publication decisions revisited. *The American Statistician*, 49(1), 108–112.

Stevens, S. (1935). The operational definition of psychological terms. *Psychological Review*, 405–416.

Stevens, S. (1939). Psychology and the science of science. *Psychological Bulletin*, 36, 221–263.

Stevenson, B. & Wolfers, J. (2008). Economic growth and subjective well–being. *Brookings Papers on Economic Activity*, 1, 1–84.

Stigler, S. (1986). *The History of Statistics*. Cambridge, MA: Harvard University Press.

Sunstein, C. (2002). Hazardous heuristics. (University of Chicago Public Law & Legal Theory Working Paper #33).

Suppe, S. (1974). The search for philosophic understanding of scientific theories. In S. Suppe (ed.). *The Structure of Scientific Theories*. Urbana: University of Illinois Press.

Symonds, P. (1939). *The Psychology of Parent-Child Relationships*. New York: Appleton.

Taleb, N. (2001). *Fooled by Randomness*. New York: Random House.

Taleb, N. (2007). *The Black Swan*. New York: Random House.

Thagard, P. (1982). From the descriptive to the normative in psychology and logic. *Philosophy of Science*, 49, 24–42

Thaler, R. (1980). Toward a positive theory of consumer choice. *Journal of Economic Behavior and Organization*, 1, 39–60.

Thaler, R. (1991). *The Winner's Curse*. New York: The Free Press.

Thaler, R. & Sunstein, C. (2008). *Nudge*. New Haven, CT: Yale University Press.

Thomas, K. (1971). *Religion and the Decline of Magic*. Cambridge: Oxford University Press.

Thompson. (1988). Review of What if there are no statistical tests. *Educational and Psychological Measurement*, 58, 334–346.

Thorndike, E. & Woodworth, R. (1901). The influence of improvement in one mental function upon the efficiency of others. *Psychological Review*, 8, 247–261.

Thorndike, R. & Hagan, E. (1969). *Measurement and Evaluation in Psychology and Education*. New York: Wiley.

Thurstone, L. (1947). *Multiple Factor Analysis*. Chicago, IL: University of Chicago Press.

Tough, P. (2012). *How Children Succeed*. New York: Houghton Mifflin Harcourt.

Tukey, J. (1962). The future of data analysis. *The Annals of Mathematics Statistics*, 33(1), 1–67.

Tukey, J. (1991). The philosophy of multiple comparisons. *Statistical Science*, 6(1), 100–116.

Tversky, A. & Kahneman, D. (1971). Belief in the law of small numbers. *Psychological Bulletin*, 2, 105–110.

Uleman, J. (2005). Becoming aware of the new unconscious. In R. Hassin, J. Uleman, & J. Bargh (eds). *The New Unconscious*. Oxford: Oxford University Press.

Van der Maas, H., Dolan, C., Grasman, R., Wicherts, J., Huizenga, H., & Raijmakers, M. (2006). A dynamical model of general intelligence: The positive manifold of intelligence by mutualism. *Psychological Review*, 113, 842–861.

Visser, B., Ashton, M., & Vernon, P. (2006). Beyond *g*. *Intelligence*, 34, 487–502

Vul, E., Harris, C., Winkielman, P. & Pashler, H. (2009). Puzzlingly high correlations in fMRI studies of emotion, personality, and social cognition. *Perspectives on Psychological Science*, 4, 274–290.

Warner, J. (2006). *Perfect Madness*. New York: Riverhead Books.

Warwick, J., Nettleback, T., & Ward, L. (2010). A response to Antonakis & Dietz. *Personality and Individual Differences*, 50(3), 416–417.

Wason, P. (1966). Reasoning. In B. Foss (ed.). *New Horizons in Psychology*. New York: Penguin.

Wason, P. & Evans, J. (1975). Dual processing in reasoning? *Cognition*, 3, 141–154.

Waterman, A. (2013). The humanist psychology-positive psychology divide, *American Psychologist*, 68(3), 124–133.

Waynforth, D. (2007). The influence of parent-infant cosleeping, nursing, and childcare on cortisol, SIgA immunity in a sample of British schoolchildren. *Developmental Psychobiology*, 49(6), 640–648.

Weber, E. U. (2006). Experienced-based and description-based perceptions of long-term risk. *Climate Change*, 77, 103–120.
Webster, R. (1995). *Why Freud Was Wrong*. New York: Basic Books.
Wegner, D. (2002). *The Illusion of Conscious Will.* Cambridge, MA: MIT Press.
Wegner, D. (2005). Who is the controller of controlled processes? In R. Hassin, J. Uleman, & J. Bargh (eds.). *The New Unconscious.* Oxford: Oxford University Press.
Wells, F. (1913). The principle of mental tests. *Science*, 972, 221–224.
Westen, D. (1998). The scientific legacy of Sigmund Freud. *Psychological Bulletin,* 124(3), 333–371.
Weinstein, N. (1980). Unrealistic optimism about future life events. *Journal of Personality & Social Psychology,* 39, 806–820.
Wentzel, K. (1999). Social motivational processes and interpersonal relationships. *Journal of Educational Psychology*, 91, 76–97.
Wiggam, A. (1928). *Exploring Your Mind.* Indianapolis, IN: Bobbs-Merrill Co.
Wilkinson, L. & The Task Force on Statistical Inference. (1999). Statistical methods in psychology journals. *American Psychologist*, 54(8), 594–604.
Wilson, T. (2002). *Stranger to Ourselves*. Cambridge, MA: Belknap Press.
Wolf, T. (1973). *Alfred Binet.* Chicago, IL: University of Chicago Press.
Yarkoni, T. (2009). Big correlations in little studies. *Perspectives on Psychological Science*, 4, 294–298.
Yarri, G. & Eisenmann, S. (2011). The hot (invisible) hand. *PLOS ONE*, 6(10). e24532.
Youmanns, E. (1867). *The Culture Demanded by Modern Life*. New York: Appleton.

Index

Allport, Gordon, 185, 186–188
Ariely, Dan, 13, 14, 15, 37
attachment, parenting, 112, 115–118
attachment, theory, 111, 145

Baumrind, Diana, 111, 112, 113, 115, 118, 120, 120–123, 139, 141
behavioral economics, 14, 15
behavioral genetics, 141–144, 174–175
between-subjects design, problems with, 26–27, 28
Big Five, personality traits, 182, 184, 188–190
Bridgman, Percy W., 64–65, 66

Cain, Susan, 11, 182
Chinese parenting, 112, 118–119
classical test theory, 151, 157, 158, 163, 164
confidence intervals, 103–104
Costa, Paul, 184–185, 188–190
construct validity. *See* validity
control, 30
correlations, problems with, 129–134
co-sleeping, studies on, 116–117

Easterlin Paradox, 88
experiment, problems with, 28–29

Fisher, Ronald, 28, 31, 76, 92, 96–99, 99, 105, 107, 113
Freud, Sigmund, 41, 44, 45, 48, 49, 51–53, 57, 70, 71, 72, 111

Gilbert, Daniel, 1–2, 75, 83–84, 88
Gigerenzer, Gerd, 18, 21, 22, 24, 58, 71, 73, 96
Gladwell, Malcolm, 13, 16–17, 45
Goleman, Daniel, 192–193, 195
Gopnik, Allison, 145, 146
Gosling, Sam, 182–183

Haidt, Jonathan, 75, 79, 80, 82–83
Harris, Judith, 123, 141
Herrnstein, Richard, 172, 175–177
homunculi, problem of, 47, 70–71

IAT. *See* Implicit Association Test
Implicit Association Test, 45, 58–60, 132
implicit attitudes, 52, 61
implicit judgment. *See* implicit attitudes

Jastrow, James, 6, 7, 8, 31
Jensen, Arthur, 172, 173, 175, 177–178

Kahneman, Daniel, 13–14, 20, 21, 23, 24, 27, 35–38, 41, 42–43, 47, 49, 55, 56, 73, 75, 76, 83, 84, 86–88, 89, 93, 123

latent variables, 158, 165, 190–191
Levitt, Steven, 13, 16
Lyubomirsky, Sonja, 75, 85, 86, 89, 108

Maccoby, Eleanor, 123, 124–127, 139–140, 141
Mayer, John, 194, 195–196, 197
McCrae, Robert, 184–185, 188–190
measurement, history, 151–155
measurement invariance, 177–178, 184
Mlodinow, Leonard, 45, 62
Murray, Charles, 172, 175–177

Neyman, Jerzy, 98–99
Nisbett, Richard, 17, 46–47
Null Hypothesis Significance Testing, 76–77, 92–95, 99–102, 104–105

operationalism, 42, 60, 63–70

Paul, Annie Murphy, 184, 193
Pearson, Egon, 98–99
Piaget, Jean, 20, 25, 54, 56, 95–96, 111, 171
power analysis, 102
pop psychology, history, 3, 6–9
priming, 52
professionalization, of psychology, 3, 9–10

rationality debate, 19–21, 25
randomization, 31–33
regression, problems with, 134–137
reliability, 157, 158
replication crisis, 34–35, 36–37, 38
representative bias, 14, 21–25, 35, 36

sampling issues, 33–34
Seligman, Martin, 75, 77–80, 81, 87, 90–91, 106–107, 107
Skinner, B. F., 41, 72
Spearman, Charles, 166, 167, 168, 169, 172, 178
Stern, William, 185–186
Sternberg, Robert, 167, 168–169
Stevens, S. S., 154–155
subliminal perception, 45, 50
system 1 versus system 2 (S1 vs. S2), 41, 42–43, 46, 48, 49, 53, 54, 54–56, 85

Taleb, Nassim, 13, 16, 17
Tiger Mom. *See* Chinese parenting
Tough, Paul, 113

validity, 63, 68–69, 158–163

Wason, Peter, 20–21
Westin, Drew, 51–53

About the Author

Robert Ausch received his doctorate from the CUNY Graduate Center in developmental psychology. He has published on a range of topics including social science methodology and the philosophy of psychology. His first book, *An Advanced Guide to Psychological Thinking: Critical and Historical Perspectives*, was released by Lexington Books in May 2015. He has worked in teacher education and currently teaches psychology at New York University and Pratt Institute.